BHAKTI KARUNA AGAPE
WITH RAIMUNDO PANIKKAR

edited by

Marko Zlomislić, David Goicoechea
Suzanne K. Tebbutt, Rajiv Kaushik

Global Academic Publishing
Binghamton University
Binghamton, NY
2003

Publication Data

Title: *Bhakti Karuna Agape with Raimundo Panikkar*

Editors: Marko Zlomislić, David Goicoechea, Suzanne K. Tebbutt, Rajib Kaushik

ISBN: 1-58684-235-8

Distributed by:
Global Academic Publishing
State University of New York at Binghamton
Binghamton University, LNG99
Binghamton, New York, USA 13902-6000
Phone: (607) 777-4495; Fax: (607) 777-6132
Email: globlpub@binghamton.edu
http://academicpublishing.binghamton.edu

Contents

Introduction

Mutual Fecundation

Bhakti

Karuna

Agape

Post-Scrypt

Introduction

Introduction: *Bhakti-Karuna-Agape*

David Goicoechea

Mutual Fecundation

Raimundo did it! He talked about love in such a lovely and loving way that we each loved it and we each loved him and we each loved each other more because of him.

Raimundo did it! He talked about *bhakti* with such play and devotion that we each delighted in the duty of its pure being—its pure consciousness—its pure bliss. He talked about *karuna* with such wit and compassion that we were each taken into the calm serenity of its embodied enlightenment—its embodied teaching-its embodied community. He talked about *agape* with such irony and self deprecation that we each were called to responsibility in the creativity of its joy—of its sorrow—of its glory. He obviously lived in the world of the good Samaritan—suffering servant with the wisdom and duty of *Krishna-Arjuna* and the enlightened sympathy of the *Arhat-Bodhisatva.*

But how did he do it? How did he captivate us? How did he so impress us that now, five years later, we are still clearly and strangely touched by him? How did he so embody and communicate the ideal that we would each like to be like him? Raimundo did it and was able to do it because he is a scientist-philosopher-theologian who has responded to the intercultural challenge with the artistry of muse-*duende*-angel to such a degree that he has the stature-authority-appeal of a hero-saint-genius.

His mother's Catalonian-Toulousian culture let there be cultivated in him not only the Benedictine-Dominican-Jesuit stock first planted by James the Apostle and nourished at Montserrat, but also the roots-offshoots-fruits of courtly love and literature which first flourished around Eleanor of Aquitaine, and stretched out into the soil of that ancient Greek-Roman-Spanish lore that form ed his language-speech-tongue. His mother's Catalonian culture received *mucho* fecundation (when he first said the word we were not sure whether he said *mucho* or mutual) from the Seville of Isadore and of the Andalusian-Flamenco, from the Granada of the *Sacra Monte* and the Alhambra, from the Madrid of Velasquez, Goya and the bulls, from the Toledo of El Greco, from the Avila of Teresa and her John of the Cross, from the primeval Basques who painted on cave walls and danced on coffins. But his city of Barcelona is not just any city from Cadiz or Cordoba to Guernica and San Sebastian. It is in fecundation with them. And Tavertet is not Barcelona. It is the primitive mountain retreat from which our world-winging falcon looks down in contemplative creativity upon his motherland and upon his world.

His father's love let there be distilled in him a love for the nature and culture of India. He loved with his father's love the sounds, the smells, the tastes, the sights and the feel of India. From infancy he smelled and ate his father's cooking. He heard and longed for his father's stories with all of their animals and peoples—with all of their images and ideas—with all of their gods and goddesses. He learned from childhood of India's dance-song-poetry, of India's painting-sculpture-architecture, of India's history-philosophy-religion. He learned of his father's special homeland and of the many regions of India—of the many kinds of Hinduism—of the six orthodox and three heterodox systems. He saw them all fecundating each other. With his father's love he came to love multiplicities and movements and organizations and classifications all according to the nine *rasas*. He identified with his mother's love and thus came to love all of his father's. He identified with his father's love and thus came to love all of his mother's. He was born and raised a child of mutual fecundation.

With Plough and Not Preservatives

Raimundo did it because he is not only a rhapsodist of love's glory and power, but also a dramatist of love's challenge and struggle. He has lived through the Spanish Civil War and the Second World War. He is very aware of nations and their nationalism. Can there be nations without nationalism? In seeking an answer to our violence he says right up front that the speaker-lover-strategist should betray himself in his fear-arrogance-ambition-vanity. That can begin a reflection upon the sword that it might be melted down to become a ploughshare. He knows full well of nature's instincts and mechanisms to invade and territorialize. Culture is usually up to its and nature's business as usual in the plunder and rape of territorial expansion. Culture plays the game of the territorial imperative. It has its center-display point-boundary. This is the dynamic structure of individual-family-clan, of church-club-society, of city-state-nation. Raimundo unmasks the self-serving preservatives that prevent fecundation between territorialized cultures. He knows that there is a contest between either fecundation or liquidation. He knows that each great love has its special strategies for negotiating with the greed-lust-power at the territory's center-display point-boundary. Poverty-chastity-obedience have been cultivated by *Bhakti-Karuna-Agape* each in its own way. Raimundo has learned the language of each-practiced the discipline of each-pursued the ideals of each. The silence of his words and the words of his silence have lingered with us like a holy feast after a holy fast. He has left us working and waiting for our poor beleaguered League of Nations. He remains with us negotiating between liquidation and fecundation.

And Yet with Preservation

Raimundo does it not only because as a teller of tales and a toiler with yokes he is a tiller of soils, but also because as the salt of the earth and the spice of life he is as cool as ice in preserving the wisdom of the ancient ways. He is one cool artist! His Sanskrit grammar lets him know the singular-the plural-the dual. And he conveys one cool dual. We may not know of the dual, but with the mime of his body and the analysis of his mind he intrigues us with its grammatical experiencing of doubt. Because he has let the dual be preserved in his experience he can invite us to wonder about the mystery between the other and me. His Greek grammar lets him know of the middle voice which is neither active nor passive. Because that is preserved within him he can bring us to wonder with him about a creative love that lives between the activity of the wakeful ego and the passivity of the unconscious me in the middle voice of myself in its creative semi-sleep. His Latin grammar lets him know of gerunds and gerundives. Thus he distinguishes and helps us distinguish the thinking of the *cogitans* from the-what-should-be- thought of the *cogitandum*. He helps us distinguish the special grace of the *ex opere operato* that is there without intention from the grace of the *ex opere operantis* that is there with intention. He helps us appreciate the late Latin *natura naturans* in the process of nature's unfolding as distinct from the *natura naturata* of perfection's completed realm. He brings us to a new reflection through the languages he has mastered. He has preserved so much of past cultures even in the deep soil of their grammar-rhetoric-logic that though he argues for the plough and not the preservatives, we know that as he takes some preservatives back with his left hand he is giving others with his right.

Bhakti: Devotion as Symmetrical Fecundation (With the Plough): My Heart has Touched Thy Feet

Within the *bhaktic* ethos of the poetry that sings: "My heart has touched thy feet" Debabrata Sinha's analysis of the unfolding of *Bhakti* takes shape according to the structure of the *Gita's* great peepal tree. The threefold root is in the *Vedas-Upanishads-Gita*. The three-fold offshoot is with *Sankara-Madhusadan-Narada.* The three- fold fruit manifests itself in the devotional poetry of Vaishnavism-Sankara-the common Indian culture.

In the Vedas, while the term *bhakti* does not appear, there is its root, the term *Bhaj* which means to resort to-to bestow upon-to share with. There are many examples of mother-father-friend to whom one can resort-who will bestow-with whom there can be sharing. In the *Upanishads* within the context of *Jnana-Atman-Brahman* the absolute is referred to as He. The metaphysical demand to make the abstract concrete brings enlightened faith to attentive devotion. The existential demand for total self involvement makes of the contemplative something practical. But it is the *Bhagavadgita* that develops the primacy of *Bhakti* in the *Bhakti-Karma-Jnana* synthesis. Arjuna in his anxious despair is graced by Lord Krishna so that after the failure of his discipline of action and his discipline of wisdom he is given *sat-cit-ananda.* In his great vision he comes to be at peace with the horrors of war and violence as he sees his place of submission within the big picture. He resorts to Krishna and Krishna bestows upon him the pure bliss of the pure consciousness of the pure being. With that he can share in the great cosmic order. In its root system *bhakti* is the symmetry of the sharing with that proceeds from resorting to and bestowing upon. In its root system, *bhakti* is the symmetry of the pure bliss of *ananda* that proceeds from the pure consciousness of *cit* into the pure being of *sat.* In its root system, *bhakti* is the symmetry of *karma yoga* and *Jnana yoga* being fulfilled in the *bhakti yoga* that flows out of Arjuna's song of despairing submission to Krishna and Krishna's vision of *Purushottoma* through *prasada* for Arjuna.

In Sankara's Buddhistic revision of Hinduism the four components of *karuna-friendliness-endurance-indifference* are distilled by fecundation into the triadic *maya-avidya-upasana* mix. Through the magic of unknowing we can focus our way through the distractions of *maya* to the intense concentration of the mind in *Jnana* on the highest object of adoration. While Sankara shoots off more from the *Upanishadic* root, Madhusudan shoots off more from the *Gita* root as he emphasizes the *rasas* of *Bhakti-Ananda.* Narada in his *Bhaktisutra* defines *bhakti* as supreme love or *paroma-prema-rupa.* His all inclusive definition takes him back to the vedic root which is the all inclusive source. He connects *bhakti* with love, the love of parent and child-the love of friend and friend-the love of lover and beloved.

Bhakti is the elevation of personal love through the overcoming of egoism into the praise of all in the Divine. In its offshoots the devotion of *bhakti* is contemplative adoration-celebratory enjoyment-comprehensive love.

The great tree of *bhakti* blossoms and brings forth many fruits. The *bhakti* cult sang forth in the Vaishnava lyrics of Bengal. Krishna and Radha were praised as the Divine Lovers loved by the eternal yearning of the human soul. Sankara himself sang of Shiva, the wave of bliss, in his devotional poetry. All across the subcontinent the *Bhakti*-Cult inspired popular culture. That culture was a religious culture filled with prayer to *Shiva* as well as *Krishna* as well as *Durga* the mother Goddess. *Bhakti* in its fruits became prayer-poetry-popular culture.

Where Being Is, There Love Is

When the worlds of Raimundo Panikkar and John Arapura meet big questions about the communication of the *agapeic* attitude and the *bhaktic* attitude begin to surface. Of course, the most important thing about John and Raimundo is that they meet as persons with great love and respect for each other. Raimundo is a *bhaktic agapeist* who was born and raised in Catalonia. John is an *agapeic bhakta* who was born and raised in Kerala. They each have a great message for all of us facing the intercultural challenge. Within their interpersonal meeting their theoretical models are at work shaping and being shaped by their interpersonal experience. Raimundo's ecumenical model of mutual fecundation is ploughed under by John's ontological model of appropriation. Questions about *mutuality* are brought into an underground ferment. John's Johannine model of appropriative unification is also ploughed under by the Pauline-Markan-Lukan elements of Raimundo's *agape* that brings him to a missionary spirit of intermarriage that implies a mutual ploughing under. But how about the mutuality? Arapura's ontology calls upon him to cultivate the depths of this notion.

Just as Debabrata explicated nine historical moments in his unfolding of *bhakti* so John unfolds nine conceptual points in his explication of love. The three-fold root of love is reality-abyss-energy. The three offshoots are contemplation-thought-*logos*. The three fruits are wonder-care-love.

The genus of all the great loves is the golden rule. *Hesed-eros-philia-bhakti-jen-tao-agape-karuna-rahim* all have in common the mutuality of the "do unto others as you would have them do unto you." John Arapura is able to find a place in thought for *agape* and *bhakti* insofar as there is a foundation for this mutuality right in the Being that is self knowing and self loving. The vedic tradition-Parmenides-Heidegger have each developed the foundation for this bond of reciprocity between, as John puts it, *res* and *ratio*. This bond is love. It is the bond that makes up *agape*-that makes up *bhakti*-that bonds them.

Being is not only a simple, stable fullness. Of course, non-being cannot be. Being cannot be only a pure identity. It is non-dual. (Panikkar raised the issue of the dual in Sanskrit grammar. In his wily guile what does he do with the dual and the non-dual?) Being as non-dual must at the same time be the abyss or openness. That openness must also be filled with *sakti* or energy.

Non-dual-open-energetic Being is a self-knowing knower. *Sat* is *cit*. Being is pure self-consciousness. Arapura shows how Parmenides and Heidegger can agree on the logic of all these propositions. This is so because there is the logic of Being or *logos*. *Logos* is the gathering that is enclosed. Being is open, but enclosed. In knowing itself

Being is pure thought. Arapura thinks against Heidegger that this need not be language.

But then comes love. Within open but enclosed Being there can be the great presencings of wonder-mystery-suffering-care-fear-love. Is this also the case with pure Being? Arapura argues (and is this not against Parmenides) that Being as loving-wonder can generate beings. Will there be then suffering only on the part of beings or is it also on the part of Being? Where is suffering when it is modified by the non-dual? Is care the care of Being in the double genitive or is it only for the suffering? Does Being care because it suffers for the suffering beings? Did Sankara bring this into his non-dualism as a result of fecundation with the Buddhists? And the suffering and the fear? Love taketh away fear? But whose fear? Is it also Being's fear? Or, does loving Being only take away the fear of beings?

Aria First: Then Duet

Ric Brown shows how the *Bhagavad Gita* itself is the outcome of mutual fecundation. Ric believes in an ideal according to which love is accounted for in terms of otherness and difference. He knows that the *Upanishadic* ideal stresses the self sameness and identity of the "That Thou Art" and "The Atman that is Brahman." So he studies *The Gita* carefully to see if it too fails to meet his criteria for true love. His argument can be seen as developing along the line of three sets of three points: the three *gunic* fruits-the three yogic offshoots-the threefold Divine root.

When Arjuna cries out in supplication to Lord Krishna that it is his duty to kill, but that he does not want to kill, Krishna says to him: know thyself. From the beginning, from the viewpoint of the *Sankhya* with its dualism of

Purush and *Prakriti,* it is made clear to Arjuna that he must act in accord with his special kind of being. (There is no longer just a logic of the genus. There is now a logic of specific differences within the genus.) The realm of *Prakriti* is further divided into the *sattvic* (those who abide in the *sat* of being) , the *rajasic* (those who abide in the raj of noble passion), the *tamasic* (those who abide in the common work). Arjuna is a *rajasic rajah* whose noble duty it is to fight and kill. He is not yet a *sattvic* contemplative who can be free of fighting. The wise man should be contemplative. The noble man should be an active hero. The common man should work. What Ric does in exploring *bhakti* is very interesting. At first, he thinks that the *sattvic* type should practice *jnana yoga* – the *rajasic* type should practice *bhakti yoga*- the *tamasic* type should practice *karma yoga.* Apparently, he does this because he does not want to associate *bhakti* primarily with the common. When he is considering the three *gunas* and especially the lowly *tamasic guna* he seems to feel the need to connect *bhakti* with Arjuna instead of the workers. That and why he does this raises big questions about the lowly commonality of love and even its mutuality.

In exploring the *yoga*s or types of yogic discipline, Ric treats four. If as Inada claims yogic practice is the key feature of all Eastern spirituality then *The Gita* is an ideal text in helping us to understand the East. For it does introduce us to and make us think about the significance and kinds of yogic discipline. In fact, each of the eighteen chapters of *The Gita* is called a particular kind of *yoga.* Perhaps the *yoga* of meditation, *dhyanayoga,* in chapter six is central to them all. But in any case there are the main three: *jnana yoga-karma yoga-bhakti yoga.* There is also as Ric shows the *sankhyayoga.* In order to understand the place of *bhakti* yoga in *The Gita,* Ric shows how Arjuna is taught first to develop *karma yoga.* This is the most proper discipline for the noble man of passionate action. He should learn how to act out of duty—in the spirit of sacrifice—without desire for the fruits of action. *Karma yoga* enables duty rather than desire to motivate action. Since desire is self centered *jnana yoga* can assist *karma yoga* because it gets rid of the illusion of self as individual. *Sankhyayoga* or non-action can also help one develop the *yoga* that lets one act but without desire for the fruits of action. Because *karma yoga* is perfected by *jnana* and *sankhya yoga The Gita* does not meet Brown's requirement of letting *bhakti* be a devotion to a different other and different others.

But then Ric shows how *The Gita* is a marvelous fecundation of the Vedanta by the Sankhyha and the Sankhyha by the Vedanta. From chapter eleven onward *The Gita* stresses a *bhakti* that has a genuine mutuality respectful of otherness. Arjuna like Ric requests a Bhakta that loves as a father loves his son-as a lover loves his beloved-as a friend loves his friend. This otherness and difference is theoretically accounted for. The roots of the upside down peepal tree are three: the root of Ishvara-the root of Brahman-the root of Purushottoma. Brahman is the womb of Purushottama. The great Purush, the being that is different from Prakriti and lets the *gunas* of prakriti be different, is more basic than and inclusive of Brahman. The Sankhya ploughs under the Vedanta in *The Gita* and lets *Bhakti* become a personified love of other personifications.

The *bhakti* of Ric's *Gita* makes us wonder how much it is like to or different from the *agape* of Kierkegaard's house. In moving from the other-destructive loves of the aesthetic basement and the ethical first floor to the absolute love of the absolute of the second floor of one's house and then coming back to the first floor and basement by relatively loving the relative, how is Kierkegaard's person like Ric's Arjuna? There is a process of transformation that reaches mystical union with the absolute and then *agape* comes back and loves all neighbours as equal and yet unique. In looking at *The Gita* with the classical *eros-agape* question Ric makes us wonder if *Bhakti* as connected with *Purushottoma* does not have to have already and always been there in letting Arjuna question and go beyond *jnana yoga* and *karma yoga*. Or putting it in Ric's last way, does not the primacy of Purushottoma suggests the primacy of a *bhakti* that is connected with otherness and difference from the beginning?

Knowledge is Nothing without Love

Martin Andic focuses on a universal problem and a universal solution. It is the problem of decision and the solution of love. An important decision always has what has classically been called the principle of double effect. To save his side of the family's values Arjuna must destroy the other side of his family. A decision has many poison gifts. I am always guilty when I make a decision. I have to choose against the goods of b when I choose the goods of a. As Derrida puts it: in taking responsibility for my cats I will be non-responsive to other needy cats.

Knowledge does not solve the problem of doing necessary violence when we decide to do one thing rather than another. If we procrastinate and do nothing we could do even more violence. Knowledge reveals a decision's dissemination into many foreseen and unforeseen evils. The more empirical knowledge we have the more weighty our decisions become. But Martin is especially interested in contemplative knowledge or *jnana yoga*. His point is that to save us from guilt *jnana* needs *bhakti*. Martin's understanding of *bhakti* as the development of *jnana* is more like John Arapura's then Ric Brown's. Martin too cites the letter of John that God is love. He argues that *bhakti* is more the preservation of *jnana* than the plough. Ric would see the Sankhya with its *bhakti* of otherness as ploughing under the Vedanta with its *bhakti* of non-dualism. Martin sees *bhakti* as a non-dualistic, mystical devotion that implicitly from the beginning lets *jnana yoga* and *karma yoga* develop and in the process it becomes explicit.

Derrida with his philosophy of dissemination-differance-deconstruction-indecidability faces exactly the problem of *The Gita.* He is concerned precisely with Arjuna's dilemma. Derrida shows why Ric finds otherness important and why Panikkar emphasizes the plough. Indecidability reveals how there can be genuine decisions that always leave one guilty. This essential connection between the decision and guilt is brought out by Heidegger-Levinas-Derrida. Derrida sees love as a taking of responsibility for that guilt and a continued working for social justice. For Panikkar-Ric-Derrida love is responsibility for the other. For Sinha-Arapura-Andic it is devotion. Devotion can save us from guilt as Andic shows. Responsibility takes the guilt and keeps working for social justice even though continued injustice will keep coming.

The Gita is a Love Story

Charles Vernoff examines the passion of Arjuna. Arjuna loves his kin. Arjuna loves his duty. But then one fine day it is his duty to kill his kin. It becomes the most terrible day of his life. Which will prevail? His love for his kin or his love for his duty? His duty is entwined with the caste system. If he forsakes his duty he will forsake the author of the caste system-the God of the universe. He tells Krishna of his passion for his kinsmen. He does not will to kill them.

The plot of the *Gita* has to do with a double movement leap. Arjuna moves from a primary passion for his kin to a primary passion for God, however, in such a way that he can still be loving to his kin. Arjuna is like Panikkar. As he converses with Krishna he is put on trial. He sees his own fear-arrogance-ambition-vanity. The *Gita* in minute depiction also puts Krishna and God on trial with Arjuna's faith in them at stake at every instant. This is the ploughing. Arjuna's old love for his kin is ploughed under. His former understanding of his duty and of Krishna and of God is ploughed under.

From chapters one to six in a detailed dialogue Arjuna gets rid of his doubts about Krishna. From chapters seven to eleven his trust is placed positively in Krishna. Chapters twelve to eighteen depict Arjuna as a man of faith in communion with and devoted to Krishna. Only with the positive transference of his highest love to Krishna can his warrior's blade be freed to perform its duty. That is because he comes to believe that even though his kin will be killed they will not perish. It is this belief in their immortality that allows him to undergo the extreme challenge. Each spirituality such as that of Job or Jesus must go through such a dark night of total passion in order to become a great spirituality.

Panikkar has undergone the ploughing-under with Jesus-Arjuna-Job-the Buddha. His ecumenism is a going-through of a variety of passions such as those of obedience-agency-suffering. Our intercultural challenge has to do with learning from each other by going through passionate underploughings with each other's sages-geniuses-saints. By discovering the glory of Krishna with Arjuna, Panikkar is better able to grow in the cosmotheandric flow.

Karuna: Compassion as Symmetrical Fecundation (By Avoiding Preservatives): Compassion is a Dynamic Human Phenomenon

Kenneth Inada shows that love has four focal points for the Buddhist. There is not only *karuna* (compassion), but also loving kindness (*metta*)-altruistic joy (*mudita*)-equanimity (*upekkha*). Each of these together with all eastern spirituality flows out of the practice of yogic meditation. For the Buddhist that meditation arrives at anatman (avoidance of self). With the voiding of self one avoids the two extremes of either substance or nihilism. Substance is the great preservative that also isolates and keeps apart. Substance is conceived of as a thing in itself and thus is not capable of full mutual fecundation with another. But if one avoids the notion of substance that could lead to nihilism. That also would despair of mutual fecundation and all the growth and transformation it enables. Thus Buddhist meditation is a dynamic process that avoids those two extremes by being the middle way between them. Ken shows how the meditation that reaches *anatman* also reaches *pratitya samutpada* (the dependent co-arising of all things). The avoiding of preservatives (*anatman)* lets there be mutual fecundation (*pratitya samutpada*). Ken shows that the fourfold love of the Buddhist fecundation can be described by nine traits. These can be ordered in three sets of three: (1) impermanence-growth-openness (2) extension-incorporation-resilience (3) mutuality-reflectiveness-uniqueness.

Raimundo acted upon the need to leave as a Christian-find himself a Hindu-return as a Buddhist because he needed in order to let his own spirituality grow to meet and learn from persons like Ken. He learned from the Buddhists the importance of and the intricacies of removing the preservatives. In practicing with them their voiding he became a Buddhist. Removing the preservatives is most of all a deconstruction of the notion of substance or thing in itself. It is thingness that is permanent. It is thingness that isolates and blocks. If there is really to be uniting then the notion of substance or atman becomes inadequate and contradictory. Avoiding the permanent permits growth. And love for the Buddhist is first of all dynamic growth. It is not first of all desire. It is not even first of all bonding. It is a movement of growth. The avoidance of desire and merging lets there be openness. No wonder Ric wanted otherness. But that otherness cannot be simply the otherness of another substance. For then we would need the magic of transubstantiation which does not meet the Buddhist test of the empirical.

Taking the preservatives out of the soil with the plough is like taking rocks out of a field after you have ploughed them up. But the Buddhist breaks down these very rocks of substance into fine, fertile soil. For Inada the dynamism of *karuna* has also to do with extension-incorporation-resilience. Meditation lets the hard, substantial rock-like things become instead something that is soft and tender. There can be mutual fecundation because we humans and all living beings and all things reach out of ourselves in an existential flow. The rocks become soil that is aflow with openness. Meditation lets all be incorporated in all. It lets all be something that is tender-soft-pliable.

When Inada describes the something that results when the substantial things are made malleable he sees them in mutuality-reflectiveness-unique becoming. The four Buddhist loves including *Karuna* are in mutual fecundation. *Karuna* is defined in terms of relationality and becoming rather than substantiality and being. We each reflect each other like mirrors of responsiveness. Each configuration is unique in the continuous flow of existence. There are no preservatives-no substances-no things-no rocks-no egos-no subjects-no persons. All is in a flow of co-dependent becoming. Seeing that gets rid of preservatives.

No Teacher was so Godless as Lord Buddha, Yet None so Godlike

John Mayer asks about the transition from Theravada to Mahayana Buddhism. John is a World Federalist and a universalist and thus like Raimundo is very concerned with mutual fecundation. What sort of fecundation happened that let Mahayana emerge out of Theravada? To explore this question John asks about the emerging in terms of Buber's model of I-Thou experience — I-It expression. Is Panikkar's cosmotheandric experience like Buber's I-Thou experience? How is the Buddhist development to be understood according to Buber and Panikkar?

I can be in an immediate, not fully articulable experience with a rock-a tree-a cat-a person. This I-Thou experience which is one of presence-wholeness-mutuality-inclusiveness breaks through to the eternal Thou. If I express this experience with any analytical thinking then it becomes an I-It relation, that is distant-partial-asymmetrical-exclusive. The mature I-Thou — I-It experience would let me be critical within the framework of sympathy. Just criticism would proceed from I-Thou experience—I-It expression together. Does John think that the I-Thou experience is common to all spiritual experience and that mutual fecundation takes place through the ploughing of the I-It expression? Does he think that the fecundation has two aspects? Is there something common in the *karuna* culture and the *agape* culture that lets Panikkar work with their mutual fecundation?

But how about Buddhism? If it is atheistic and does not break through to an eternal Thou is it an I-Thou experience? If it denies the substance of man-God-world how can it be cosmotheandric? John gives two arguments to show that in spite of these difficulties Buddhism is very much an I-Thou experience. By arguing against the substantial existence of Atman and Brahman, Buddhism is showing the dangers of the mere I-It expression. Buddhism's denial and silence is just a more strict application of the Hindu neti, neti (Brahman is not this and not that) and the Christian negative theology. If there were no I-Thou base there would not be such concern to point out the limits of the I-It.

Secondly, John argues that the transition from Theravada to Mahayana has to do with a growing awareness of an I-Thou loving responsibility for others. This love must be both vertical in its absolute love for the absolute and horizontal in its relative love for the relative. Buddhist meditation arrives at the cosmotheandric experience in a very sophisticated way that gets beyond any self-loving preferences. Buddhist argumentation sets world-God-man in a non substantial framework. But then Buddhist *karuna* cares for the thou of every being in the mix of its becoming. Being lamps unto themselves as non-substances allows Buddhists to become lights for others as non-substances. For the arhant there is already the I-Thou experience with no I-It expression. But the *Boddhisattva* adds to that pure I-Thou a care for this Thou and that Thou in their unique suffering. The pure I-Thou of relation with no substantial I and no substantial Thou was ploughed under by the unique Thous who live in the I-It world. For the sake of those in the I-It world the Bodhisattva also lives in the I-It world, but in an I-Thou way.

Agape and *bhakti* need the plough of *karuna* to question and clarify further the I-thou—I-it distinction and relation. What happens when each is non-substantialized? If the Mahayanist is like Buber was there some *agape*-like attitude that ploughed under the Theravada?

When We Scan Kuan Yin's Innumerable Helping Hands

Richard Berg visited five Mahayana temples. He took pictures of the beautiful images. He made slides and showed them to us. He wrote his doctoral thesis on Michel Dufrenne's phenomenology of *The Aesthetic Experience*. Richard spoke to us as a philosopher of religion—a philosopher of ethics—a philosopher of art about the temples and the works of art within them. He brought us to reflection about how the work of art works on us.

Panikkar grew up in the world of the most beautiful art. He knew well the sacred space of Montserrat and the beautiful black Madonna. The nuns who taught him and whom he taught were always clothed as works of art. *Agape* was taught him by countless works of art. Murillo-Goya-Velasques-El Greco-Dali-Picasso were all his fellow country-men. Sacred song and dance even in its secular flamenco form was always pulsating in his world.

So Richard brought us to new reflection about mutual fecundation-about cultivating with the plough-about preserving with or without preservatives. Our besouled body is like field soil. Beautiful bodily images can plough it-harrow it-furrow it-plant it just as can beautiful sounds-gestures-movements. Mutual fecundation can take place when beautiful works of Buddhist art work on our soul soil. They can touch us, perhaps especially when we are young. They can inspire us to imitation. Panikkar knows much of the art of the muses-of the angels-of duende. The art of the Duen de la Casa is the art of the imp and of death. Art is of good taste and it teaches and embodies good taste. Panikkar has plenty of the imp within him.

In the temple there are the celestial Buddha's amida and Maitreya. There is Sakhyamuni, the earthly incarnate Buddha. There is Kuan Yin who rescues victims of disaster and illness. There is Ti Tsang who takes trips to hell to deliver sentient suffering beings. There is the unnamed myriad that typically line the temple walls. The Buddhist Pantheon might manifest a trinitarian theology-a moral metaphor-a temporal locator-a spatial locator-a cosmology-a rational monism-a personal monism-a somatic monism-an impersonal monism. But none of this is enough to explain the fecundation. As Mayer would say, it is all at the I-It level without getting to the I-Thou. All of this needs the wider ethos of the voluntary suffering for others that is the *karuna* of the *Boddhisattva* vow. Buddhist art can have a glory that can help the Mahayanist undergo the double transformation of enlightenment and compassion. This art can take him or her away from an involuntary, passive and egoistic experience of suffering. It can help him or her approach his or her own suffering as voluntary, active and altruistic.

Compassion is the Great Mystery of Ethics

When Timothy Madigan and Raimundo Panikkar meet at the crossroads there is immediate satisfaction. For in both of them the sacred cows of science and religion have already met as they did in Arthur Schopenhauer.

Imagine the great Irish moralist, Professor Timothy Madigan, the great German theorist, Herr Professor Arthur

Schopenhauer, and the great Spanish mystic, Fray Raimundo Panikkar meeting at a Vietnamese restaurant in San Francisco. After a round of Tequila and then of Saki, Arthur begins to loosen his gravitas. He tells them of a dream he recently had: "There were three cows pulling three ploughs in three wheatfields that were next to each other. One was a fine Brahma cow; all white, strong and glorious. One was a noble Spanish bull; all black, wild and spirited. One was a lovely Holstein; all black and white with udders full of milk. They each with stately bearing pulled their shining plough. Their sheer plod made plough down sillion shine. They approached each other from three directions. They met at a point where the three fields meet, at a crossroads. They turned into three poodles: a black one, a white one and a black and white one. I awakened."

Timothy and Raimundo both burst into a friendly, good humored laughter. And all of a sudden, at least for Raimundo, they became Tim, Art and Ray. They were being Americanized. Ray asked Art what he thought it meant. Being well trained by Freud, Art went at once back to the dream day. He said he didn't know. But yesterday after being at the university with his fellow theorists he was so glad to get home to his new poodle puppy that he named him "Mensch." Tim and Ray laughed again and so did Art. Ray said: "I'll bet your dream is about mutual fecundation at the crossroads. You see, when the plough pulling cow of compassion meets the plough pulling bull of devotion it is the clash of the ethical and the aesthetic. And when the plough pulling Holstein of science meets the two of them they can bring forth offspring of *mucho* satisfaction. The science can make the religion more ethical and aesthetic and that is a more satisfying religion. The ethics can make the science more honest and more pertinent to compassion. The religion can make the ethics and the science more mysterious. Art, you are at the crossroads.

You see the limits of epistemology. You see that it is like hunting. You aim at one and block out the rest. But you with Kant know the fascinating mystery of the starry sky above and the moral law within. Your dream of crossroads fecundation gave birth to poodles instead of German Short-Hairs because you love playful mystery rather than dangerous epistemology."

Tim for some reason thought of James Joyce, Pablo Picasso and Albert Einstein dining together in Paris. But he let that pass. He had to try to get serious and make some sense of all this. Raimundo's interpretation was wilder than Arthur's dream. "Art and Ray," he said, "I think I see what is happening. I think I understand Art's dream and your interpretation, Ray." He was still under the influence of Dr. Panikkar's playful mixing. He sat up like a more serious moralist and said: "Dr. Schopenhauer, I have always admired you for your humour and your good sense. In short, I have admired your secular humanism. I think that makes you a man of the crossroads. Kant's *agape* is such that he would not be here learning from the Buddhists and the Atheists. He would cultivate his *agape* at the center of the field like the good Holstein. Even Hegel would not go out to really learn from the other. From his display point he would appropriate others rather than really learn from them. But you, Dr. Schopenhauer, you learn from science and modify your religion to get a better ethics. You learn from the compassionate Buddha how to better appreciate Jesus and *agape*. In fact, you see Buddhism as a learning and a changing. Deep down in your dreaming heart I suspect that you suspect that the Mahayana moved from the Theravada by learning from the self sacrifice and the voluntary suffering of Jesus. After all, the Mahayana came after Jesus. Dr. Schopenhauer, you seem to have the *agape* of Luke's Jesus rather than that of Paul or John."

"And Dr. Panikkar, I really appreciate your appreciation of the sacred-secular and of science and Atheism. I know your father was a chemist and I appreciate your genuine openness to not the sacred cow of science, but to a humble, curious, hardworking, playful science. You do really love in such a way that you learn from the Buddhists as did Dr. Schopenhauer. While Kant has an *agape* like Luther's and John's, and Hegel's *agape* is like Augustine's and Paul's, I see yours to be like that of St. Francis and Luke. That is probably why we are here in San Francisco. You explore the periphery and the crossroads of the spiritual territory. Your St. John of the Cross is as much a Buddhist as is the begging St. Francis. Your interpretation emphasized a learning from each other at the crossroads. It takes a special *agape* to learn from others rather than to ignore the other or to appropriate the other." And with that the three friends of the crossroads were ready for desert.

The Priest Functions as a Living Symbol, A Person Ontologically Changed To Mediate in Service, the Mercies of God

Stephen Frost is a man after Panikkar's own heart, the heart that pulsates through the art of his symbolic body. We now begin to see why Raimundo left us with such satisfaction, the satisfaction of bliss-ecstasy-love.

For the sake of mediating God's mercies to mankind Stephen is a wandering-errant- saunterer on a pilgrimage . He is a priest-a Benedictine-a Trappist-a Tantric Buddhist-a Byzantine Monk-a Shaman-a Forest Dweller. He has read Raimundo and studied with him. His vocation has been to cultivate the shift of consciousness into the spiritual with the many methods of mankind. He like

Raimundo is the living embodiment of ecumenism. He has given himself to the masters of each tradition that they might re-plough his embodied unconsciousness in order to bring about shift after shift of consciousness.

With Raimundo, Stephen sees us as living in the fourth stage of human history. We humans have: (1) sought to appease the gods (2) sought to kill the tyrant (3) sought to tame nature (4) and now we seek to be free through meager machines. Are they not each but ploughs? With the Benedictines and Trappists he let the community-the rule-the novice master-the spiritual director cultivate within him not only the spirituality of poverty-chastity-obedience, but especially that of stability. But then his vocation called him away from that very stability into the wanderers way's. He relived history. The Benedictines taught the barbarian hordes the stability of the agricultural way. But with the new urbanization of the 12th century there came the new spirituality of Dominicans-Franciscans-Carmelites-Servites. They learned wandering from the Buddhists just as the Buddhists became Mahayanists after Christ. The spirituality of Raimundo and Stephen has to do with the stability of Montserrat being ploughed under by the play of wandering Troubadours, especially of the Cistercian type. Now they are surfing the net. Meager machines of global communication have succeeded the technology that sought to tame nature.

But these meager machines are mixed blessings and ecumenists like Raimundo and Stephen take it as their challenge to cultivate our embodied consciousness as we use them with a conscience that demands satisfaction for all at the level of bliss-ecstasy-love. But, this demands a creativity of the spirit that is so beyond us that it is satisfying. How could a stable Benedictine become a professional wanderer? How can a Benedictine surf the net? Is not computer communication a threat to monastic stability and silence? What kind of *agape* can go out and learn from other loves even by abandoning its own way. Would *bhakti* or *karuna* do that? Are there different models of *agape*? Some that would encourage such radical ecumenism and some that would not?

Agape: Love that Preserves with Asymmetrical Mutuality: The Flawed Legacy of John's View of Love

William Klassen like Raimundo is a thinker and a scholar of vast proportions. He like Raimundo is also a lover of more than vast proportions. His thinking and his scholarship because of his love have taken him beyond the simple symmetry of proportion. Bill too has lived out what Raimundo calls love's mutual fecundation with the plough and without preservatives. Bill knows that the legacy of *agape* is rich and diverse. It is so mysteriously rich that it cannot fit within an *ethos of logos*. It can only exceed itself within an ethos of glory. It is so frighteningly diverse that it is self contradictory. For the sake of fecundation it ploughs under its own flaws. They must not be preserved. And yet fecundation could only mean that the bitter choke cherries must go through the fecundation process in becoming the sweet preserve of choke cherry jelly. The bitterness lets the jell preserve without preservatives. Bill Klassen focuses on the asymmetry of the mutuality that lets *agape* fecundate. Is it the bitter flaw that preserves love?

The Jesus of Q and Luke loved all especially sinners and enemies. His *agape* was universal. But the Beloved community of John condemned the enemy and did not love Judas. Paul loved gentiles, but he expected them to get over their otherness and become Christians. His apocalyptic Christ was a severe judge and in Pauline communities as well as Johannine communities sinners were to be shunned. Augustine's *City of God* would be an exclusive Johannine community. Luther, who set in motion the flaws of Nygren, would think, with Paul, that faith alone could save.

But Bill ploughs under the flaws of John and Augustine and of Paul and Luther. With Francis and the existential postmodernists he wants to preserve an all inclusive Lukan *agape* that does not shun. And yet it is most of all in terms of Paul's hymn to love that he ploughs under the flaws of John and Paul. I Corinthians 13 shows that love preserves faith and good works and even self-immolation and lets them be the works of love even though by themselves they are nothing. Luther's faith and James' good works and the glorious Indian self immolations are by themselves only vainglorious. But *agape* is the bitter love that lets them last. Jesus' suffering and death for others is asymmetrical. He gives but does not get. He redeems the flaws of others. Without their flaws he need never have become flawed man. Just as Paul through his thorn in the flesh loved others, just as his communities through their thorny, flawed factions could love with Christ's love so William and Raimundo think it necessary not to shun but to love the flawed.

If the Personal Emphasis of Love Is Preserved

Katherine Young continues with Panikkar the dialogue between those who love with *bhakti* and those who love with *agape*. She meditates on the love of Jesus and the love of Antal. Antal was a maiden of the Tamil Nadu tradition, the same from which Panikkar's father came. Panikkar in the dialogue into which Katherine enters throws light on *bhakti* by showing how it can be love even without the dualism which Vedantists avoid. Dualism implies for them individuation, the gulf between the two and the selfishness of each. But persons need not be individuals. Persons can be interpersonal in such a way that the relating precedes the *relata*. Especially in the Tamil tradition the denial of individuals need not mean the denial of the personal and personal love. Both Raimundo and Katherine want to preserve the personal as it is found with Antal and Jesus. The individual can be ploughed under in order that the personal be preserved. That has been the case with Antal's *bhakti*. Vedantists can teach Christians that they must do that. Defining the person as an individual substance of a rational nature is not nearly good enough for *agape* as the Vedantist's *bhakti* shows.

This Tamil poetry with its multiple female voices is great art with a potent and beautiful mix of sex, death and religion just right for fecundation. Antal says: "I could not live if men enjoy my breasts that grow (as I grow up). It would be like a roaming jungle jackal who pollutes the oblations of the forest sages set aside for the celestial gods." From *The Song of Songs* to Origen to Bernard of Clairvaux to St. John of the Cross there has been the image of these flowery breasts kept wholly for him alone. *Agape* is adoration and devotion and what could enkindle its awful reverence more than the secret fruition of this female mystery. *Agape* as adoration like Antal's *bhakti* is composed of a fearful asymmetry. Antal saves herself for him alone. But will he ever come? Mutual fecundation here is not yet reciprocal. She adores asymmetrically. Others are brought to adoration by her asymmetrically.

And yet Katherine argues that Antal is more than a saint. She is a female Jesus figure. She enkindles more than adoration. She dies for justice just as Jesus did. In the situation of arranged marriages she wanted to be Krsna's bride and no one else's. Where there was a lingering but strong caste system she used the hunger strike against the injustices of the mighty institution of arranged marriage and its caste system. She would be Krsna's and no one else's. She rebuked her father that he was a hypocrite for speaking of the love of God, but giving her to a man. The intense pain of separation fueled her love of God and her contempt for God for not coming to take her as He promised. She plaintively addressed her female relatives: "Have you seen the Lord?" They say: "Yes, He is coming." He is coming to bring justice to all young women and to all women and to all lower castes and all outcastes. Her suffering and her death from her holy fast let all who are touched by her be fed with a holy feast. Her spunk aims to energize a system that saps energy.

Katherine even argues that Antal is a Mary figure. Her love is not only a *bhakti* of devoted adoration and a *bhakti* of protest for justice, it is also a *bhakti* of religious bonding. Her love is the flow-line of God's mercy to mankind and of mankind's supplication to God. Antal is not only the adorable virgin, but she is also a nourishing mother like Holy Mother Church. She is in mutual fecundation with Holy Wisdom as a created creatrix of playful delight-a word breath mediatrix-a mirror image radiatrix-a death defying redemptrix. Antal as the spirit and the bride says to us: "Come!" She invites us to adoration-justice-church. She warns us against being a jackal-man and a tyrant-father with a jackal-tyrant God.

Unless the Grain of Wheat Dies

David Goicoechea seeks to better appreciate Raimundo Panikkar's ecumenism by reflecting on how the practise of *agape* develops within the New Testament. *Agape* is not only a fundamental attitude that gives direction to our preferences-feelings-thoughts-words-deeds. It is not only a fundamental attitude that gives direction to our affections, friendships and erotic loves. It is most of all a movement. It is a process of the person's continuous change through the mourning of loss. "Unless the grain of wheat falls into the ground and dies it cannot bring forth new life." We are always dying to the old and awakening to the new. Panikkar's notion of ecumenism is based on this. The person is always in process and the great forms of spirituality cultivate this process through spiritual reading, spiritual direction and spiritual exercises. The person needs to go through spiritual transformations toward a more and more healthy attitude or his or her attitude will become more and more diseased. The question is: "How can each disease be turned into a greater health?" Panikkar's ecumenism is an answer to this question.

Goicoechea shows how *agape* is in process in the New Testament itself. *Agape* is like the grain of wheat that is constantly falling and being ploughed under and bringing forth new life. This process of *agapeic* growth takes place within the first Christian communities as they meet in prayerful conversation. The *agape* of Q is a process. Mark works out the direction of *agape's* process. Matthew sets that process within the movement of the wider ethos of the growing church. Luke gives it a universal and all inclusive ethos beyond horizons. John cultivates it within communities of glorification. Paul cultivated the wheat germ of *agape* in co-operation with the Holy Spirit's energies. Panikkar's ecumenism is rooted right in this process of *agape*. Only through mutual fecundation can there be growth beyond disease and through disease. This fecundation needs the plowing under of the seed. It needs germination from the other which is not easy. This mutual giving to each other is asymmetrical. To emphasize this asymmetry is the gift of *agape*.

Bhakti and *Karuna* are also fundamental attitudes in process. *Karuna* with Heidegger reveals the process of the attitude. *Bhakti* with Derrida reveals the fundamentality of the process. *Agape* with Levinas reveals the historical direction of the fundamental attitude in process. The revealing has to do with glory and the task of glorification. For glory is the manifestation of the unmanifest even in its unmanifestness. Process implies a manifesting revealing connected with a concealing. Glory is the test for love so that as vainglorious it does not succumb to disease. Love is the test for glory so that in its process of revealing-concealing it does not mislead into death without life. Love must be stronger than death or it is not glorious love. Panikkar's ecumenism demands the uneasy asymmetry that believes in interpersonal personhood and preserves it through all of its fallings and underploughings in the worth of its equality and uniqueness.

Relating Without Revealing Is an Artificial Act

Young Chan Ro, who as a student of Panikkar has thought long, hard and deep about his ecumenism, sees it as rooted in the *agape* which is the spontaneous being of God. Jesus revealed God as a dynamic interpersonal becoming that explodes forth in creation-incarnation-reconciliation. This explosion is not emanation. God is a big bang that just keeps banging along giving birth to new beings just as new stars are born. But the birthing is personal. Fecundation has to do with the "dare" of giving. It has to do with the "cum" of togetherness. Panikkar's fecundation is not only rooted in our need for growth, but it is rooted in the very spontaneity who bubbles forth like boiling water giving birth to the new.

Jesus with his *agape* of the good Samaritan and the suffering servant is the glory of God. His twofold *agapeic* loving reveals that fecundating God. God is relational and in process. But relating is mechanical if it does not reveal. It reveals a constant law if it is organic. But if it is personal it reveals the new and the unique. Persons as new are each unique and thus are of equal value under the law of ethics. Jesus with his love revealed the glory of all persons as well as the birds of the air and the lilies of the field. Persons are relational and should reveal each other to each other. That is, mutual fecundation is an obligation given by the interpersonal God of mutual giving. It is unethical to break apart relating and revealing. Any individualistic attitude or activity is vainglorious. We should live in a way that we want revealed and that we can reveal.

Spontaneity is especially dear to the Taoist and the Zen Buddhist. Young Chan Ro stresses it in order to bring out an important feature of *agape-bhakti-karuna* and the fecundation within each and between each. Dogen said: "If you want to obtain a certain thing, you must first be a certain man. Then obtaining that certain thing won't be a concern of yours any more." Of course, you will obtain it better that way. That is always the point of the Taoist-to succeed by not directly trying to succeed. We have to be a certain person, that is, get our attitude just right. We need to get the attitude of unconditional-sacrificial-creative love and then without concern all will be taken care of. The right attitude is one of fecundation that relates and reveals. That should happen with spontaneity. The lack of spontaneity is artificiality. Panikkar said that he got himself ready before his presentation. He did not worry about getting his talk ready right then. He had been doing that for a long time. He was getting ready for spontaneous fecundation as Young Chan Ro describes it.

Triangultion or Triadic Fecundation

Scott Eastham who has had a near thirty year bonding with Panikkar as student-translator-editor-friend makes clear the deep triadic logic of Panikkar's ecumenical mission-practise-theory. Besides revealing the triadic logic of Panikkar which takes him beyond the logic of non-contradiction emphasized by the ancients (Plato and his) and the logic of contradiction emphasized by the moderns (Hegel and his) to the postmodern logic of the paradox, Eastham offers a very helpful summary of the historical unfolding of Panikkar's thinking. Panikkar moved step by step to-through-with his all inclusive third logic which took him beyond the monistic law of the jungle and the dualistic jungle of the law to the jingle-jangle-jungle of a new rhythm of an omni-triangulation that prevents strangulation. Eastham presents the three step rhythm of Panikkar's journey as follows:

> bridging the gap between traditional ways of knowing and modern science taking ecumenism beyond its in-house Christian varieties to the unknown Christ of Hinduism reaching out from the religious atheism of Buddhism to the secular atheism of the West toward a sacred secularism studying the triadic symbolism of Christian-Hindu religiosity studying the rules of the game in

> the dialogical theatre studying for the modern reader the religious experience of the vedas meditating on truth from within as the inter-religious challenge meditating on peace from within as the inter-cultural challenge meditating on ecology from within as the global challenge. Finally, as an epilogue Panikkar loves wisdom, not as the opposite of folly, but as the opposite of polymathy.

This map that Scott provides with its three sets of three and its threefold epilogue suggests the flow of this volume. First, we can observe just as in Raimundo's thinking an unfolding of *bhakti* then of *karuna* and then of *agape*. Then we can question the mutuality of their mutual fecundation. Mutuality-reciprocity-symmetry may seem like synonyms. But does not *agape* force upon us the primacy and ultimacy of asymmetry? Emmanuel Levinas has demonstrated clearly the asymmetry of suffering-servant responsibility. Buddhist enlightenment may plough under atman-Brahman-substance-individuality, but as Raimundo shows *agape* demands that the notion of personhood be preserved. Mutual fecundation is an activity of asymmetrical relating between interpersonal persons in process. Would the ecumenism of mutual fecundation have any urgency without *agape*? Would it not be greatly lacking in ardor without *bhakti*? Would it not fall into the traps of substance and causality without *karuna*?

Mutual Fecundation

Bhakti-Karuna-Agape: An Inter-Cultural Challenge

Raimundo Panikkar

Generally, introductions are made to make it easy for the speaker. Tonight he makes this difficult because he has raised such high expectations that we are bound to be able to find just a simple man, sharing with you his doubts, his anxieties, his love. My role tonight is not to read a paper, but to deliver a lecture. This means that I have been preparing myself more than preparing what I have to say. The paper is an organized system of words conveying a sort of meaning. A lecture, I think, has to betray the speaker, and I say betray, because in spite of the screen that he, himself/herself has made, he has to come forth out of silence, fear, arrogance, ambition or vanity. But all these come through.

I should try to begin by saying that what I would like to say will remain unsaid to all. It all depends on you, on your sympathy—*karuna,* how I am going to succeed in conveying the title which was only for me, because the title for you was different. For me, it's an intellectual challenge indeed. The official title, which through electronic media gets sometimes confused, because artificial intelligence is only artificial and nothing else was *Bhakti Karuna, Agape: An Intercultural Challenge*. I would like to stick to the intercultural challenge, which has to do WITH a Buddhist Chinese saying that in rough translation says: "They are not words which allow man to understand." Professor Inada might tell us the original source of this. We must prior to words become a man in order to understand the words. In old classical languages these words are not sexist. "Man" stands for the human being throughout and I would like to say man and not human being. Most classical languages have not fallen into the procession of defining things and putting everyone into one compartment or another. When I want to evidate my theological beliefs a little, I say that if you want to kill Christianity, make of it a religion of the book. Christianity is an original word not a book. The word is a word when it is spoken by somebody to someone saying something with some material: voice, ways, matters.

Now to speak about love is as difficult and contradictory as to speak about silence. Silence does not speak but lets the word emerge as in the saying: "If your words are not more valuable than silence, shut up." Love does not speak either, but impulses the words to appear. The words are only vagal to something different. If I say: "I love you, j'a vous." It's nothing. If my heart is full and I look into your eyes and you feel that there is something there, "I love you" is an original word which has never been said before. So I would like to ask you to have this kind of new innocence, to try, well, to re-enact, to understand the topic of this presentation. The real word, I said, comes out of silence, and is threatening with love when it is a real word and not just a sign, an arrow—not a living symbol. Any living symbol has a relative power. Otherwise, it is only information. Now my topic then will be this cross-cultural or intercultural challenge between these three rich notions crystallized in these three words which are the title of this beautiful lecture series.

Let me begin. If I am successful, I would like to stick to my sacred nummery—nine points which I would like to sum up or that I would like to convey. The first point is that the three words are irreducible, in a certain way incomparable. Once I have said that there is still the temptation and I befall to it to use love as a synonym for the three. But to do this is an impoverishment of the human experience. In a harsh sense it would produce the three universes which breathe through these three words into one single notion. One needs two eyes to have a bifocal perception of the physical things. One needs three eyes to be in real contact with reality. And the third eye is not just an invention of the present day diaspora Lamas of Tibet. The third eye, as some of you will know, was the most normal thing of the Victorines in the 12th century, who spoke of the third eye without which reality is flat, monocolored and lifeless. To be attentive to the many dimensions I have developed the notion of *homeomorphic equivalence* which is a kind of third order analogy. In this case *agape, bhakti* and *karuna* are equivalent homeomorphically. They are not the same in their meaning and force. On the other hand *agape, karuna, bhakti* are not like saying *elephant, psycho* and *post office*. So they have something. But they do not have the same thing and not even a similar thing as is seen in the third degree analogy. They are performing in respective universes a role which is equivalent. A simple example, before I get to my topic, would have to do with *Brahman* and *God*. When you read Brahman, do you translate God? That would be a very bad, faulty translation. But you cannot translate Brahman as a piece of paper or God as a commander. They are not the same. Brahman is neuter. God is masculine. God cares. Brahman couldn't care less, etc., etc. One is creator. The other doesn't need to create, etc. So, they are not similar. They don't even perform the same function. They perform an equivalent function within respective universes each of which is felt to be unified by its own kind of reverence or whatever you want to call it. *Bhakti, karuna, agape* are homeomorphic equivalents. They are not simply three different notions of one and the same thing.

When speaking with philosophers I am not confused. As Professor Inada did this morning we can speak of an underlying Platonism in the West. We can speak of the modern mind as crypto-Kantian. Crypto-Kantianism thinks of the thing in itself as there. And at the same time it thinks of it as nominal. We say one thing and another. I think the same thing is here. Then I displace it and think it does not exist in itself. If you simply believe all the paths leading to the mountain then the mountain will collapse. The way you go is part of the reality and not an abstract thing over there. Then you call it *karuna*. You say you are meaning love. Then you call it *bhakti* and I say I know what you mean. No, you need the third eye to respect and allow things to be what they are.

There are not three different notions, but three different symbols of three different universes. That is very hard to re-enact when since for four or five centuries the dominant civilization of the world has been crypto-Kantianist. That brings us to make believe that from one single perspective we can embrace the wide range of the human spirits. That is frivolous to say the least and phenomenologically speaking it is using a politically heavy word—colonialism. Colonialism is not a bad thing. The colonialist people were highly respectable and had the best intentions and the best everything. Colonialism is the belief in a mono-culturalism of man, that with one single culture we can do everything. And the symbols stick more forcefully than just concepts. If I would say: "one king, one empire, one God" that's *passé*. Now we say: "one world government, one world bank, one world market, one United Nations" and we fall into the same trap. This need not mean anarchy. Perhaps, it could mean more freedom and respect for the uniqueness of every single being. If the single being is unique then it is incomparable. If it is incomparable then that is its value.

There are three different universes. *Agape* is mainly monotheistic – mainly. It is mainly the experience that God loves us. The initiative comes from the divine. You have the feeling that you are loved and that you are capable to respond, to re-create, to enter into that beautiful bride imaginary of which we heard some beautiful examples this morning in Tamil literature. God loves you. He takes the initiative for you. You allow yourself to be loved. And by this allowance you are purified. And then you respond in the most passionate ways to his love which may have human or not human figures and incarnations, but which is that which leads the individual with affection. God loves us first and then we can understand how to use our "love your God with all your heart and all your soul and all your strength," without analyzing what heart, soul and strength mean. And without this mono-theistic, explicit or implicit, idea *agape* is not totally understandable.

Bhakti belongs to a different universe. To use words of English origin, and if the medical profession can do that without sounding preposterous so can philosophers, notwithstanding all of that we can say that we love him as part of him, as his sparks. We are sparks of the play of the divine and we take part as partners. And we don't need to say who loves first. You enter into the loving dance. You belong to one of the movements of Nataraja and you respond accordingly. We love him because he loves us and the two are on the same level. The ignorant say that love and God are different, not knowing that they are the same. When they know that love and God are the same, they rush to God as love.

Karuna is more cosmic. It implies a universal sympathy. It is not individualizable and not personifiable either. *Karuna* is, let me put this way of translating it, the revelation of the loveliness of everything and it is up to you to discover the radiant, hidden plans that, perhaps because you are in a hurry or selfish or full of desire, you were not able to detect, to discover and to fall in the sympathy with everything.

Tempted as I am to make a more detailed analysis and to get a lot of Greek and Sanskrit words, and give a whole list and make classifications that would not classify everything, I would rather introduce us into the mystery conveyed by these three holy and sacred words. So I will avoid the temptation of more analysis and instead go further in the general presentation of love as a formal concept embracing the main experiences behind the riches of these three religions, three universes within which you can make all the necessary distinctions. *Bhakti* is not prema. *Philia* is not *agape* etc. Incidentally, the kiss of which we heard this morning is in Greek *philema* from *philia* and *philanthropia.* Within each universe there are a number of distinctions. The *bhakti* of one tradition in India is not the *bhakti* of another. I will use the word "love" in a formal way which tries more or less to stand for this triple, the three-fold and almost infinite division which humanity and our ancestors have had when using these words.

We find a certain type of general aspect which I would like to underline when I speak of inter-cultural fecundation which is not multi-culturalism. Multi-culturalism is the word which is officially used in Canada. But with all due respect I would like to challenge this notion. Quebec is proud to be a multi-cultural society. I don't think a society can be multi-cultural. "I am multi-cultural and you have only one single culture. You poor man. What do you know? I am, I mean I have the control of everything. We, the multi-cultural fellows, are above all the anti-cultural fellows. We are multi-cultured because we stand above everything. We have made of this multi-culture another culture which is perhaps even more empirical and more dangerous than all the other little ones which are satisfied only with their uni-culture." What we have today, however, his inter-culturality which means that no culture today stands alone. No man is an island. We cannot be satisfied with the pleasure of a splendid isolation, with a wretched solitude. We need cross-cultural fecundation. We need to learn from one another. We have to be open to the lessons of the other. It may very well be that another culture cannot teach us anything. But it is imperative for us to learn from the other one. The burden is on the learner and the responsibility is not on the teacher. It is the disciple that makes the guru and not the guru who picks up the learner. And whom do I teach? I think we have these experiences all over the world today.

Inter-culturality means and lives through this mutual fecundation of cultures which is imperative for hard times. But allow me, as we are now here in a very sympathetic room, to say that I feel that there are still a lot of cultural preservatives which impede this mutual fecundation. So fecundation would be the plough and not the preservatives. And the preservatives are: "Well I am better than you. I have a bigger part in truth that you. I am more or less more developed." It is a sign of Western hubris in the political world today to think of three quarters of the world population as underdeveloped. We wonder how these people have the guts to call the others underdeveloped. When we wanted to correct this we called it "on the way to development." "On the way." Ah, be satisfied. "On the way to development." You have all those computers and artificial intelligence and you come to bankruptcy because the debt of the United States is three times more than the debt of all the other nations of the world together. But as for credit and atom bombs, we go on playing the game—"on the way to development." If the world became like the developed world in seven years the planet would be barren. If the world should consume the amount of paper that the developed world does in two years no single tree would be left on the planet. You know the situation of the atom bomb in the Himalayas.

But think of love. Love is not just the passing acceptance of family. Love is passion. And passion can ultimately challenge you. Mutual fecundation is the conveyance of learning. Let us now try to describe briefly and in elementary fashion some of the features that concur in the three kinds of love without entering into an analysis of any of them. First of all, I think that the three traditions or groups of traditions as presented by these three words consider love as central and basic. It is not an accident that *agape* stands or falls with Christianity. You take *karuna* from Buddhism and Buddhism collapses. You eliminate *bhakti* and Hinduism may set things out but they get scribbled in a very serious way. So the loves are basic. They are not accidental. They are not something which you can have or not have. They are not there because you love this or that person, because it is better for your digestion. No, no, no! The central or basic love, sympathy or whatever it is for the three traditions or groups of traditions, presents the three universes to this world.

It is more. Love is ultimate and that's a challenge. It is an intellectual challenge if you want to use the unintended word. But it is much more. If it is not ultimate then love has no life. Love has no meaning. There would be meaning only from something behind love. That meaning would then be more ultimate than love. If someone asks: "Why do you love me?" and you cannot give an answer then your love is finished. If I say "I love you because you are young" then that will not last. If I say "I love you because you are rich" then the rest of you is not so valuable. If I say "I love you because you are good" then what happens when I get irritated. "I love because." It is not "because." Respond to goodness, health, intelligence, service, etc., but love me. There is no "why?" Love is the ultimate meaning. The question for the meaning of life is a loveless question. It destroys love by the very fact that it asks for something beyond the ultimate. We sometimes lack intellectual humility. Its like asking your wife everything. Its like sending stuff to the Buddha that he might give us a favor when it may not be good for us, when he may have better things in store for us. Brother you cannot ask for that because you don't know what you are asking. You don't know the limits of the question. If you do not know what you ask you had better keep silent. Love has no why. It is nothing beyond itself. It is irreducible to other values. It is irreducible to humility. It is meaninglessness and sometimes we are scandalized by meaninglessness because we approach reality only with cold reason and a lifeless intellect. Sometimes young people and sentimentalists ask: why? But love has no why? That's why something else does not motivate it. That's why it's free. There is no reason for love because reality, as we heard this morning, does not need to be teleological. It's self motivated. There is not a motivation behind. It's the ultimate force. You need a poet to say: "Love moves the sun and all the other stars."

Third feature. Love is a centrifical force in the universe and in the human being. It's a dynamic aspect of reality. Love is centrifical. It goes, jumps, embraces, kisses, hates, goes out, does not let you be reduced to yourself. I am reminded about the professor's talk this morning about the narcissus myth. But love is dynamic, centrifical, does not stop at you, does not move with you, discovers something beyond, maybe your own self even that is over there. Love pushes you, drags you, pulls you. Maybe that is why

Aristotle would say that the prime mover is the *Eromenon*. As the erotically beloved it attracts everything. Eros is something that loves and attracts. There is a great temptation in the East and in the West to place love on the second level because love does not allow any reduction to the mono-lithic doing. In order to love you need, I'm not going to say to split, you need the complexity of reality. You need the other as other and non- as other. Let me put forth just a simple example for the philosophers. Fichte, Schelling and undoubtedly Hegel and all idealists discovered the power of the I. But from there to Marx is only a simple step. He puts in front of it the not. They posit the I. He posits the not-I. But they forget something which even philologists should know. To me it is a sign of the times that most of the languages, more than languages, have forgotten an extraordinarily rich revelation of human wisdom. And that is the dual. The dual is not singular and not pluralized. The dual is the grammatical experience of the *Tao*. The *Tao* is not the non-I and it is not the I. The *Tao* is neither the non-I, the thing or *esse* as they say, but the *Tao* is part and parcel of the very I when the I is completed. The I can really say I when it discovers its I immersed in the words, in the love of the *Tao* and vice-versa. What I am saying I can put in different language. Love is not inferior to knowledge. The dichotomy between love and knowledge has been lethal for many a tradition. Lethal because it has reduced love to sentimentalism, to passion, to promotion, to a certain type of intuition and liking and disliking and the intellect to a cutting instrument. But as Tagore says using the words of the poet: "A man of intellect alone is like a knife without a handle. It wounds the hand of the person who uses it." Love and knowledge belong together so that if there is not knowledge there is not love and if there is not love there is not knowledge. It is not that one is the ingredient of the other. They are constitutively and inherently the same human, basic experience. You are able to be inasmuch as you receive and you are able to receive inasmuch as you are ready to be. If love is centrifical, knowledge is centrifical. The two belong together. You cannot be exhausted in just loving if your love is full of intellect. And you cannot be exhausted by just receiving if love is also there because you transmit what you have and have received.

The highest love is the highest knowledge within all these three positions. And the highest knowledge is the highest love. There is not one without the other. This is not only psychological. It is much more basic and radical. You cannot really know without the other. If you go to the *Upanishads* or wherever, you find that to know is to become what you know. Both are integral parts to one and the same fundamental human act by which the human being is renewed and by which every being is built up.

Love is a saving power whatever we may mean by the word salvation. It leads to mukti, to moksa, to nirvana. It leads to heaven, to beatific vision, to fulfillment of one's life. Love has an intrinsic saving and liberating power. It gets rid of all fear and anxiety. Here again the three traditions in their corresponding ways tell us about this power that saves us. This goes against the grain of our modern civilization. It is independent of our way. We think that by willpower we can love. We think that by conviction we can get love. So we make a nuisance of ourselves and give others a hard time. If love is not spontaneous, it is not love.

If love is not for the sake of the other it is not love. One of the most important and healthy aspects of the Western population is the nuns. Sociologically speaking the nuns are one of the healthiest groups in the Western world. But, when I meet with them, I tell them, well you see little sister, all that you do for sweet Jesus will not count for you in any way. It has no value for you whatsoever. Only what you do not for the sake of Jesus, but for the sake of this wretched fellow to whom you give a glass of water, or for a real friend to whom you give five minutes of your conversation, or for that one to whom you offer a smile, only that counts and for him. Not what you do for Jesus, or for God. Spontaneity, not will. It is not through the I. Capitalism doesn't enter here. When pressed for a very important, more academic word for gift it is grace, prasada, ruah, etc. Love has to be a gift. It has to be given to you. When you are given that gift you feel important to love. You cannot command it. It either comes or it doesn't come. If you have a pure heart it flows without asking why, without saying "For the sake of Jesus, for the sake of God, for the sake of whatever." It sometimes works that for the sake of my career, my prestige, my ambition, I do good things and I end up sad. Unless my left hand does not know what the right hand has done then it was just propaganda. When love asks for such and such then there is no love. Life, knowledge and love go together. They are self-motivating. They have no why. They have no reason. They don't stand under the will to power, our power and our will. We are important. We are like children whose is the kingdom.

Today, the three are intermingling in the modern world and I would like slowly to recite a passage of a person quoted this morning, the Dalai Lama. When in 1993, there were the long lasting horrible things in Bombay, the Dalai Lama gave a message reproduced in the newspapers. I quote from the Indian papers, "undiscriminative, spontaneous and unlimited compassion for all sentient beings. This is obviously not the usual love that one has for friends or family which is alive with desire, attachment and ignorance. The kind of love we should advocate is this wider love that you can have even for someone who has done you harm, your enemy." If I would not have said the author of these lines, probably many of you would have said this was a Christian saying or a gospel or that it is pure *bhakti*. Even for your enemy. A love which is not aligned he says with desire, attachment and ignorance, which again falls in with the classic distinction that there are two loves.

The Latin Mediaevals had a beautiful expression that love recoils; that it does not go straight. When I am proud of you there is selfishness. Take care. This beautiful sentence, untranslatable I think into English unless one makes it a long paragraph can be distorted. We approach it trying to say that we haven't forgotten the history of the world. And when in St. Catharines we recall Katerina of Sienna. Here is an Italian, untranslatable idiom that bears on the recoiling love: "In you, I think of you. But to think of you means I care for you." That is love and that means that love is inseparable from the feelings of being love. Otherwise, there is no love. It's not one-way traffic. Love is the opening which goes the two ways.

Now this leads me to the contemporary challenge. I said that *agape* implies the supremacy of the divine, that *bhakti* and *karuna* are cosmic, more or less. In our present day we have, I was going to say an epitome, I retract it—I don't want to be nasty. I will say that we have an ingrained self-understanding of every one of us as separated individuals, individualism. That's why love has been degraded, either to gratification or to psychological models or to erotic options or to a second degree of things which lead to your fulfilment, which leads you to feeling better. That is neither *karuna* nor *agape* nor *bhakti*. That may be selfishness, that may be a desire for self-fulfilment or that may be simply individualism. That's why these words of the Dali Lama say that just discriminately to love, with attachment and desire and ignorance is not the love which we need to live in peace and to live fully. It is not a self-centered love. It's not individualistic love. These lead to anger. That is certainly not *agape*, not *bhakti*, not *karuna*.

Now, is it not true that we have a certain innate resistance in the contemporary world toward universal love? This morning an important question arose which was not sufficiently taken care of. How can I have an indiscriminative love? Would I not be inhuman if I felt that my child would be different from any other child in the world who is dying? And here, the middle way is needed. If I am incapable of loving in this universal way, my love for my child would be a selfish attachment which could give me some little pleasures, but certainly afterwards much friction and many headaches. Many bad things will happen because the child is not going to live up to my standards or what I would like him to be. To combine the total universal love with the concrete love, that is wisdom. And wisdom is the inside that discovers in the concrete in my child all the children of the world; in my wife, in my husband, the entire manhood and womanhood of the world; in that flower, the infinite beauty of the entire creation; in that conversation, all the gusto of being.

If we do not live up to this kind of insight and experience then the last step will be like the one before it. Then everything is a telos, then everything is final, definite. If everything is not irreducible and incomparable, then we have lost love in our lives and we reduce ourselves to thinking machines. I must say that I feel that one of our most important tasks, and we are here in a philosophical room for philosophy, is to re-introduce love into the so-called external world. I don't want to go now into epistemology. I think epistemology is the wrong thing, but that is another question. When love is seen as an intrinsic part of knowledge then knowledge is put in its own place, because you feel that the union with the known is never ended, never fulfilled, because the very nature of reality is polarity, is love, is this moment. If we re-integrate love with knowledge, we would overcome the gap of subject and object in epistemology which otherwise cannot be overcome. Love is trinitarian, neither one nor two. It is the very experience of the warp and woof of the very nature of reality. This for me, is the cross-cultural challenge, to overcome our individualism. Then we can discover through experience the way that love permeates us. We can discover that this love and knowledge to quote *The Gita* are precisely two aspects of this complex, fantastic, beautiful reality.

Transcribed from a recording by David Goicoechea

Bhakti

Bhakti: The Twine in the Spectrum

Debabrata Sinha

When Blaise Pascal observed, "The knowledge of God is very far from the love of Him,"[1] he was already hinting at the way of "the heart" over the way of "reason" in his universe of discourse. Should that necessarily imply a juxtaposition of the two—i.e., reason and knowledge, on the one hand and love and faith on the other? Or does it simply mean a submission to the truism of human nature in its tendency to believe and to love, independent of the question of truth value with regard to the objects to which they are directed—a point, by the way, also hinted by Pascal. Whatever may be the outcome of the issue, irrespective of Pascal we are here envisaging a dimension of human experience (and edification) which, though diversely embedded in and through varied culture traditions, is yet distinctively characterized by the predominant thrust of the heart. In speaking of *bhakti* (or the *bhakti* tradition) we refer presumably to that dimension as it has come to be typified across a broad and rich spectrum within the folds of the Indic tradition at large.

Picking up from the panorama of India's religio-philosophic-*cum*-literary tradition relating to the broad-based perspective of *bhakti*, let us start by citing—not necessarily in any historical order—a mediaeval mystic named Kabir.

> Oh my heart! the Supreme Spirit, the Great master, is near you: wake, oh wake! Run to the feet of your Beloved: for your Lord stands near to your head. You have slept for unnumbered ages; this morning will you not wake?[1]

This is just one of the gems from the hundreds of Hindi songs (or rather hymns) of Kabir, born a so-called low caste weaver (of Muslim origin) in 15th century India; his devotional songs have been sung through all these centuries, and even today are among the most favorites of devotional music in India. Also it is interesting to note that the translation of the original poem just cited was done by the poet of modern India, Rabindranath Tagore. Spanning over the centuries, Tagore, it seems, expresses in essence a comparable sentiment or perception in a profoundly aesthetic mode in many of his verses and lyrics and songs—some thousands of them composed by him in Bengali. To cite, as an example, from one of those:

> Yes, I know, this is nothing but thy love,
> O beloved of my heart—this golden light
> that dances upon the leaves,
> those idle clouds sailing across the sky,
> this passing breeze leaving its coolness
> upon my forehead.
> The morning light has flooded my eyes—
> this is thy message to my heart.
> Thy face is bent from above,
> thy eyes look down on my eyes,
> and my heart has touched thy feet.

At this point one could wonder: aren't these two instances—Kabir and particularly Tagore—much too aesthetically oriented to exemplify the typical mode that is *bhakti*? To respond quickly, in Kabir's case, he uses the simplest metaphors from everyday life of the common people. He appeals to needs, passions, relations which all men understood—such as the bridegroom and the bride, the guru and the disciple, the pilgrim, the farmer, the migrant bird, and so on—in order to drive home his intense faith in the reality of the soul's intercourse with the Divine. However, it is not exactly my concern here to dwell on Kabir or on Tagore as such, but to focus, through these preliminary illustrations, on what I consider to be a significant dimension and issue in the many-splendoured spectrum that is encapsulated by that one word *bhakti*.

Now to come back to the general question just posed: What is the essence of *bhakti*? How to understand its distinctive character—unless, of course, the term gets lost as a buzzword which can mean anything and nothing? In the first instance, it is a *praxiological* concept—one that is embedded in the life-praxis permeating the cultural milieu of the Indian humanity, and now far extending its original ethno-geographic borders. True its modus operandi has been bafflingly heterogeneous, infinitely complex and richly diversified. The said praxiological mode meets and combines at various levels, explicitly or implicitly, myths, symbols and legends drawn from Hindu mythology. But along with the mythico-ritual orientation, the theological (or rather, onto-theological) and metaphysical perspectives have had considerable role to play in widely divergent but yet closely interacting ramifications. However, even behind the apparent straightjackets of the respective religio-philosophical systems and creeds, we can find a broad-based stratum that lends itself to be hermeneutically identified, as we proceed to explore the area, tangled as it may appear to be, generally in a phenomenological mode of inspection.

But to put the whole tradition of *bhakti* in perspective, we have at this point to flash back to the early stage of the *Upanishads* to trace the distant origins of this cluster of ideas that *bhakti* stands for (a ride on the time-machine, as it were, through the millennia of cultural history.) In one of the principal but relatively later *Upanishad*, viz. *Svetasvatara*, we come across a couple of verses as follows:

> Aspirant for liberation (*moksa*), I am taking refuge in that Supreme Being, who is of the nature of self-effulgent consciousness. Taking recourse to that Supreme Godhead, who is without parts, transcendent, changeless and tranquil, totally unaffected, the highest bridge to Immortality, who is like the glowing flame.

One who has some acquaintance with the *Upanishads* would recognize here a different note in the centrally dominant thrust of the *Upanishads* altogether for *Jnana*, i.e., 'Knowledge' in the sense of spiritually enlightened integral understanding of the Self, nay of the nature of things and beings in their Totality. Call it *Atman* in the self language, call it *Brahman* in the language of the Absolute, the principle of all principles has been commonly referred to in impersonal terms rather than the personal *per se*—that is, in terms of "That" or "It" etc., and even verging on the totally "Indeterminate." In other words, it is the language of Reality that tends to prevail in respect of the ultimate source of things, which grounds and sustains all, but is *per se* Ineffable.

Yet at the same time we can hardly overlook that the *Upanishadic* Absolute has also been referred to as "He." So there is this rather indefinite usage of "It," "That," "He" in indicating Supreme reality. In fact, if we glance a step further back into that massive storehouse of the *Rig-Veda*, we find *Brahman* had been addressed as the "Father," as the "Mother," as the friend. The ancient Vedic mind does not show any sign of being inhibited by monotheistic rigidities. On the other hand, the *Vedic-Upanishadic* drive for the One ("That One," as it says) need not too easily be branded as "monistic" in an abstract speculative sense either—Parmenidean or otherwise. Irrespective of the attempted characterizations of this pre-classical pre-system era—monistic, pantheistic or even "paentheistic"—the most crucially significant point is the equation of Self and the Absolute (*Atman* and *Brahman* as equivalent), of the subject principle that is finite but most intimately inward and the World-ground that is Infinite, though putatively outward.

This brings us to the dynamics of religious experience in its phenomenological roots—I mean phenomenology not in a rigid Husserlian sense of fixing apriorities. Rather what is in view is a more flexible approach in opening up to what presents itself back within the stratum of experience, as far as the latter could lend itself to description, and further to a deeper (hermeneutic) understanding. Thus two originary demands have to be taken into account—which may otherwise be viewed as two interactive aspects of the same ideal component. (a) The need of the striving mind for *concrete* reality—the "metaphysical demand," as Kierkegaard might call it, for concrete reality. To put it conversely, the mind is no longer satisfied with an abstract principle of theoretic reflection to be speculatively posited as the ultimate ground of being. The mind demands at some point of intuitive reflection a deeper equation of the highest principle of being with the underlying truth (or truths) of the realities of life-world. (The concreteness attributed to the notion of "Concrete Universal" in the Hegelian panlogistic system, for example, would not meet with this said demand.) (b) Coming to the other component within this original drive for the source of things, we could hardly fail to notice the demand of consciousness to *relate*. What I mean here is not exactly *connecting* facts and events into uniformities of rules and laws, leading on to higher unities, in terms of which individual facts can be interpreted. Relating here goes beyond the purely cognitive attitude of understanding things in their dissociated contexts, where one can have, and sometimes obliged to have, a value-neutral emotively indifferent attitude towards the object. There is a felt need to be *involve*d in an *existential* manner with the contemplated reality—that is, with the whole being of our person. And such relationship—at whatever level of human experience, whether in regard to ordinary realities of life-world or to higher contemplative insights—would be possible only in respect of the real viewed as concrete, and not just in terms of "bloodless categories."

These two correlative demands that inherently condition the search for the ultimate and unconditioned Source of things and beings—the *Arche*, the *Nous*, as the Greeks would have called it—may give us a clue to the move that the *Upanishadic* mind tends to take, as illustrated in the quote. But the very logic of the drive, it seems, pushes on further towards the shaping of a more definite focus. And that is the focus which eventually found its formulation in the broad-based concept of *bhakti*. The word came to signify the attitude of devotion or devotional love towards the godhead. The polysemic etymology of the root *bhaj*, however—like many Sanskrit terms—offers a significant range of correlated meanings, some of which contribute towards the profoundly rich connotation of the concept in its eventual orientation. Thus, importantly enough—besides loving faith or worshipful adoration, the root also bears the meanings of (a) "taking resort to," (b) "to bestow" and (c) "to share with." All these elements, as I will try to indicate, go to constitute the many-faceted complex that is called *bhakti.*

It was with the *Bhagavadgita,* the next significant landmark (i.e., after the *Upanishadic* era) in the evolution of the religio-philosophical culture of ancient India, that the transition from the *jnana*-oriented *moksa*-centered climate of the *Upanishads* to the central recognition of *bhakti* made itself felt. What lay somewhat ambivalent behind the *Brahman-Atman* language of the *Upanishads* came into fore-front—though not at all in exclusion of the former *jnana*-drive, but rather in inclusive harmony with it. (In fact, even the *Svetasvatara Upanishad*, in its very concluding verse, does use the word "*bhakti,*" in emphasizing the necessity of genuine devotion to the Supreme Being (as well as to guru) for obtaining higher enlightenment. Thanks to the corpus of literature called the *Bhagavata*—centering around the myths of Krishna, the Divine Incarnation (*Avatara*)—the epic scenario was set for the *Gita* to introduce the theme of *bhakti.*

There, in the *Gita,* we come upon the pair of interrelated elements which crucially mark the attitude of devotion to God incarnate in the person of SriKrishna, the Supreme Person (*Purusottama*). On the one hand, total surrender or resignation to godhead is insisted upon; on the other hand, as the necessary counterpart, the element of favour (*prasada*)—or call it "grace," as in Christian theology—on the part of god to the devotee. The one cardinal statement of the *Gita* runs as follows:

> Abandoning all duties (*dharmas*), take me and me alone (that is, Srikrishna) as the resort; I will deliver you from all failings and miseries, so do not grieve.[2]

In this final appeal to Arjuna, the representative man, by Krishna, his friend, philosopher and guide in the actual world of living (and fighting too), the apex of *bhakti* is crystallized in the note of total unconditional self-giving, with the assurance of faith in the elevation of the spirit. No wonder many of the theistic (*Vaish-nava*) schools of Vedanta - like Ramanuja and others—look upon this verse as the very final note of the whole text (i.e., *Gita*).

However, keeping in view the total perspective of the *Gita* very much as a work of *synthesis*, we have to remind ourselves that the said *bhakti* is not put forward as a pathway in exclusion of the pathway of knowledge (*jnana-yoga*), nor of *Karma*, but rather as the alternative approach which is necessarily complementary at the same time. After all, it is the enlightened devotee (*jnani-bhakta*) who is most extolled, rather than a simple infatuated *bhakta*.

It is this interface between the two fundamental attitudes of the mind—*bhakti* and *jnana*—that poses a challenging issue in an in-depth understanding of the *bhakti* mode itself. In the non-dualistic (*advaita*) framework of Sankara's *Vedanta*, to take a conspicuous example, *bhakti*, it may appear, finds a rather secondary place in the overall centrally dominant accent on *jnana*—liberation (*moksa*) being understood entirely in terms of integral apprehension of the Self-essence (*atman*). Sankara concedes to *bhakti* only a subservient instrumental role in the purification of the aspiring mind in its onward progression towards the highest goal. To know the truth of one's being would be the only way to attain spiritual freedom, and the discipline primarily lies in the way of Knowing, and secondarily that of willing (i.e., *karma*) and feeling (i.e., *bhakti*). But the position, often formally so stated, need not be considered the whole truth about the Advaitic spirituality, as we would presently see, but rather the half-truth!

It would be appropriate at this point to take a quick look at the allied world of Buddhist thought and culture—especially in the Mahayana (Sanskritic, and subsequently, Tibetan) tradition of Buddhism. For there we could notice conspicuously a compresence of the two elements of Wisdom (*prajna*) and Compassion (*karuna*). Of these the latter definitely signifies the dimension of devotional love in a tradition which had originally been oriented to the predominant ideal of Enlightenment (*nirvana*). But even in early Buddhism, where spirituality came to be defined in terms of a profoundly based psychological ethics, *karuna* was not at all a stranger. For it was counted as one of the four components constituting the ideal state of a perfectly edified mind (*brahmavihara*)—along with friendliness, endurance and indifference. But with the introduction of the notion of *Bodhisattva*, who incarnates Enlightenment and yet goes beyond it in the exercise of infinite love and compassion for the redemption of all beings moving in the cyclic orbits of suffering (*dukkha*)—there was a giant move towards the *bhakti* fold. But while in its praxiological intent Mahayana tends to be theistic (not in a strict doctrinaire sense of theism though)—or rather, polytheistic in its worship of the pantheon of divinities (gods, goddesses, *bodhisattvas* etc.), its ontology of the Absolute as totally uncategorisable (*sunya*) is worked out mainly through a negative dialectic.

To take a closer look again into the Vedantic model, devotional worship that constitutes religion in practice, is, on the one hand, pushed back to the practical-pragmatic level of nescience (*avidya*) in the general ontological scheme. But, on the other hand, it is recognized to be an aid, a valuable aid, in the preparation for higher illumination. For it helps in the formation of that inner attitude and frame of mind with which the aspiring subject can plunge into the spiritual quest *per se*. But further, it is more than a means of preparation; it constitutes the quest itself. For with progressive transparency of the mind effected through the discipline, the innermost essence would shine in, though not necessarily in the intellectual way. The knowledge in the context of spiritual freedom is spiritual being in its totality, rather than the detached consciousness of a spectator. After all, *bhakti,* in the best of its tradition as drawn from the *Upanishads,* indicates *upasana,* i.e., intense focusing of the mind on the highest object of adoration; and as such, it essentially serves as the *bridge* to that forward movement of the soul. We are in a way reminded at this point of the notion of "Intellectual love of God" (*Amor Dei intellectualis*) in Spinoza's philosophy—a conjunction of knowledge and love of God together as the highest good and the highest virtue.

The transition sought for could best be envisaged as enlightened faith, rather than as the so-called "leap of faith." In fact, in many a text in the Hindu tradition of spiritual culture, the terms *jnana* and *bhakti* have been used synonymously—that is, to signify experience in the highest stage of immediacy (*anubhava*). *Narada,* for example, describes love (*prema*) as of the nature of "subtler," deeper and more intimate *anubhava* than ordinary experience. In the paradigm of *bhakti* the essence of all knowledge merges with the essence of all bliss. What is indicated as the enjoyment of bliss absolute in the elevated experience of love is the translation in the language of *bhakti* of basically the same experience which in the idiom of *jnana* stands out as the highest immediacy in experience. In one case, viz., the latter, the standpoint of pure consciousness (*cit*) prevails, whereas in the former that of bliss-full delight (*ananda*).

This move towards a kind of hermeneutic reconciliation of the two strands within the fold of Vedantic thinking takes on subsequently—at least in the case of one outstanding thinker, called Madhusudan Sarasvati—a definite edge in favour of *bhakti,* with a twist on the *jnana*-model. Madhusudan had produced the most formidable dialectical critique of the concept of "difference" in order to establish the supreme validity of the concept of Identity (or rather, "non-difference," to put it in terms of the transcendental logic of Advaita Vedanta). But at the same time he offered a significant about-face in his religio-philosophical works. One is his interpretative commentary on the *Bhagavadgita,* with a conspicuously "theistic" turn, departing from Sankara's. The other work I have to mention, curiously enough, bears the title, *Bhaktirasayana*—discourse on that intensely enjoying state of mind (*rasa*) which is imbued with *bhakti.* In expounding the discipline of *bhakti* (i.e., *bhakti-yoga*), he presents it as the consummation of all the *rasas*; or if regarded s an independent *rasa* by itself, it marks the highest end of human being. But then he moves on to observe that even *jnana-yoga* has as its end *bhakti-yoga,* because without the latter there is no fulfilling satisfaction of the mind.

This brings about the moment of "enjoyment" essentially, though implicitly, embedded within the drive of knowledge itself. At certain points of our cognitive or reflective life, that moment may surface, and come more into focus. Be it as an accompanying overtone, be it as the hidden *telos* or inherent demand of ongoing reflection, our understanding (or self-understanding) immanently contains a moment of enjoyment. (Bertrand Russell, it seems, uttered perhaps a half-truth when he proposed his formula of wisdom as "guided by knowledge and inspired by love"—as if the two are completely independent faculties!)

So to come back to the said element of enjoyment, it could rightfully be translated in the emotive language of love and delight. However that need not mean an equation with a naive stage of blind ecstasy nor with a state of mindless infatuation; by the same token it should also be clear that we are not here speaking of the dry exercise of empty ratiocination. Neither spurious emotionalism, verging on irrationalism, nor self-enclosed sterile intellectualism could hold that promise of "enjoyment." For if we could refer to spiritual experience meaningfully, not as a cliche, then we have to recognize in that context an experiential paradigm where intellect, will or feeling do not just operate piecemeal and separately, but the whole human being is involved with the entire dimension of his or her existence.

The move for devotional love, it is true, might sometimes have taken a more radical shape of pure unalloyed *bhakti* to the exclusion of cognitive understanding altogether—as it might have been the case with certain extreme forms of Vaishnavism (one wing of Bangal Vaishnavism, for example). The unique aspect of the devotional model as such, put forward as the self-fulfilling *modus vivendi* and the ultimate ideal, owes, however, its original formulation to the aphoristic source traditionally attributed to the sage Narada, viz. *Bhaktisutra.* The latter lays down right at the outset a straightforward statement on the essence of *bhakti*, that it is of the nature of supreme love (*paramaprema-svarupa*).

Although the nature of Love *per se* as the ideal end is admitted to defy any definition, Narada nonetheless describes that paradigmatic state to be identified as the realization that is *bhakti*, in ecstatic terms. Along with such epithets as "intoxicated," "enchanted," he also uses, almost in an Upanishadic vain, such phrases as "enjoying the bliss that is *atman*." The *Upanishads* have harped on the note of *ananda* (bliss) on the ontological as well as the subjective dimensions, where the two, of course, are not viewed as different. "Self-fulfilled," "self-delighted," "self-enraptured"—all these phrases have been used to describe the nature of *atman*. On the other hand, *Brahman* in its turn is also referred to as "*Rasa*" — "He is indeed *rasa*," so runs a statement.

All these, again, would hermeneutically signify a link, at least implicit, between the mainstream *Upanishadic* tradition and what eventually took the shape of the *bhakti* cult down to the Vaishnava lyrics of Bengal. From the original Krishna legend were drawn the allegories of Krishna in the aspect of the divine Lover, the embodiment of beauty and joy par excellence, and Radha, who symbolizes the eternal yearning of the human soul. And these were evoked in expressing *bhakti*, devotion and selfless dedication, as the only approach to the supreme source of giving and receiving of joy. The Bengali Vaishnava lyric poetry, which reached its creative efflorescence in the 16th and 17th centuries, is as much a part of living tradition—and so are the innumerable hymns of mediaeval India (Kabir, Nanaka. Mirabai etc.)—as some Christian hymnody of the same period in Europe. In the Judeao-Christian tradition, we could trace such orientation of love in the devotional context certainly as far back as the "Psalms of David" and more expressly, perhaps, in "the Song of Solomon." The essential sentiment (*rasa*) behind Solomon's utterance: "I *am* my beloved's, and his desire is toward me" may well find its resonance across the bounds of age and culture in a Bengali Vaishnava lyric, for example:

> When the sound of your flute reaches my ears it compels me to leave my home, my friends, it draws me into the dark toward you.[3]

Moving from this image of devotional love in its utter completeness, we can turn once more back to Sankara—but interestingly enough, with a different face (considering his uncompromising stand on Identity). And that is the face of *bhakti*—not in any way as an apology for its place in the scheme of knowledge-oriented faith, but as expressed in his numerous hymns addressed to Siva, as well to Mother Goddess (Durga). For instance, he prays to Goddess: "You, the supreme goddess, you alone are the recourse." One of his famous hymns to Siva, contains verses like this:

> O Siva! Thou bearest the responsibility for the welfare of all beings; Thou art intent on giving all that is good; Thou dost teach the way to all desired ends, seen and unseen; Thou art all pervading, inside and outside; Thou art omniscient and merciful; to Thee, what should I make known? Thou art my inmost self: thus do I always think in my mind.

The devotional attitude for him is not just a concession to the popular demand of practical religion, but far deeper a slant, in keeping with the authentic theme of Vedantic self-realization. Devotion that has an important place in the scheme of spiritual discipline, essentially means directing the mind, in its cognitive, emotional and volitional modes, to flow constantly towards God and getting them absorbed there.

Moreover, the very title of Sankara's hymn referred to could be cited as a point of significance in this context; it is called by him "*Sivanandalahari,*" which means "Siva, the Wave of Bliss." The recognition of *ananda* at the core of spiritual ontology (or the phenomenological ontology of the spirit) is central to the *Upanishadic-Vedantic* insight. Bliss or delight constitutes the essential dimension of pure consciousness (*cit*), and is that which renders self as the dearest of all—not in any egoistic sense, but on the contrary, in the sense of universal essence. In that perspective the divine as ideally the repository of absolute joy and beauty, also becomes the most desirable. *Bhakti* would thus serve as the paradigmatic meeting ground for the different streams of emotion: the aesthetic turn to beauty, the erotic drive for love and the urge for surrendering. Along with that the cognitive aspect of mind—i.e., reflection and contemplation—and the resolve and the strength of will also join the chore.

However marked the aesthetic overtone of *bhakti,* and for that matter any tradition of devotional love, may be, the distinctive element of "grace" or "compassion" often shows up, in some form or other, as a necessary counterpart to surrender or resignation. It is recognised by almost all the *Bhakti* schools that it is the Grace of God that alone can elevate the aspirant to a state of ultimate edification and beatitude. The accent on the total dependence on Divine mercy (*vis-a-vis* the devotee's effort and disciplinary state) may vary from school to school, sect to sect. But coming to the essential philosophical point about the notion of Grace, leaving out its institutionalized ritualistic contexts, it may possibly lend itself to a phenomenological-ontological (rather than onto-theological) translation. Thus it may, in ontological terms, mark that twilight ground where the aspiring human *Dasein* (to borrow Heidegger's term), in the progressive ascent of consciousness, meets Being (or the Divine, to use the locution of religious faith) in the latter's unfolding. (The Heideggerian usage of the Greek word *Aletheia,* i.e., "unconcealment" may be relevant in this regard.)

In more than one *Upanishad* we come across a note of receptive submission in a profoundly spiritual-ontological context, from which perhaps a only fine line of distinction could otherwise be drawn from the notion of "grace" in a purely religious-cum-theological context. One conspicuous *Upanishadic* statement runs as follows:

> That *Atman* (the Universal Self) is not to be obtained through scriptures, not by intellect, nor by scholastic pursuits; Only whom He (or That) accepts (or receives), by him\her alone is *Atman* attainable, and whom *Atman* reveals His own nature and glory.[4]

It brings into focus the quintessence of spiritual experience *per se*, in which the ascent of the human soul, of human consciousness, meets as its counterpart, as it were, the "Descent" of the Divine. Here behind this metaphorical language of "ascent-descent" we could comprehend a common ground of spiritual ontology where the Mahayana Buddhist notion of "*karuna*," the Christian doctrine of "*agape*" and "*grace*," and the Hindu tradition of *bhakti* could all meet in meaningful resonance and dialogue.

However, I have here no intention of pushing further the possibility of an ontological equation of the idea of "grace." But I share in a way the caution spelt by Paul Ricouer against what he calls the "'crypto-philosophical temptation' of religious faith of taking over the vacant role of ultimate foundations." One need not join the ranks of avowed post-modernists to see that an authority-instituted faith – be it in Hindu, Jain or Buddhist traditions, be it in Christianity, Islam or Judaism – could carry the unhealthy possibility of self-foundational claim to philosophical solutions that the "cogito" of the sovereign thinking subject would exercise.

Now to wind up the net of my discourse rather widely spread out, the question that I am prompted to pose in conclusion (not so much answering though): where do we stand today – I mean philosophically (or say, philosophically-culturally) in the face of the *bhakti* tradition in broad – irrespective of geo-cultural – diversities? From the ground of our present-day philosophizing, does that model bear any relevant significance for us in the contemporary world? The response I will leave to you, but I may only suggest briefly a few points to consider. As we look to the history of the movement, one feature is conspicuous: namely, the path of devotion has carried an undeniable appeal to the common man for its directness, relative simplicity, kinship to natural human interests of love and beauty. Unlike the rigorous path of contemplative reflection or of the rigorous self-culture of *yoga*, in the path of devotion one is not called upon to go against one's grain. On the other hand, without the intellectual discipline of contemplative reflection and understanding, which can distinguish and interpret, a bare emotive move of the mind could simply lead to an irrationalism of a self-enclosed faith.

Yet what the broad-based paradigm of *bhakti* could demonstrate to us is the essential place for openness, sensitivity and submission to what is revealed in and through the depths of our everyday life and the lived world. It is a call to our tired intellect to come out of its confines of barren ratiocination and "false rationalism" (as Husserl perhaps would have said), and to open up to the dimensions of love and beauty. They have either been too trivialized in our generally prevailing pragmatic attitude or too etherealized in conceptual hypostatization. The moment of joy, of playful delight, has so often been undermined, if not obscured, in our thinking practice as well as in common perception. If *bhakti* were to mean anything philosophically and culturally significant to us today, it is the recognition of this intrinsic moment of joy in the texture of our thinking and perception of reality. It is not meant to be an escape from the humdrum of living, but an ontological insight that self-fulfilling delight lies in the heart of reality, it constitutes the essential dimension of Being. "The hidden Yea in you is stronger than all the Nays and Perhaps, of which you and your age are sick" Nietzsche exclaimed.[5] *Bhakti* represents that affirmation of life and existence—a call for expansion and inclusion, not only to the heart but also to the head. But it is an affirmation which is to make its way in all spontaneity through authentically submitting oneself to the nature of things in reverence and in wonder.

Notes

1. Cf. *One Hundred Poems of Kabir,* No. XIX, Translated by Rabindranath Tagore (Assisted by Evelyn Underhill), Macmillan, 1915/1985.

2. *Bhagavadgita*, 18.66.

3. In Praise of Krishna: Songs from the Bengali, translated by Edward Dimock & Denise Levertov, Anchor Books, 1967.

4. Cf. *Katha Upanishad*, I.2.23.

5. Friedrich Nietzsche, *Joyful Wisdom*. (#377) New York: Frederick Ungar Publishing Co., 1973.

A Scheme for Receiving *Bhakti* and *Agape:* Two Forms of Love into Thought

John G. Arapura

My topic is worded "A Scheme for Receiving *Bhakti* and *Agape*: Two Forms of Love Into Thought." However, I would first of all down-play the term "scheme," as I have not used it in any technical way, nor in the sense of *schema*, favored by some philosophers. Even so, I have a connected plan in mind.

Also, in order to understand my standpoint, it may be useful to say a word about the intellectual corner I come from in dealing with this and other similar topics as we all come from our respective corners. Mine is defined by my life-long involvement with Non-dualist Vedanta in the first place, qualified by a very deep interest in certain aspects of Western philosophy, especially those that tie in with the metaphysics of Christianity. To this another element is added, namely, my own inclination to go to the roots of things by myself. This last no doubt defines most people of our calling. And we all come from corners which hold such mixes, though of varying kinds according to the individuals.

A Brief Sketch of the Plan

Now, as my topic stipulates, thought on one side and *bhakti* and *agape* on the other figure as the principal terms, and the connection sought between them is expressed by the term *receiving*. Clearly, between the two sides, the more problematic issues would concern the term "thought," inasmuch as it is not one of customary use in dealing with *bhakti* and *agape*. Hence, I will take up the issues concerning thought first, to be followed up with reflections on *bhakti* and *agape*. However, reception of these latter two is of crucial interest, and so in order to discuss it intelligibly they have to be expressed by a common term which can accommodate them both. The choice without any doubt is the English word *love* or the word of any language that is able to convey its general meaning. And as for *bhakti* and *agape*, because they are very deep in their own special ways, a term of very general import such as *love* will have to take their place for the most part. But certainly, we will return to the two special terms at appropriate times so as to be assisted in our movement to the end, which, however, must not be called conclusion.

Some Observations on Issues of Thought

First of all, permit me to say with some apology that it is felt expedient to drag up a rather wider base than would seem warranted. However, it is found to be unavoidable if one has to make one's point. But I ask for your indulgence and forbearance.

That there are some important inquiries into the nature of thought as well as a few profound reflections on the subject is well known. However, even the greatest of the reflections, those by Heidegger most of all, have only an oblique relation to what I am presenting. I mark here the main point on which difference is felt to exist. It is generally assumed that thought is something that a human thinker does, in whatever manner resulting in such disastrous formulae as "I think, therefore I am," "a small step for man, but a giant step for modern mankind over the edge of the cliff." On the contrary, we must start with no assumption of a being—human or divine. Rather, it is important to make thought transparent to its own essence and only base so that the question formulated on the basis of thought continues to be there even if there were no humans and no world. That base we must call, for want of another word, by the name "reality," which I use an extrapolation from the *Upanishads* as they refer to it non-descriptively as *he/it*, and say that there is no other thinker but he/it. We go further and stipulate that Reality alone is thinker, Reality alone is thing, Reality alone is essence of thought. This position parallels and in fact extends the Non-dualist view of Sankara that Ultimate Reality is that A in which there is no difference between knowledge, known and knower *(jnana-jneya-jnatr-bhedarahitam).*

As for the word "reality" it is chosen not for any positive virtue it possesses, but rather for the negative ones, as the one worth risking. The root of this word, *res*, tells us nothing. And as the word gained currency, such misuses as in making contrasts between "real" and "ideal," "reality" and "appearance" became stock-in-trade. But they too must be ignored. However, the word of itself tells us something of unique importance, given in the presentational immediacy of the physical, essentially time and space, although the Reality there lies not so much in what is presented or in what is concealed as in what is revealed in the inherent contradiction between the necessity for them (i.e., time and space) to be bounded and yet not to be bounded. Thus time and space also begin to serve as symbols of all contradictions constitutive of Reality, experiential, moral, metaphysical, spiritual and existential. One has to go some further length on this in order to arrive at some clarity as to what thought is based on this view of Reality, the objective at present being to see how love can be received into it.

So then we turn again to the view of Reality as we have set forth and to what is revealed in its contradictions, and there is only one word by which we can hope to express it, however inadequately, and that word is *Abyss*. This word too can be misleading in a number of ways, not the least on account of its association in mystical literature with Godhead, especially celebrated in the writings of Dionysus the Areopagite, and I have no such thing in mind. On the contrary, we may consider it as a very bland concept based on the simple image of the Abyss as that which excludes everything and every notion otherwise included in a conception of Reality, and includes everything and every notion otherwise excluded. And then the image may be further advanced by viewing it as what it is without contrast, without contrary, without an other and without comparison, inasmuch as the Abyss swallows them all up. In the words of the *Mandukya Upanishad* , it is that which is unnameable (*avyapadesyam*), unable to be dealt with (*avyavaharyam*), sign-less (*alaksanam*), etc.

Nevertheless, there is something crucial: Reality as Abyss also turns around, and thereby contours itself, wherein lies that which is, i.e., Being. But in order for Being to be, ancient sources (e.g., *Chandogya Upanishad,* 6.2.1-2), and Parmenides contrast it with Non-Being/Nothing (See for example, Parmenides, *Ancillia to Pre-Socratic Philosophers,* a Diels Work, translated by K. Freeman, Harvard University Press, pp. 41-46). That, no doubt, affects our first rule against contrast, i.e., that Reality is without Contrast. Parmenides further saw Necessity holding the illimitable in the bond of Limit, which constrains it round about. Now, while this stipulation upholds the necessity of limit, it sets aside the equally important necessity of no limit for Reality, the two opposing necessities generating the contradictions that are descriptive of the Abyss. Parmenides' objective is to get on with Being, moving on to its extension into thought. Hence for him Being is like the mass of a well-rounded sphere, equally balanced from its center in every direction. On the other hand, the Abyss as we describe it remains the Abyss even when contoured; there is no cut-off line, or fixed periphery. Being is that which is without boundary or periphery, and is there by virtue of the contours of the Abyss. And its essence is purely interior to itself.

Some Observations on Issues of Thought Continued: The Idea of the Open

Insofar as a cut-off line between Being and the Abyss as such is to be rejected, when we come to the question of thought we must be able to see it as in no way predicated on any cut-off line. The Abyss pervades Being itself, right within the contours, and yet without in any way affecting the interior essence of Being.

Reality, the Abyss, is by definition *the* open, even in terms of Being as what is within the contours. Accordingly, thought may be grasped as Reality, the open, entering itself, the open. Not only that, as stated earlier, Reality alone is thinker and it alone is thing. In that way only is it possible to say that the questions formulated on the basis of thought continue to be there even if there were no humans and no world. But then, what about humans who invoke the prerogative of thought? The answer is that humans who do so are to understand themselves as but adjuncts of Reality's own thought, and as catchers of the image. For humans, then, to think is to so enter as adjuncts that they be where Reality is, which is everywhere and nowhere: and yet somewhere, that is, in terms of the contoured Abyss, which is called Being (*sat* in Sanskrit).

This *somewhere*, which is Being, however, comes to view in an all-important manner. That is to say, although it is by no means constricted by any cut-off line or limit that marks it off from the Abyss as such, it takes over as thinker, thing and thought. And so it may be truly said that Being thinks, Being is thing and Being is thought. And yet it never cedes or surrenders the open of Reality. So then, as for the human thinker, a unique relation with Being, destined to be identity, emerges into view.

Much has been said by persons who have deeply pondered the subject of thought in terms of openness to Reality, and rightly so. However, it may be added that openness to Reality must translate as being in *the* open of Reality, quite appropriately under the species of Being. Such openness alone can qualify as releasement, and it is hard to see how language has a place there as sometimes construed by persons of great stature, meaning someone like Heidegger.

There is here a word of an exceptional bonus. This comes in respect of the connection between the human thinker and Being, and beings as well. We are released, spared, from having to formulate some appropriate philosophical anthropology for that purpose. Heidegger describes it as philosophical, that is, thoughtful doctrine of man's essential nature, to which he attaches what one may call a game-plan of making that nature identical with Being/beings (see *What is Called Thinking*?, E.T.J. Glen Gray, New York, Harper and Row, 1966, p. 79). We are released from this onus, rather thought is released from it, because it is now possible to see that Reality (no doubt, under the species of Being) is alone thinker. However, just as there is no need for human or other beings to be at all but Reality ordains that they be, so too Reality ordains that they think, be thinkers without any need. Thought so construed is free from strain, free from constraint of necessity.

Now, there is the other side to release from any philosophical anthropology: that is the avoidance of de-ontologizing the human being, which has been forthcoming generously from the techno-scientific end of things. That has been a happy excursion for many, among whom are those who generate contrived thought for that purpose. Contrived thought may be defined as that kind of thought which cannot square with itself, because it cannot square with Being. And the trouble with this kind is that it is totally incapable of self-criticism which has the potentiality to remove the block to the entry into the open. By contrast, any genuine philosophical anthropology retains that potential capability.

The Issue of *Logos* in Thought: In Anticipation of Reception of Love

The issue of *logos* (*Vak* in Sanskrit) has immense importance for reception of love into thought. That which has brought us to Being will take us further into Love, mediated by the proposition where Being is, there Love is. One pre-eminent way in which the Vedic-Vedantic tradition considers Being is to figure it in terms of Energy (*Sakti*), which generates beings, meaning, "The All" (*ta panta, sarvam*), freely and without necessity, likened to the breath of the *Self-originated* (*Svayambhuh*). Energy has an assignation with itself, as that which brings to pass "The All" from Being, and that assignation may be explicitly stated as Love, which, however, is a word never expressly used in the central portions of Vedic-Vedantic literature, while expressly spelled out in the New Testament Johannine texts as *agape*. In the Vedic-Vedantic tradition it is carried over a tangent by the word *bhakti*. And although *bhakti* has been generally apportioned to the soul in its striving towards God, there is a connecting link in the Divine itself, i.e., as *Sakti*, meaning the inherent Power by which something is. *Sakti* is creative Power, which is to say, that it has no need for any other Reason for it to be but itself, and be what it is, and it eventually translates as Love.

Shifting back to the open, which is Reality (Being) into which itself enters and as such is thought, it may be pointed out that *the* open is altogether illuminated by what is central to Vedanta, i.e., Absolute Knowledge, or *jnana*; as a translation for it we shall use the word *gnosis*, though not in the Gnostic sense. Thought thus is to be understood as *the* open that is so illuminated. Into it Love, that is *agape/bhakti*, is to be received.

Now let us consider how *logos* (which in part is identical with the Vedic *Vak*) stands with regard to the entry into the open. The striking fact that comes to view is that *logos* was needed to stake out an Enclosed, a fixed form, marked by a limit, even according to Parmenides. We learn from great authorities that *legein*, as also its counterpart *noein*, works within the Enclosed staked out in *the* open, although *the* open is certainly still there, which is a fact that no thinker would deny.

Heidegger's celebrated extrapolation from, and extension of, Parmenides' original sayings are extremely instructive in that they reinforce our perception that there is such an Enclosed within which *logos* works, and generates thought, and is itself thought. And that thought is the receptacle for all things which accord with it. Scholars have agreed that the word *logos* came from the root *leg*, evoking the act of gathering, eventually destined to be the intellectual operation of perceiving similar data in the body of an immense mass of facts, and ultimately of perceiving the reigning unity in the cosmos itself. Obviously

Heidegger, while not disagreeing with this finding, simply transposes it to meditative thinking, and very appropriately so. This line is specially mentioned here because it is so close to what we have in mind and yet so far.

The important lesson we learn, from all this, is that the Greek *Noesis*, i.e., thought, operates in an unbreakable bond with *logos*, a fact elaborately expressed. We have such statements (in *What is Called Thinking?*) as: *legein* precedes *noein* (Harper and Row, 1966, p. 208); *noein* unfolds out of *legein*, *noein* is kept within *legein* (p. 211), thinking happens by their *ratio* (p. 210) etc. Unfortunately, at last, thought is squeezed into a tunnel, that of Western civilization and a special brand of historicism, where Being too must suffocate. Whether this should have been so, we do not know.

But the redeeming feature of it is that great depth is both promised and delivered. However, it has undeniable affinity with what keeps unfolding itself on the other side of modern thought, namely, techno-science, which produces both mind-boggling cosmologies and equally mind-boggling micro-discoveries of all kinds such as particles, quarks or whatever. However, the Enclosed is inevitably there, no matter how far its boundary is pushed conceptually as well as physically. And no doubt, the Enclosed is illuminated either by profound meditative thinking or by mathematics and empirical procedures. But the difference between the Enclosed either way and thought as *the* open of Reality altogether illuminated by *gnosis*, into which Reality (Being) itself enters, will remain as ultimate.

Thought and Reality's Primordial Presences, with Love as the Supreme One

In order to expand what has been said, the idea of "Presences of Reality" may be introduced. The term "presence" is employed as a translation of the Sanskrit *sannidhyam,* as in Sankhya of the *sannidhyam* of the Spirit (*purusha*) which is the source of all happenings.

In our list, the primordial presences are: Wonder, Mystery, the twin of Suffering and Care and the dark one, Fear. In the Enclosed, under the dominion of *Logos*/Logic, the twin, Suffering and Care, may get a vogue or are ignored, as also Fear, while Wonder and Mystery give way to presentational and representational data, signs, significations, symbols, leading the road down to techno-science. The presences belong with Reality, and do not need anyone else. Wonder, for instance, does not need Parmenides or Plato or you and me to do the wondering.

As for Love the supreme presence, its natural place of entry is the open illumined by *gnosis,* where it is received. Love as the supreme presence of Reality grounds itself in an equation of identity, which in the language of St. John of the New Testament is expressed as "God is Love" (*ho theos agape estin,* 1 John, 4, 8 & 16). What is grasped and expressed as Love by St. John is grasped and expressed differently in Vedanta, i.e., in terms of Energy (*Sakti*) and its own radical essence, *Sat,* which is translated as "Being" but it is Being as well as that which "makes be" (*sat karoti*). That is *Sat* which "makes be" (*sat karoti*), makes itself be (*svayam sat karoti*), of its own accord (*svena*). There is solid ground for taking the view that within such a framework *Sat* is the same as Love, the ultimate creative power, which needs no other but itself to be and to make be. There is here a natural, which means not strained, correspondence between this and thought as the open of Reality into which Reality itself enters, not affected by its own self-contouring by way of its turn around, to which we have referred before. And we always bear in mind that Reality is Abyss.

Here then we view again the other primordial presences in light of the Supreme presence of Love. The truth is, Love appropriates them, and so appropriating, it transforms Wonder into contemplation; Mystery into ever deepening and boundless fascination; transforms Suffering, (*dukham*), the very stuff of Existence, into Redemptive power; deepens Care into compassion (*karuna*), but casts out Fear as it is said perfect love casts out fear (*he teleia agape echo ballei ton phobon*, 1 John, 4, 18). Which is why in Love there is *aphobos, abhayam*.

Reception of Love into Thought

The verb "to receive" has been subjected to some important philosophical treatments. Heidegger's way of associating it with the verb "to perceive" is rather entrancing. However, he connects them both, in fact equates them, with the meaning of *noein*, leading to the sense of "taking to heart" and more (*What is Called Thinking?* p. 203). But we will turn to the much profounder meaning of it that lies in the Sanskrit *svikaram, svikaranam*, which according to sources such as the *Nirukta* and *Yajnvalkya Smriti*, comes from *svi*, a mode of *sva*,self, with *kar*, to make, so that the word means making (something or someone) one's own. And it does have the nuance of taking to heart as well, rather taking into heart. It has a strong association with love in the sense of human love. Its social usage was to express a bride's entry and reception into the new home, leading to her being made at home and the home in turn made hers.

Its religious, i.e., Vedic, usage is parallel. It refers to the gods being received as guests and guests as gods. The saga begins with invocation (*amantranam*), continues in welcome (*svagatam*), and then on to reception (*svikaranam*, *svikaram*). Love makes itself be of its own accord (*svena*) and so made, it is ready to be received into thought so that thought makes it its own.

Love as *Agape* and as *Bhakti*

In general, *agape* and *bhakti* are placed at two ends of the same line, namely, Love. But we have noticed the link between them in Energy (*Sakti*) and its radical essence, *Sat*, which is not just Being but that which makes be of its own accord, leading us to the conclusion that that which so makes be is translatable as Love. And we have called attention to the natural correspondence between Love in this sense and thought. Hence the fact that we cannot say that God is *bhakti* in the way it is said God is *agape* is no longer a dominant problem because that which stands behind *Bhakti*, i.e., *Sakti* and its radical essence, *Sat*, take the place of *Bhakti* and it is figurable as God.

Bhakti, generally understood as devotion, has a more original meaning, i.e., "division," from the root *bhaj*, "to divide." Accordingly, *Bhakti* at its source stood for the division of Divine Energy (*Sakti*) (comprehending its own radical essence, *Sat*) between itself and the soul of each being in a timeless assignation, enfolded in *Sakti's* own assignation with itself. By reason of this, the soul moves towards the Divine on a journey of longing, in order to reunite with it. It partially reads like the story of the *Eros* of Greek Mythology (not found in Homer, however), where it is the apotheosis of the Divine essence and Power that proceeds from the desiring subject. It is a part split-off from the whole. In *bhakti*, on the other hand, at least in Vedanta, the division between the part, particle (*amsa*) and the whole (*amsin*) is only an assignation one of love, no doubt,between *Sakti* and itself. The yearning soul is already located in that relation; only it must dispel the ignorance that conceals that fact. This is the way non-dualist Vedanta deals with it, anyway.

The knowledge that reveals this fact is the *gnosis* which illumines thought, i.e., *the* open of Reality into which it itself enters and the humans too as adjuncts and image catchers. In essential non-dualist Vedanta, *gnosis* is not one thing and thought another. For at the risk of frequent repetition, let us say that thought is *the* open illumined by *gnosis,* answering to Reality as such, along with all its presences, and most of all the supreme presence, Love. *Gnosis* naturally extends itself into thought which stands with Reality. There is no question of any way (*marga*) in this, although in conventional terms "the way of *gnosis*" (*jnana-marga*) along with "the way of *bhakti*" and "the way of *karma*" are spoken of. However, standing with Reality, it may be said that there is no way but thought and thought is no way, not even a way of non-way. Does this fact act as a boundary? No, because there is no boundary to Reality, and hence thought is never helmed in although it eternally realizes itself within the contours.

Now in thought is commenced the final passage of the saga which began with the invitation (*amantrana*), as celebration of Love. *Agape* has been well-known as Love-celebration. This is also *satkara,* which has the connotation of honoring and feasting, held in reserve, that goes with "making-be," which is its essence. *Agape* that began its career in the New Testament as Love-feast has been well-known as celebration based on the principle that God is Love. Tradition, however, confined the Love-feast to the *ecclesia,* those called together. But by being so confined, its practice both retarded its true purpose and yet at the same time preserved it as a symbol of an endless celebration in which all beings (*sarva bhutani*) will participate. However, as for Love's reception into thought, it is quite clear that in respect of the Love-feast tradition of *agape,* it has to be lifted at that end for its entry.

Vedanta conceives this celebration in terms of *bhakti,* an ever advancing internal act of the soul, always gathering momentum, and on the way of traversing the infinite distance between its own destiny ever accomplished (*siddham*) and yet-to-be-accomplished (*sadhyam*), entirely in accord with Reality itself. But it is the procession that is part of the celebration that never ceases. The Energy that is at the back of it keeps replenishing it. In the words of the *Viveka-Cudamani* (verse 32), it is the highest among the things that can move one on the way to the goal (necessarily defined as), liberation (*moka-sadhana-samagryam bhakti-reva gariyasi*).

And now by marking the end of this discussion not to arrive at any conclusion, as stated at the beginning a final word may be said, rather repeated, with regard to thought, lest it be ever construed as having anything to do with "I think" (*cogito*). For, thought belongs entirely with Reality, so much so that even in our experience of thought we are but adjuncts, and hence are beneficiaries of release from what thought would be if it were to be "I think." And as such it is unbounded plenitude, disposing us to go in a number of directions from there, not the least that of action, and quest for justice by action, but to be in a way thoroughly consistent with Love. For, Love is the supreme presence of Reality.

"*Song of the Lord*: Aria or Duet?"

Richard S. G. Brown

Consider the young man who, at the age of eighteen, thought that his father was rather stupid. The young man then went off to the university. After three years of diligent study, he received his diploma and was simply amazed to discover how much his father had learned in the interim. Like that young man, I would like to see just how much the *Gita* has learned since the last time I read it. But if a little knowledge in general is a dangerous thing, a little knowledge of the *Gita* might prove to be even more dangerous. I brought to my reading of the text this time around a host of preconceived ideas of what the text had to say. I was therefore afraid that when I read it through again, I would only be trying to confirm my prejudices. I thought that I could avoid this eventuality if I tried to approach the text this time somewhat scientifically, by drawing up, in advance, certain hypotheses, which my re-reading of the text would either prove or disprove. I then decided to conflate these two approaches in the following fashion: while others were very keen and busy distinguishing the content and message of the *Gita* either from the *Anugita* (from Chapter 14 of the *Mahabharata*) or from the so-called *Urgita* (the original *Gita*),[1] I decided instead to see exactly how the content and message of the *Gita* compared to what I thought the ideal *Gita* ought to be.

The Ideal *Gita*[2]

It seemed to me that the popular appeal of the *Gita* had to rest full square on its sensitivity to the fact that there are different personality types and that these different personality types entailed different *yoga*s or pathways. In other words, unlike essentially all Indian thought, the *Gita* was exceptional precisely because it set aside, at least in part, the generic Indian standard that knowledge and only knowledge is the exclusive means of obtaining liberation or *moksa*. Beginning with the divine ordering of the castes (XVIII, 41-48), the ideal *Gita* would distinguish between personality types according to their dominant quality or *gunic* mix (*sattva, rajas, tamas*). If we follow Sankara's assessment of these mixes, in their various combinations, the highest caste or Brahmins would be primarily *sattvic* and hence would be able to be contemplative and follow *jnana-yoga* or the path of knowledge; warriors, like Arjuna, on the other hand, who are basically passionate or *rajasic* albeit with some *sattva* admixture, would have to follow another route best suited to them; and so on down the *gunic* line, as it were.[3] The ideal *Gita*, I thought, would map each of the three personality types corresponding to the three *gunas* on to the three *yoga*s or pathways: *sattvic* or contemplative types being ideally suited to follow *jnana-yoga* or the path of knowledge to Absolute *Brahman*; passionate or *rajasic* types, like Arjuna, would obviously be singularly unsuited for contemplation, but, because of their dominant *gunic* quality, would nevertheless be perfectly suited to follow *bhakti-yoga* or the path of love and devotion to a personal God; and *tamasic* types would then be ideally suited to follow *karma-yoga*, the path of works, which means they would do the duties (*dharma*) which were prescribed to them according to their class (and their nature) but to cast off or sacrifice the fruits of their actions so as to avoid their karmic consequences, for good or bad.

So far, so good, I thought. Something for everyone. Universal appeal. However, my ideal *Gita* still required something special to set it apart from the rest of Indian philosophy, especially the *Upanishads* and the tradition, which prioritized knowledge. What the ideal *Gita* needed to reconsider were the various goals, since there had to be more than one, which would be appropriate to the three *yogas* respectively. Obviously, the *sattvic* or contemplative types who used the *yoga* of knowledge had becoming one with *Brahman* as their goal. However, for *sattvic* or contemplative types at least, what the ideal *Gita* had to say about *jnana-yoga* and the goal of *Brahman* did not differ from the overwhelming message of the *Upanishads*: to know *Brahman* is to become *Brahman*. But just how many *sattvic* or contemplative types are there who could actually come to know *Brahman*? Not too many, I guessed. And my ideal *Gita* is, after all, a dialogue, a dramatic exchange, between God and Arjuna, a passionate or *rajasic* warrior who, very much like the rest of us, is confused about what he ought to be doing—and why. I surmised that since God chose the passionate and thoroughly confused Arjuna to be his one and only interlocutor in the *Gita*, he would not burden Arjuna with an essentially Upanishadic message heavily laden with abstract concepts relating to knowledge of *Brahman*. In other words, in my ideal *Gita*, God would not speak to Arjuna as if he were Yajnavalkya, the paradigm of the *sattvic*, contemplative Upanishadic sage. By this single criterion alone, in my ideal *Gita* at least, God would have to relate to Arjuna something quite special about the relationship between Arjuna's passionate or *rajasic* nature, on the one hand, and the appropriate path of love and devotion to God, on the other hand. After all, what could the passionate and thoroughly confused Arjuna understand about the imperishable, absolute, impersonal, and borderline incomprehensible *Brahman*? And since talk of love and devotion to *Brahman* made no sense, the ideal *Gita* would have to be fraught with the kind of love and devotion between Arjuna and God which would basically obviate any need on Arjuna's part to know *Brahman* or to invest time and effort in acquiring the knowledge required to attain *Brahman*. Last, but not least, *karma-yoga* or path of works or disinterested action would be left in reserve for the tamasic types who could simply do what they had to do and sacrifice the fruits of their actions to God.

In itself, the picture I have just painted of what my ideal *Gita* ought to be, even to this point, is a radical departure from the "single path—single goal" model of the *Upanishads*, that is, knowledge—*Brahman*. However, from the point of view of a passionate or *rajasic* person like Arjuna, the path of love and devotion to reach God could never really be ultimately satisfying or liberating if the *sattvic* or contemplative knowers of *Brahman* were able to play their metaphysical trump card and insist that, in the ontological scheme of things, the personal God (Ishvara, Krishna) is subordinate to the impersonal absolute *Brahman*; *Brahman* being, of course, the only reality. Not only do love and devotion to an impersonal absolute make no sense, but it makes even less than no sense when knowledge of *Brahman* demands identity in difference, or finding the one in the many. Love and devotion, by their own internal logic, would seem to demand some genuine otherness between the lover and the beloved, between devotee and the object of devotion. A difference within unity, so-to-speak. So the ideal *Gita* would have to alter Upanishadic metaphysics, as a minimum, in order to guarantee that the "single legitimate path—single legitimate goal" trump card of the *Upanishads* could not be played out because it would push passionate or *rajasic* types, like Arjuna, with their special path of love and devotion to a distant second place if, in the immense design of things, they would continue to have any legitimate place at all. So I estimated that the ideal *Gita* would not only demonstrate that *bhakti-yoga* or the path of love and devotion to a personal God was superior to *jnana-yoga* or the path of knowledge to *Brahman* because a) it was easier; because b) it would be available to a greater number of people (including women!);[4] because c) the devotee could be straightway[5] or immediately delivered to God rather than have to face countless rebirths in order to become increasingly *sattvic* and wise but, far more importantly, because d) the impersonal absolute *Brahman* would be rendered ontologically subordinate to God. So, while knowing *Brahman* and thereby becoming *Brahman* and achieving moksa the hard way still remained a legitimate goal for *sattvic* types, in the ideal *Gita* the highest goal could be reached without knowledge simply by loving God.[6] The individual in the ideal *Gita,* as the "Song of the Lord," would then be singing a duet with God in the otherness of love rather than an aria in the identity which characterizes *Brahman.* And what, I ventured to think, could be more ideal than this? The only question, which now remains, is whether the actual *Gita* lives up to any of my ideals.

Multiple Personalities and Multiple Pathways

Perhaps the best place to start testing the actual *Gita* against the ideal one is Chapter XVIII (41-48) where Krishna lists the four social classes: "The four-caste system did I generate with categories of 'constituents' and 'works' (IV, 13) and describes each one of them in turn insofar as "they arise from the nature of things as they are" (XVIII,

41).[7] What must be remembered throughout, however, is that Arjuna is a *rajasic* or passionate warrior so the descriptions which Krishna offers in the text which review the *rajasic* category are meant to describe Arjuna exactly as we find him at least in the opening pages of the *Gita*: on a battlefield in profound confusion. There may be some good reasons to suspect that by the end of the *Gita*, Arjuna has literally undergone a miraculous change.[8] However, in marked contrast to the *rajasic* description of Arjuna as he is, we are also given detailed accounts of how Arjuna ought to be, if he follows the collective message of the *Gita*, namely, descriptions of the *sattvic* person of contemplation: the perfect yogin who receives long, countless, and extraordinarily glowing descriptions throughout the *Gita*.[9] In chapter XVIII, 42, for example, the highest social class, the Brahmins, is characterized in the following terms: "Calm, self-restraint, ascetic practice [renunciation of actions], purity, long-suffering and uprightness, wisdom [*jnana*] in theory as in practice...."[10] The description of Arjuna's warrior social class, which immediately follows in the text, certainly describes Arjuna or Arjuna's type but, quite rightly, it makes no mention of the stuff of *sattva*.[11] But, after all, Arjuna and his type are *rajasic*. Similarly, the description of the *sattvic* intellect as one who "... distinguishes between activity and its cessation, between what should be done and what should not, between danger and security, bondage and release ..." (XVIII, 30) is to be contrasted with the intellect of Arjuna's *rajasic* type who "what should be done and what should not, are untruly understood ..." (XVIII, 31). And lastly, the *sattvic* agent is one "... who, from attachment freed, steadfast and resolute, remains unchanged in failure and success and never speaks of 'I ...'" (XVIII, 27). One is immediately reminded of Arjuna's announcement on the battlefield, "I will not fight" (II, 9) which Krishna quotes Arjuna at XVIII, 59.

These *sattvic* accounts do not, and cannot, describe *rajasic* Arjuna as he is. Only the *rajasic* accounts could as one might expect. But all of the *sattvic* accounts describe the perfect yogin or wise man Arjuna ought to become.

However, none of this should come as a surprise to us in the *final* chapters of the *Gita* because the relationship between personality type and appropriate pathway was initially made halfway through the second chapter. Arjuna, who is confused about what he ought to do, asks Krishna, "... which is the better course? Tell me [and let your words be definite and clear]" (II, 7). Krishna then draws one of the *Gita*'s most important distinctions. It seems there are two quite different paths which could be taken (II, 37): *Samkhya,* defined variously as "rational analysis" (Radhakrishnan), "theory" (Zaehner), the "exercise of wisdom" (XVI, 1) and, ambiguously, as the renunciation of works (V, 2), and *yoga,* defined as "spiritual exercise" (XIII, 10), "sameness-and-indifference" (II, 48), "how to caste away the bondage of works [karma, action, deeds]" (Radhakrishnan) or "practice" (Zaehner) (II, 39). Samkhyan theory, as the name suggests, requires wisdom or knowledge; it is contemplation (*buddhi-yoga*). Yogic practice, on the other hand, is the unselfish or disinterested performance of works but without regard for their fruits. Krishna insists that the fruits of all actions, which are performed, ought to be offered to God as a sacrifice. Although *Samkhya* and *yoga* seem to be separate and distinct paths, the *Gita* also claims that the wise do not see a difference between them (V, 4). They are, in fact, the same at least insofar as their goal is concerned, namely, *Brahman* or liberation (V, 2, 5; VI, 6). But Arjuna, upon hearing this distinction, says to Krishna, "You confuse my soul and intellect [*buddhi*], or so it seems, with distinctly muddled words: so tell me with authority the one [simple way] whereby I can attain the better part" (III, 2; Cf. V, 1). Krishna proceeds by telling

Arjuna that the path he ought to follow is dependent on his particular personality type, *gunic* mix, or social class (since they basically amount to the same thing). Krishna says, "Of old did I proclaim the twofold law [that holds sway] in this world,—for men of theory the spiritual exercise of wisdom, for men of action the spiritual exercise through works" (III, 3). This means that *sattvic*, contemplative persons should follow the path of knowledge or *jnana-yoga* while *rajasic* and passionate persons, like Arjuna, should follow the path of "spiritual exercise through works" or *karma-yoga*. Then Krishna's yogic prescription to Arjuna is grounded in the principle that "[All] creatures follow [their] Nature" (III, 33). However, the relationship between the theoretical *vis-à-vis* the practical, renunciation of works (*Samkhya-yoga*) is still unclear to Arjuna. Arjuna says, "'Renounce [all] works': [such is the course] You recommend; and then again [You say]; 'Perform them.' Which one is the better of the two? Tell me this [in clear,] decisive [words]" (V, 1). Krishna offers Arjuna the following answer: "Renouncing works,—performing them [as spiritual exercise],—both lead to the highest goal; but of the two to engage in works is more excellent than to renounce them" (V, 2). At first blush, it would appear as if Krishna has just tipped his hat in favour of *karma-yoga*, which happens to be the path Arjuna is obliged to take as a *rajasic* man of action; that *karma-yoga* is indeed a better pathway than *jnana-yoga* or the path of wisdom since it was initially defined as the renunciation of works.[12] But this may not necessarily be the case. The "renunciation of works" is an ambiguous expression. Krishna could also be referring negatively to a person's futile attempt not to act and thereby not to accrue bad karma. While the practice of *yoga* in this instance appears to be better than the renunciation of works (*Samkhya*), at II, 49, Krishna said that the renunciation of works (*Samkhya*) was better than *yoga*: "For lower far is [the path of] active work [for its own sake] than the spiritual exercise of the soul [*buddhi*]. Seek refuge in the soul!" (II, 49).[13] But does it really matter? Krishna continues: " 'There must be a difference between theory and practice,' so say the simple-minded, not the wise. Apply yourself to only one whole-heartedly and win the fruit of both" (V, 4). Arjuna now knows that, as a passionate warrior, he ought to apply himself whole-heartedly to the practice of *karma-yoga*. But if Samkhyan theory and Yogic practice achieve the very same goal, how could Krishna claim that one was better or higher than another (V, 2)? Once again, Krishna seems to be acutely sensitive to Arjuna's needs as a *rajasic* warrior-type for whom the Samkhyan renunciation of action which requires wisdom would be more difficult (if possible at all) than acting unselfishly (V, 6). "But hard to attain is [true] renunciation without [the practice of some] spiritual exercise: the sage well integrated by spiritual exercise right soon to *Brahman* comes" (V, 6). Krishna's main point is that if you do not accept the fruits of your action as your own, you cannot reap the fate, which would follow upon the particular desire or attachment. Therefore Arjuna is told not to desire or to attach himself to the fruits of his action. But this does not mean do not act; it means do not desire. Arjuna is to act but to act from desirelessness or even-mindedness. This is precisely the *Gita*'s definition of *yoga* (II, 48). Renouncing the fruits of action will give Arjuna a reward greater than heaven, namely, *Brahman*, *moksa*, or liberation. But not, it would seem, without his first gaining knowledge, that is, without his eventually incorporating the theory with the practice and becoming the perfect yogin who engages in what might appropriately be called *praxis* since the mutual entailment of *jnana-yoga* and *karma-yoga* seem to destine them to collapse into a single path. Zaehner[14] contends, quite rightly I believe, that in the *Gita* the practice of *yoga* is only a necessary preparation for Samkhyan contemplation and wisdom; Samkhyan theory is the proper culmination of the practice of *yoga*. They are, in effect, ultimately inseparable as paths.[15] "[True], the men of contemplative theory attain a [high] estate, but that [same estate] achieve the men of practice too; for theory and practice are all one: who sees [that this is true], he sees [indeed]" (V, 5). "What men call renunciation is also [spiritual exercise] (practice): you must know this. For without renouncing all set purpose, no one can engage in spiritual exercise" (VI, 2).

How *Bhakti-Yoga* Relates to Personality Type

In chapter IV, *bhakti-yoga* or the path of love and devotion to God is introduced for the first time as a distinct *yoga* having a distinct goal and a distinct set of prerequisites.[16] God says, "In whatsoever way [devoted] men approach Me, in that same way do I return their love" (IV, 11). Also in chapter IV, we find Krishna telling Arjuna that "A man of faith, intent on wisdom, his senses [all] restrained, wins wisdom; and, wisdom won, he will come right soon to perfect peace" (IV, 39). So having faith or desiring the kind of wisdom which is required for liberation seems to result in wisdom but then it is only by means of this wisdom or knowledge that liberation can be achieved. Sacrifice and faith are necessary conditions for wisdom and wisdom is a necessary condition for liberation.

But what I find to be most extraordinary about the *Gita*, and where it differs most markedly from the ideal *Gita* I earlier described, is that liberation or becoming *Brahman* through knowledge is itself a necessary condition for loving God and attaining to God's particular mode of

Being which the *Gita* offers as a new and distinct goal.[17] Liberation through knowledge precedes loving God and makes it possible. *Jnana-karma yoga* then, taken as a single path and *bhakti-yoga* represent quite distinct steps in a two-step process.[18] Remember the exchange between Arjuna and Krishna at the beginning of chapter XII. Even though Arjuna has already heard about God's powers first hand in chapter X and has actually seen God's powers through his celestial eye in chapter XI, Arjuna still wants to know who is higher or better: those who are ever-integrated (the perfect yogins) who also serve God with devotion or those who only revere or know *Brahman* (XII, 1)? Krishna's answer is not surprising when the question is rephrased. Arjuna is asking God who God thinks is better: the person who is liberated through spiritual exercise who subsequently loves God or the person who is liberated through spiritual exercise but stops short at becoming one with the impersonal *Brahman*? God, as might be expected, opts in favour of the first alternative not only because the latter is subsumed in the former but also because the *Gita* takes the unique stand that *Brahman* is ontologically subsumed in God. Since God is ontologically higher than *Brahman*, liberated devotees and *bhakti-yoga* are going to be higher than those liberated non-devotees who have become one with *Brahman*, stopping at part one of a possible two-step process.[19]

Bhakti-yoga is only a necessary condition for knowing God; it is not a requirement for knowing *Brahman*.[20]

> By love-and-loyalty he comes to know Me as I really am, how great I am and who; and once he knows Me as I am, he enters [Me] forthwith (XVIII, 55). Whoever thus knows Me, unconfused, as the Person [All-] Sublime, knows all and [knowing all] communes with Me, with all his being, all his love

> (XV, 19). But by worship-of-love addressed to [Me], none other, Arjuna, can I be known and seen in such a form and as I really am: [so can my lovers] enter into me (XI, 54). (Cf. also IX, 13 and XIII, 18)

God gives the liberated yogin-devotee knowledge of Himself through his divine grace (*prasada*)[21] but only after the individual is first liberated and subsequently loves God. It is not completely clear whether or not God gives knowledge of *Brahman* to those who strive after liberation but, in chapter X, Krishna does say that "To these men who are ever integrated and commune with Me [who must be liberated devotees], I give that integration of the soul (*buddhi*) by which they may draw nigh to Me" (X, 10).[22] However, it does not make any sense to me for God to give his devotees, who are already liberated, the same kind of knowledge or insight, which they required to be liberated in the first place. So the kind of integration or knowledge which God gives to the liberated devotee or perfected yogin upon reaching liberation must be unique; it is knowledge of Krishna himself as God.

First problem

Arjuna, at least as we find him in the earlier chapters of the *Gita*, is the paradigm of the passionate *rajasic* type; he does not believe that he is able to draw away completely from his senses and his desires, as the perfect yogin should.[23] Arjuna recognises the difficulty he has with his "roving senses" (II, 67), that it is exceedingly difficult to be indifferent to all things. Indeed, Arjuna practically apologises because his "mind is very fickle" (VI, 33-34). Arjuna says to Krishna, "Suppose a man of faith should strive in vain, his restless mind shying away from spiritual exercise: he fails to win the perfect prize of spiritual exercise—what path does be tread then?" (VI, 37). In other words, Arjuna wants to know if there is another route, besides the praxis of jnana-karma, something perhaps like loving God and being straightway delivered I should imagine, if he should happen to fail at spiritual exercise, through no fault of his own, given the fact that he is a passionate warrior. But Krishna makes it abundantly clear to Arjuna that spiritual exercise, becoming a perfect yogin, a man of steady wisdom, and becoming *Brahman* or achieving liberation is a necessary precondition for loving God and achieving the highest ontological and spiritual goal. If this is true, Arjuna is certainly asking a very important question for all *rajasic* types. How can Arjuna and other *rajasic* types perfect themselves in the integration of the self if this ultimately requires a *sattvic* personality? How is Arjuna going to achieve this? Krishna's answer seems rather cold-hearted: Arjuna can do this "little by little" (VI, 25), by being reborn in circumstances which are more conducive to achieving success (VI, 40-43) by "perfecting himself" (XVIII, 45), becoming more and more *sattvic* and wise. So Arjuna, if at first you don't succeed, or cannot succeed because you are not *sattvic* enough, then try, try again.

Second problem

Clearly, Arjuna's becoming the perfect yogin or the man of steady wisdom is modelled on the *Upanishadic* principle that desire is obviated when there is no otherness. In chapter XVIII, Krishna distinguishes three kinds of action, agent, and knowledge according to the three constituents of Nature (*gunas* of *prakrti*) which correspond appropriately to each of the three personality types. *Sattvic* knowledge, which we must assume the perfect yogin or man of steady wisdom requires, is described as follows: "That [kind of] knowledge by which one sees one mode of being, changeless, undivided in all contingent beings, divided [as they are] ..." (XVIII, 20). *Sattvic* knowledge is ideal for seekers of *Brahman* because it knows identity in difference. *Rajasic* knowledge, on the other hand, is quite different. It is described in these terms: "But that [kind of] knowledge which in all contingent beings discerns in separation all manner of modes of being, different and distinct,—this you must know is knowledge born of Passion (*rajas*)" (XVIII, 21). *Rajasic* knowledge is ideal for lovers of God because it knows difference in unity. So while the *sattvic* personality type would have the ideal *gunic* mix to become *Brahman* and attain liberation, on reaching *Brahman*, he would then lack the appropriate *gunic* mix and type of knowledge which would seem to be required for his subsequent love and devotion towards a personal God. Liberation demands de-detachment from desires and the world while love and devotion of God require attachment.

The *Gita* certainly assumes that the love relationship between the devotee and God is one of otherness. We are told rather strenuously that the devotee does not lose his identity, dare I say lose his individuality[24], on loving God. While the prerequisite of becoming one with *Brahman* is modelled on an aria with but a single voice, the love which exists between the devotee and God is decidedly a duet. As Krishna says, "Who sees me everywhere, who sees the all in Me, for him I am not lost, nor is he lost to Me" (VI, 30). So what we find in the *Gita* is not so much a philosophy of love between a personal God and his devotees, which replaces the philosophy of knowledge of the impersonal *Brahman* which we find in the *Upanishads*. On the contrary. Not only does the *Gita* basically acknowledge the *Upanishadic* message wholesale, albeit with a powerful and poignant ontological alteration,[25] but it supplements the path of knowledge with of a philosophy of love which can only begin where the philosophy of knowledge ends. The *bhakti-yoga* or the love and worship of God is in addition to, rather than in lieu of, knowledge of *Brahman*. It is not that God loves the liberated person especially; God loves the liberated person exclusively just as long as the liberated person becomes God's devotee (Cf. XII, 14). So while my ideal *Gita* would prefer to agree with a commentator like Dasputa, for example, who believes that, in the *Gita*, "One may seek to attain this state [of perfect equanimity of mind] ***either*** by philosophic wisdom ***or*** by devotion to God" (Emphasis mine.), he seems to be rather wrong-headed.[26] But Sharma too is wrong-headed for thinking that, in the *Gita*, "Absolute monism is ... the completion of the dualism with which the devotional consciousness starts."[27] Radhakrishnan, commenting on the monistic tendencies in the late Vedic hymns, said, "The mind of man is not satisfied with an anthropomorphic deity."[28] The *Gita* would seem to be a demonstration to the contrary. To give the *Gita* itself the last word, Krishna says, "Of these the man of wisdom, ever integrated, who loves-and-worships Me alone excels: for to the man of wisdom I am exceedingly dear and he is dear to Me" (VII, 17).

Notes

1. See Chandradhar Sharma, *Indian Philosophy: A Critical Survey*, p. 27 for a brief account of the "*Urgita*."

2. Throughout, I have used the translation of R.C. Zaehner, *The Bhagavad-Gita* (London: Oxford University Press, 1973).

3. See Zaehner, op. cit., pp. 187, 392.

4. "For whosoever makes me his haven, base-born though he may be, yes, women too and artisans, even serfs, theirs it is to tread the highest way" (IX, 32).

5. "By love-and-loyalty he comes to know Me as I really am, how great I am and who; and once he knows Me as I am, he enters [Me] forthwith" (XVIII, 55).

6. "Be it a leaf or flower or fruit or water that a zealous soul may offer me with love's devotion, that do I [willingly] accept, for it was love that made the offering" (IX, 26).

7. See Surendranath Dasputa, *A History of Indian Philosophy,* Vol. II, pp. 468-470, for a complete account of the three gunas in their various relations in the *Gita.*

8. If Arjuna does move from being confused in the early chapters of the *Gita* to having all of his confusion destroyed by the end (XVIII, 72-73), it was primarily because he has had a prolonged encounter with God. In chapter XI, for example, Arjuna had the unique experience of seeing God as he really was, an experience we are told which no one ever had before (XI, 45, 47) and, upon seeing God's divine form, Arjuna said, "at last I understand" (XI, 18). Krishna also told Arjuna that he had a "godly destiny" (XVI, 5) and is told, by Krishna of his salvation (XVIII, 64). And God directs the following comment specifically to Arjuna out of his personal love for him: "Bear Me in mind, love Me and worship Me, sacrifice, prostrate yourself to me: so will you come to Me, I promise you truly, for you are dear to Me" (XVIII, 65). Then, through God's grace (prasada), all of Arjuna's doubts were completely dispelled (XVIII, 73). Indeed, Arjuna seems to fit the description of the *sattvic* man of self-surrender (XVIII, 9-10) and no longer the *rajasic* man of self-surrender (XVIII, 8). Arjuna therefore seems to have moved rather miraculously from confusion to understanding, in the course of his encounter with God, and I would venture to guess that he might have moved from a *rajasic* to a *sattvic* nature without having had to satisfy the

requirement of multiple rebirths in order to perfect his spiritual exercise to win liberation.

9. Descriptions of the perfect yogin and the man of steady wisdom abound in the *Gita*: man of steady wisdom (II, 56-7); the "man God loves" (XII, 13-19). These are essentially the same descriptions although it is clear that God returns love and gives knowledge of himself as God only to those liberated devotees who love Him first.

10. The person whose wisdom or knowledge is manifested ***both in theory and in practice*** is precisely the person Arjuna needs to become in order for him to be liberated and thus in a position to love God.

11. Most of Chapter XVII and much of Chapter XVIII are dedicated to the application of the three gunas to such specifics as food, sacrifice, asceticism, and the giving of alms.

12. Zaehner's gloss (p. 147) makes little sense to me although his translation seems to clarify the point. The path of active work *for its own sake* , i.e., in active and selfish pursuit of their fruits, is not what the text means by the path of *karma-yoga*, the unselfish performance of prescribed actions.

13. This is why at the beginning of chapter III, Arjuna says, "If you think that [the contemplative life of] the soul (buddhi) is a loftier [course] than [the mere performance of] acts, then why do you command me to do a cruel deed?" (III, 1) "You confuse my soul (buddhi) [and intellect], or so it seems, with distinctly muddled words: so tell me with authority the one [simple way] whereby I can attain the better part" (III, 2).

14. Zaehner, p. 203.

15. See Zaehner p.218. One must practice *yoga* in order to be able to contemplate (*Samkhya*) and renounce works (See VI, 2). Compare Sharma, *Indian Philosophy: A Critical Survey*: "*yoga* bereft of

knowledge is an impossibility.... The culmination of action is in knowledge" (p. 22).

16. The prerequisites for *bhakti-yoga*, which alone serves as the pathway to God, will be the other two *yoga*s (theory-practice; *jnana-karma*) which will merge into a single *yoga* of praxis. While Zaehner claims that "Throughout the *Gita jnana*, 'wisdom,' is contrasted with *karma*, action" (p. 162), I would be much more inclined to follow Sharma: "*Karma-yoga* is not opposed to *jnana-yoga*" (p. 23), though not for his reasons. Sharma believes that "Karma and *Bhakti*, understood in their proper senses, are only manifestations of *jnana*" (p. 25).

17. That God's mode of being is not the same as liberation or becoming *Brahman*, see IV, 10; VIII, 5; XIII, 18; XIV, 19.

18. Zaehner refers to the "progressive stages on the way to liberation" (p. 173. See also pp. 195, 384). Compare the hierarchy of *yoga*s at XII, 12 which excludes mention of *bhakti* as well as XIII, 24-25. *Bhakti-yoga* is obviously possible at all stages (Compare Zaehner, p. 398) but they differ in kind not by degree. Sacrifice (*yajna*) to other gods which Krishna guarantees would be the lowest kind of *bhakti*. One kind of knowledge wins liberation which allows for one kind of devotion to God. Being devoted to God then wins the devotee a different kind of knowledge, namely, knowledge of God as he truly is, which then affords the devotee a new and higher kind of devotion which is the ultimate and highest goal in the *Gita*.

19. This is the reason why God says that those who revere the impersonal *Brahman* only will reach or attain him (XI, 3-4) though it is difficult (XI, 5. Cf. V, 6). Zaehner (p. 324) says the reason for this is because becoming *Brahman* and drawing near to the transcendent God are essentially the same thing; there is no real distinction between the two (Z. 325). But if there is no real distinction between the impersonal *Brahman* and Krishna as personal God, why is the pursuit of the former said to be more difficult? It is because there is no personal element of love and devotion which makes it easier for human beings to understand.

But even this makes little sense if the need to be an integrated self (liberated or attain moksa or becoming *Brahman*) is a necessary precondition for being devoted to a personal God. One would think that learning to be detached and indifferent to all things would make learning to be attached and devoted to a personal God all the more difficult. Zaehner (p. 326) claims that the seeker of *Brahman* is able to attain God because he receives bhakti "the lamp of wisdom" from God. However, there may be another metaphysical explanation. To know *Brahman*, the only proper object of knowledge (XIII, 12) is to know God's body therefore, in some sense at least, to know God (XI, 38). See Zaehner, p. 340.

20. In much the same way that the *Upanishads* distinguish two kinds of knowledge, a higher and a lower, the *Gita* seems to be doing the same thing. Lower knowledge in the *Gita* at least would refer to jnana- and *karma-yoga* taken together which are required for the individual to win liberation and become one with *Brahman*, the impersonal absolute. Higher knowledge in the *Gita* would be the unique knowledge which God gives only to the liberated devotee, through his grace, in return for the devotee's love.

21. For grace (prasada), see XVIII, 56–57, 62, 73.

22. Chandradhar Sharma, *Indian Philosophy: A Critical Survey* cites this passage and says that "Even the devotees are granted knowledge by the Lord so that they may realize the goal" (p. 22). What Sharma has failed to realize is that the knowledge which God gives is subsequent to, and other than, the knowledge required to be liberated.

23. Krishna continuously re-describes throughout the *Gita* the perfect yogin or man of steady wisdom of chapter II, that is, the person who is even-minded, without desires, who has renounced the fruits of his actions; a mind untroubled in the midst of sorrow, free from anger, desire, and pleasure, having no passion, fear or rage or any affection one way or the other, neither loving nor hating. He is indifferent to what might happen to him either for good or bad having drawn his senses and thereby his desires

away from the objects of sense as a tortoise would draw its head into its shell. He has "no love for any thing" (II, 57). The perfect yogin does not seem to have the prerequisites for loving and attaching himself to God.

24. I say this because of Krishna's comment at XV,7: "In a world of living things a minute part of Me, eternal [still], becomes a living [self], drawing to itself the five senses and the mind which have their roots in Nature." This passage might suggest that while a non-dual *atman* metaphysics is appropriate for *jnana-yoga* and becoming one with *Brahman*, a metaphysics which has a plethora of purushas might make more sense of *bhakti-yoga* with its difference in unity.

25. I think that the three different persons passage at XV, 16-17 coupled with Krishna's claim: "For I am the base supporting *Brahman*, – immortal [*Brahman*] which knows no change ..." (XIV, 27) are sufficient to make a case that the personal God is ontologically superior to *Brahman*. See Zaehner, p. 339.

26. S. Dasputa, *A History of Indian Philosophy*, Vol. II, p. 503.

27. Sharma, op. cit., p. 25.

28. A Sourcebook in Indian Philosophy, edited by S. Radhakrishnan and Charles A. Moore (Princeton: Princeton University Press, 1957), p. 17.

Love and Knowledge in *The Bhagavad Gita*

Martin Andic

The *Bhagavad Gita* addresses the question how can one act *freely*, free of guilt, in a situation in which there is evil in whatever one does. In explaining this secret of secrets to Arjuna, Krishna mentions the ways of work, knowledge, and love—dharma, jnana, and *bhakti*—and seems to say that they are all equally ways to God and truth and freedom. Nevertheless, does one of the ways come before the others? I will explore the idea that although at their highest and fullest they really are equal, even one and the same, nevertheless love does come first. In developing this I will refer to respects in which activity is passive and passivity is active,[1] related respectively to Taoist *wei wu wei* or non-active action, and to passion or suffering for a cause such as justice or truth; and I will show some links to the themes of knowledge as becoming and realization or incarnation of what is known, as in the medieval notion of connaturality. In closing my remarks I will point out some parallels in New Testament Christianity and in the writings of a major poet of our own century.

I

The *Bhagavad Gita* presents a conversation taken from the middle of the pre-Buddhist, sixth century epic of

Great India, the *Mahabharata* (6.13-40) which recounts the conflict between the families of two royal brothers, Dhrita-rashtra and Pandu. Dhrita-rashtra was the elder but because he was blind it was agreed that his brother Pandu should be king; in time Pandu died and left his five sons in the care of his blind brother, who raised them in the palace along with his own hundred sons. Dhrita-rashtra's eldest son Duryodhana was wicked; he hated his cousins for their heroism and piety, and persecuted them. For a time the two families shared the kingdom, but the Pandavas twice lost their portion by gambling. Eventually the whole of India was drawn into a civil war, which the poem presents frankly as a conflict of good and evil. Arjuna is the third of the five sons of Pandu and belongs to the side of good; Krishna is his charioteer, his brother-in-law and cousin. The conversation begins as the two armies are drawn up for a great battle.[2]

The poem's title, *Bhagavad Gita*, means "the song of glorious God." The conversation is narrated by Sanjaya to King Dhrita-rashtra, and Sanjaya says that he was granted the supernatural power to see and hear from a distance all that happened on the battlefield in order to report it to the blind king.[3]

It has been said that the real battle is a spiritual one. And it is true that the battlefield, the field of the Kurus, a sacred place of pilgrimage near Delhi, is called the field of *dharma*, justice, truth, in the sense of our task or work in life (cf. 3.35, 18.47). Moreover, Krishna occasionally calls Arjuna to war on self, on selfish desire that leads to wrong and evil doing, by destroying faith in goodness and God.[4] And he goes on to explain that when we know the divine Self that is deathless and indestructible in all of us, we cannot kill or cause another to kill (2.21), we cannot hurt ourselves by hurting others (13.28, cf. 12.13, 18). We must destroy selfish desire[5] and find peace (2.48, 55, 60, 70-72).

On the other hand, Krishna is explaining to Arjuna how he can war on his enemies, fight for justice, fulfil his duty as a *warrior*, with peace in his soul (2.31-38). He must fight for right against wrong, though he must first destroy wrong within himself,[6] overcome what is merely human, in this sense titanic, by what is divine. He must first fight free of egoistic worldly desire that blinds him to the truth about how rightly to live, and so keeps him from fulfilling that truth. But he has to fulfil it by making war, leading his soldiers into slaughter. Thus if the inward and spiritual battle for justice is the real battle presented in the text, it is fulfilled in the outward and bloody battle for India that presupposes it.

With this qualification it could also be said that the Pandavas and Kuravas are the divine and titanic elements respectively both in man and in the soul of India. Arjuna and Krishna are another human and divine pair, but of a different kind; Arjuna is not opposed and alien to Krishna but receptive and akin to him. The last line of the poem says that "wherever Krishna drives and Arjuna bends the bow [with him], there is beauty and victory, prosperity and justice"; thus in the person who masters himself we see the beauty and victory, the joy and the righteousness of God himself. For Arjuna is related to Krishna as in the *Mundaka Upanishad* 3.1-13 the fruit-eating bird is related to the Atmanic bird that does not eat but looks at and with Brahman, where the first bird is unhappy until it sees the other and what it sees, and likewise ceases to eat the fruit and is fed instead by the vision of God.[7] Within the poem Krishna is a human being like Arjuna, who drives his chariot, hears his lament, offers advice, then gradually reveals himself as the supreme God himself, wonderful and terrifying, before resuming his gracious and gentle human form, and spelling out the secret of secrets to answer the question in Arjuna's heart. Thus almost the first thing we learn about the two is that Krishna is "the Lord of the soul" and Arjuna is "the winner of treasure" (1.15). Krishna then is both man and God, in that Krishna is a free man who sees God and knows himself to be one with him, and who calls Arjuna to be and do what he is and does, someone who does right in sacrifice of self for the good of all.[8]

II

Arjuna causes his chariot to be driven between the two armies and speaks his heart to Krishna. Seeing kinsmen and teachers facing one another on both sides, he is overcome with pity and despair. What good can come of such a fight? he asks. For who can desire victory, kingdom, pleasure, or life at such a cost, when even those for whom we desire it must give up their own life? I would rather be killed myself than kill my kinsmen and teachers; for evil reaps evil, especially when knowingly done; and destroying a family destroys all customs and society. Why then destroy my own people for merely earthly kingdom, and not let them kill me without a fight? (1.21-47). Krishna tells him to get a grip on himself and be a man. Yet Arjuna repeats, how can I kill those I owe reverence even if they would take my kingdom? I would rather eat a beggar's food than a king's smeared with blood. For who knows whether killing or being killed is better for us? I am weak with pity, and cannot see my duty: show me. Neither kingdom nor heaven will do me any good until I am healed. I will not fight (2.1-9).

Krishna treats Arjuna's doubts as merely materialistic and self-centered, as sentimental self-pity, and goes on to explain to him that what is truly alive in him and in everyone else is divine, deathless and indestructible;

Arjuna must do his work, as everyone must, even God, and his work is to make war; but he must do it in renunciation of selfish desire and surrender of selfish rewards, as a sacrifice to God whose work is sacrifice and who is sacrifice.[9]

Krishna mysteriously says, however, that a man cannot avoid action to which he is driven by the forces of nature (3.5, 33, 18.11, 40, 59-60), and that it is selfish delusion to think he himself is the agent (3.27), he ought to think that it is only his body that works (5.11); similarly, God only watches the work of nature and man, and is not bound by it (5.14-15, 9.9, 13.22, 29, 31). Nevertheless we must *do* the work to be done (3.19, 35, 5.10, 6.1, 18.7, 47); God himself works, though he has nothing to do, and unless he did all would be chaos (3.22-24), we should be only the means of *his* work, here on the battlefield, these men are already slain by him (11.33), *his* hands and feet are everywhere, his power is measurelessly great (13.33, 11.16, 40).

This is not exactly determinism or fatalism or predestination, a view that I must do whatever I do because I am naturally caused to do it, or because God knows that I will do it or has already done it himself; nor is it a dualism whereby God has abandoned the world and mankind to the amoral forces of nature, and even less a divine voluntarism by which whatever happens, right or wrong, it is God who does it. What Krishna is driving at belongs not to metaphysics so much as to religious ethics.

Our clue is the emphasis on sacrifice. Krishna says in the name of God that he has nothing to do and yet he works for the good of the world, in selfless beneficence that is sacrifice, in which he is recipient, giver, and what is given. He means that he has no worldly object to get since he has everything, being the God of all; and that (if we may put it this way) he is nothing but love that loves nothing but love: a love that is righteousness or justice, working always only for what is good for all (3.20-25, 4.7-8, 14.27). We for our part cannot avoid the compulsions of nature and duty, but we can obey them with free consent; we can love God and his love and righteousness, and let these be our whole and only action, in surrender and passivity to him as his instruments (4.17-18).[10]

Thus when we are so placed that whatever we do we must do harm—more particularly when we cannot fulfil our duty, do right, without harming someone, and so cannot avoid the greatest evil without committing a lesser one[11]—we can act free of blame nevertheless by pausing to weigh up selflessly all the demands on us, taking everything relevant into account and giving each its due weight, and then doing what right thing there is to do, regarding the good as accomplished by God, and the inevitable evil as done by nature. Thus the secret of secrets is to love God, and do what we will.[12]

If the right thing to do, our *dharma*, the work God wants us to do, his will, is what offers itself when we look selflessly, there is perhaps room to ask how we know that we are looking selflessly enough; or that we love God enough, or purely enough, to look quite selflessly. I think Krishna would say that there is no criterion and whatever seems right really *is* right, so long as we have faith that God directs the hearts of those who love him, so as not to let their hearts be defiled by the evil they do or suffer.

It is generally true that we cannot do what is right and good without failing to do some other thing that is good; and it is certainly true that whenever we deal with *force*, whether by using it like Arjuna or suffering it like Christ, we feel a loss of contact with God, goodness, and truth. We doubt ourselves, feel degraded, *cursed* by the evil we do or receive, at least fear that we may be only calling our own heart God, or resenting and hating our oppressor and the God who allows us to be harmed, and wishing to return evil for evil and wrong for wrong. A Christian like Simone Weil would say that all we can do—to save ourselves from the spiritual delusion of David Koresh and the Branch Davidians, or the Brotherhood of the Solar Temple—is to *ask* that the harm we do may fall on no one but ourselves, and that the evil we receive we may absorb without passing it on.[13] But this is *to love justice*, to love God.[14] I think that this is what Krishna is calling the secret of secrets: love me, and you may do as you choose; fear not, for I will free you from all sin (18.63-66).

III

He goes on to say that he wants to be worshiped by the knowledge of him who studies this sacred dialogue of theirs; though he too is freed and finds his joy who only hears but has faith in it. Arjuna says that he has heard it with a single heart, and it has destroyed the delusion of his ignorance, so that he will *do* Krishna's word (18.70-73); and thus it seems that the knowledge that is true worship is active acceptance in practice. Now all through Krishna's discourse it has been said that we are united to God in *work* rightly done as a sacrifice of God (3.11, 19, 30-31, 4.23-24, 5.6-7); in *knowledge* of God (4.33-35, 5.16-24, 6.29-31, 7.17-19), and in *love* of God (6.31, 47, 9.29, 31, 34). All three—*karma, jnana, bhakti*—seem to be a union of subject with subject. But it is *love* that comes first (8.22), and God is especially responsive to our love of him.[15] It seems to follow that our best and entire work for God and knowledge of him is love: it is not merely a result of love, but love itself.[16] It is adherence and contact and union, with an active dimension of surrender and a passive dimension of transformation and embodiment. It is what Thomas calls a *connatural* knowledge that consists in obedience, practice, becoming what we know. Like is known only by like.[17]

There is a similar thought in New Testament Christianity, e.g., in *John* 14 where Christ tells his disciples that the one who does his word is the one who loves him and is loved by him and the Father, and to whom Christ will manifest himself, to whom Christ and Father will come to live with him. In other words, it is by practice that shows our own love that we acquire the love and the knowledge of God, a love that is itself acknowledgment, and a sharing of life. He is to be the vine and we the branches, and (in brief) he and his Father are to be in us, so that what they have done for us, we shall do for one another, and for the world. Likewise in *1 John* 4 only that person knows God who loves God, for God is love. Paul says that knowledge is nothing without love, and that it is not he himself who lives but Christ in him. He prays that we too may know the love of Christ that surpasses all knowledge [but *his,* Christ's], and so may fulfil every law.[18]

The last letter of the poet Yeats formulates a comparable thought.

> I will begin to write my most fundamental thoughts ... I am happy, and I think full of an energy ... I had despaired of. It seems to me that I have found what I wanted. When I try to put all into a phrase I say, 'Man can embody truth, but he cannot know it.' I must embody it in the completion of my life. The abstraction is not life and everywhere draws out its contradictions. You can refute Hegel but not the saint or the Song of Sixpence.[19]

Man can embody truth, but he cannot otherwise know it. This is a truth of which we have our best and entire knowledge by passive action and active suffering: learning it by surrender to it that passively lets it change us into it to give it flesh and blood, and that actively endures for it faithfully whatever comes. Yeats does not say that to learn the truth we must *love* it, but perhaps that is implied, for he is speaking of a truth it gives him joy and energy to know.

This knowledge is personal, one might say existential in Kierkegaard's sense that it comes by our existing in what we understand, basing our thoughts and actions and thus our life and existence on it. Krishna can be understood as a human being who has realized it; or as the higher element of a man who has fulfilled it. But it is also impersonal, in that it is selfless and unworldly, and is present *wherever* or in whomever it is fulfilled or in whoever wants to fulfil it and loves it. But in this sense it is individualizing, realizing, so again personal.

IV

The poem is a miracle. It shows a man who does the impossible, or anyhow what is impossible without God, namely to do *right* even when one has to do evil. And it explains how what this man does, any of us can do too, with the love of God. If the poem is right, then the evil that we *do* can be purified, just as if the Gospels are right then the evil that we *suffer* can be made pure. The two accounts complete each other. The world can be redeemed. It is a miraculous world. This is a miracle play. Who wrote it? Surely not a human being?[20]

Notes

1. I take this way of putting it from Marina Barabas.

2. When the conversation is complete the battle resumes and lasts for eighteen days, with total victory for the Pandavas and the death of Duryhodhana. Arjuna's eldest brother Yudhisthira becomes king of all India and rules for 36 years. The poem closes with the death of Krishna, the brothers' renunciation, and their entry into heaven.

3. 18.7; 1.1-2.10 & ff, 11.9, 35, 50, 18.74-78.

4. 3.41 "slay sinful desire, the destroyer of vision and wisdom," 43; 4.42 "Kill with the sword of wisdom the doubt born of ignorance in your heart." Thus Rama Coomaraswamy, "The *Bhagavad Gita*," *Studies in Comparative Religion* 10.3 (1976), pp. 175-87.

5. There is also self*less* righteous desire that is good and leads to vision and freedom: 7.11, 20-22 "I am desire when this is pure, not against righteousness ... if a man desires with faith to adore this or that god, I give faith to that man ... [and from that god] he attains his desires; but whatever is good comes from me," 11.3 "my soul is yearning to see your form as God of this all," 12.8 "Set your heart on me alone, and give me your understanding, and you will in truth live in me hereafter," 13.11, 15.9-10, 18.37.

6. It might be argued that the *Gita* presents a struggle for the soul of man – a struggle between right and wrong, where *wrong* argues that the cost of right in unavoidable evil makes right impossible, even though the cost of wrong is even worse – and *right* replies that nevertheless right is right, and that the evil it involves is necessary and blameless if one does right for the love of God.

7. In the *Rig Veda* 1.164.20 it is the Self that *eats* the fruit of Divine Knowledge that is greater than the self that does not yet do so; while in the *Upanishad* it is the Self that does *not* eat the fruit of worldly knowledge that is greater than the self that does; for the

Veda the Self is immanent or humanly realized, for the *Upanishad* it is at first transcendent only. In *Katha Upanishad* 3.1, there are two in the secret high place of the heart, but *both* drink the wine of life in the world of truth; in 3.3 the Atman is Lord of the chariot, and if reason is the charioteer and the body is the chariot, then the man himself is the one who reaches the goal. Krishna's name means "black one" whereas Arjuna's means "white one." Krishna's name is also explained by some as "draws the heart," or again as "earthly happiness." This last meaning is especially appropriate, insofar as he is showing how a man may live the life of God in the world, in Buddhist terms how to live in Nirvana in Samsara, even a warrior, even a man of *rajas*, like Arjuna. Thus BG 2.54, 3.1-2, 6,33, 37, 14.5-27; 6.31 "He who in this disciplined oneness of love, loves me in whatever he sees, *wherever* this man may live, truly this man lives in me"; 18.55-56.

8. Thus 1.15, 5.24, 6.27, 7.18 "the man of vision and I are one," 9.11, 11.50-51, 13.30, 34, 14.26, 18.54-55, and 4.6-9, 3.10-25. This is the state of non-dual vision and love and sacrifice in which Al-Hallaj spoke as a human voice of God, somewhere between Socrates (*Apology* 23ab) and Isaiah and Jeremiah, on the one hand, and a full *avatar* or incarnation like Jesus, on the other. See 4.7-8 rendered by Peter Brook in his film version of *The Mahabharata* (1987) as "I was born to destroy the destroyers, and I became your friend for love of the world."

9. 3.10-25, 4.9, 24 "Who in all his work seeks God, he in truth goes unto God: God is his worship, God is his offering, offered by God in the fire of God," 8.4 "In this body I offer sacrifice, and my body is a sacrifice," 9.16 "I am the sacrifice ... the holy fire, and the offering that is made in the fire," 11.19 "I see your face as a sacred fire that gives light and life to the whole universe in the splendor of a vast offering." This is the sacrifice of Nachiketas in the *Katha Upanishad*. It may well be the fire of Heraclitus (Diels B 30, 67). Thus M. L. West, *Early Greek Philosophy and the Orient* (Oxford 1971), page 201: "The *Brhadaranyaka Upanishad* alone throws more light on what Heraclitus was talking about than all the remains of the other Pre-socratics together." Cf. the fire of Prometheus in Hesiod, *Theogony* 500-613, *Works and Days* 45-104.

10. Obedience can be a kind of rest: 4.18. Cf. *Lao Tzu* 16, 20, 37, 45; *Matthew* 11.28-30, *Jeremiah* 6.16.

11. Thus Aristotle remarks (in *Nicomachean Ethics* 3.1) that the sea captain *unwillingly* throws his cargo overboard, for to lose it is an evil, but he *willingly* does it to save himself and his crew and passengers and his ship, because that is a lesser evil. The actress Mae West is supposed to have said: "Whenever I have to choose between two evils, I always pick the one I never tried before." Cf. Simone Weil: "The serpent offered Adam and Eve knowledge. The sirens offered Ulysses knowledge. These stories teach us that the soul becomes lost by seeking for knowledge for pleasure.... But it is right for us to seek for knowledge in suffering." (*Notebooks*, tr. Arthur Wills, page 216.) This is knowledge through practice, taking a stand and enduring every consequence: it is learning through suffering, the return to the cave.

12. 18.63 "I have given you the secret of secrets; think of it in your heart, and do what you choose." Cf. Dante, *Purgatory* 27.139-143 "Expect no more of me in word or deed: here your will is upright, free and whole, and you would be in error not to heed whatever your own impulse prompts you to do: lord of yourself I crown and mitre you"; behind this is Augustine, "Love and do what you will" (*On John's Letter to Parthos* 7.8, commenting on *1 John* 3.6, 9, 5.18 "no one born of God sins"); in the Old Testament there is already Nathan's word to David in *2 Samuel* 7.3 "Go, do all that is in your heart; for the LORD is with you," see further *1 Kings* 8.17f. To love God and do what you will, that means, Love God and do what right thing you must, for that is what He wills and your best and only freedom, not from dying but from doing wrong and fear of doing it.

13. This is perhaps the star example of active suffering: a passion of innocent goodness that so loves right that it will *never* do wrong even in defense or return, thus ever receive wrong rather than do it, like Socrates, and like Christ.

14. I am following Simone Weil in her *Notebooks* 25 ("The *Bhagavad Gita* and the Gospels complete each other"), 53-58, 285-

286, 418. But Christ seems more fully human, more fully incarnate, than Krishna, who seems not even for a moment to share the horror of the defilement of *doing* wrong that Arjuna feels, as Christ must feel that of *suffering* wrong. Christ is closer to Arjuna than to Krishna at this point.

15. Thus 4.3 "Today I reveal to you this eternal Yoga, this supreme secret, because you love me, and call me friend," 7.1 "you will have the full vision of me, if your heart is set on me," 7.17 "The best is the man of vision, who is ever one, and whose love is one; for I love him and he loves me," 10.1 "I speak for your true good, because you rejoice in me," 10.10 "To those who love me and worship me with love, I give the Yoga of vision by which they come to me," 11.55 "Only by love can men see me, and know me, and come unto me," 18.55 "By love he knows me in truth and enters into my Being," 18.65 "Give me your mind and your love and your sacrifice and your worship, and I promise you will come to me because I love you." (Cf. *Svetasvatara Upanishad* 6.23).

16. Love is not all you need, is not enough, when it is contrasted with knowledge and work; but love is fulfilled in knowledge and work, and perfects them. It includes them.

17. 10.15 "Only your Self knows your Self; " 11.8 "You will never see me with your own eyes, I will give you divine vision, see my high glory," 38 "You are the one to be known and the one to know it." The "only" and "never " are, however, an acknowledgment of transcendence: love's knowledge lets the other go as not fully knowable otherwise than by love, lets it be in its mystery, its *reality*.

18. *1 Corinthians* 8.1-3, 13.1-13, *2 Corinthians* 5.11, *Galatians* 4.9, 2.20, *Ephesians* 3.14-19, *Romans* 13.8-10.

19. *The Letters of W. B . Yeats*, edited by Allan Wade (MacMillan 1955), page 922, a letter to Lady Elizabeth Pelham, January 4th 1939. The Song of Sixpence sings of king, queen, maid, blackbirds, each with its own part to play, just as Arjuna must play his. I

thank Kathleen Raine for this reference, and Wendy Hamblet for the suggestion about the Song.

20. See Harold Goddard in *The Meaning of Shakespeare* (1951), Chapter 1, page 14, and Chapter 29, page 171 (on *Lear*); Fyodor Dostoevsky, *The Brothers Karamazov* (1880) 1.6.2d, page 356 in McDuff version, Penguin Books 1993.

The Passion of Arjuna

Charles Elliott Vernoff

I
The Passion Situation

Insofar as a religious tradition is a finite construction of cultural elements, it is in principle subject to destruction by one of the infinite challenges time can put to it. The supreme test comes through a crisis wherein the structure of existence threatens to overcome the structure of norms and a tradition appears to fall into contradiction with itself under the weight of a turbulent reality it cannot contain. So overwhelmed, man becomes radically aware of his passivity in the face of an aroused cosmos which has emasculated his sense of orientation to his experience. This situation, forcing upon man ultimate consciousness of has passivity, his contingency upon the conditions of his existence, may be called the situation of passion.

A religious tradition emerges as great when it weathers the radical doubt engendered in the passion situation, and incorporates within its principles the crisis. By so doing, a religious tradition transcends its own parochialism of historical conditioning and becomes infinite and universal; a religion must transcend its own structure to achieve the highest level upon which it merits the attention of everyone in the human situation itself, of all mankind.

Three great religious traditions, Hinduism, Judaism and Christianity, classically develop the norms of response for the roles which man may assume in the human situation of passivity; respectively, these are agency, sufferance and obedience. Each tradition contains a passion situation in which religion stands on trial by existence and vindicates its universal relevance radically.

All norms, secular or religious, have as their purpose the furtherance of life. For a norm to recommend annihilation is to become inconsistent with itself, to fall into a contradiction in terms. Even in Buddhism, the "annihilation" wrought by nirvana is a dialectical term, the object of which is an ego-less spiritual recreation. Passion situations arise when religious duty seems to require self-annihilation, repudiation of the ground of one's own being: this is not only paradox but categorical impossibility. Suicide itself represents a final desperate attempt to protect the self from an overwhelming reality by destroying in principle the possibility of intolerable experiences. The self can do naught but wish to save itself, even when that salvation entails an apparent destruction; it can no more wish itself into nonbeing than can the heart wish to stop beating, for its nature is to exist.

In the passion of sufferance, acceptance of the inscrutable agency of the God of history seems to require Job to acquiesce in his own annihilation, moving Job to question the justice of God. In the passion of obedience, Jesus questions the faithfulness of the God whom he has agreed unfalteringly to serve, asking at the height of his agony why that God had forsaken him; obedience seems to demand separation from Him whom Jesus recognized as the ground of his being.

On the plain of Kurukshetra, Arjuna undergoes the passion of agency. Religious duty, as a member of the warrior caste, calls upon Arjuna to slay beloved kinsmen with whom he identifies himself. Arjuna cries in anguish to his charioteer, Krishna, "Though they should slay me, how could I harm them?" and the *Bhagavad-Gita* unfolds.

II
Dramatic and Ontological Structure of the Passion

Commentators both Western and Eastern have more often than not despaired of detecting any real structure in the *Bhagavad-Gita*. In the general view, it consists of a medley of philosophical ideas—appealing or confusing depending on the individual taste—loosely, artificially and even suspiciously attached to the dramatic structure of an epic narrative with a life and direction very much its own. The two protagonists become little more than mouthpieces to promulgate the syncretistic thinking of the author, regarded as more likely than not an interpolator, and the dramatic situation becomes nothing but a painfully protracted stitch in time while opposing armies are amassed eager to commence battle—an "absurdity" according to Edgerton.

And yet the Indian people have taken the *Gita* to their heart and canonized it with centuries of devotion not accorded so powerfully to any other single sacred text. Now, the most cursory investigation of the popular religious taste anywhere and at any time reveals that straight philosophy only weakly if at all titillates the palate of the common folk; only other people, people in dramatic situations of tribulation and victory, excite the perennial interest of the mass. The *akeda* of Abraham and Isaac, Israel in Egypt, the temptation of Adam, the Christmas and Easter narratives—these Biblical accounts have captivated the popular Western imagination for centuries. In our own experience, they give ample indication of the flavor of faith that thrills the body of believers. And why should it be different in the East? On the contrary, the undying acclaim afforded the Ramayana and the Mahabharata serve notice that the heart of the people, stronghold of any faith, is everywhere reliably dedicated to the moments of passion and grandeur, of dramatic and cosmic intensity, in the annals of religious tradition.

Consistently enough, therefore, the *Gita* is the heart of the Mahabharata. This would suggest that, in the minds of the people where the depth of faith generates, the *Gita* embodies—rather than a tranquil hiatus of philosophical babble in the midst of fascinating cataclysm—the very apex of this monumental epic's dramatic action. Why has this possibility not occurred to generations of commentators? There would seem to be but one explanation: the gulf which yawns historically between the religion of the people and the religion of the philosophers. Philosophy, I suggest, found within the rich folds of the *Gita* much with which to preoccupy itself and never bothered to take interest in or account for the nature of popular devotion to the same text, a devotion which in all probability sprang from entirely different roots. Western students, themselves stepped in the classical philosophy of the Westernmost branch of the Aryan invasion, easily took their lead from the Hindu philosophers. Indeed, it is only very recently that the West has begun to realize the existence of great and profound theistic traditions in India; even now the vast bulk of interested Occidentals identify the loftiest attainment of Hindu piety with the cerebral doctrines of the *Vedanta* and *Yoga* schools.

It is my conviction that the *Bhagavad-Gita* represents a dramatic denouement whose impact achieves a force fully comparable to the most dramatic peaks in the Western tradition. Moreover, I suggest that as a passion situation it exhibits a generic structure shared with its sister traditions in Judaism and Christianity as well as a unique configuration of dramatic elements adapted to its special nature. The generic structure has two aspects: a dramatic or existential depth, related to the emotional core of religious experience; a theological or ontological breadth, related to the conceptual framework of religious thought.

The dramatic structure of the passion situation has four moments. First, the specter of a crisis of contradiction throws its shadow over a preestablished dramatic canvas. Secondly, the protagonist succumbs to the existential tension—which has thrust him out of cultic provinces into the naked light of universal interest—and in an agony of doubt questions the very ground of his being wherein he has wholeheartedly reposed total commitment, in which he has inextricably planted the foundations of his existence. Third, possible solutions are developed and explored in a speculative interlude. Fourth, a theophany provides the answer which it alone can render. In the passion of sufferance, these moments appear as the irrational subjection of Job to increasingly evil circumstance, Job's plea for an explanation from God, the orthodox justifications and rebukes of his friends, and the voice from the whirlwind betokening a direct experience of God which assures him of the incomprehensible reality of transcendental Divine justice. In the passion of obedience, these moments appear as the unanticipated depth of Jesus' agony on the cross, Jesus' bewildered cry for an explanation of why God had forsaken him, the uncertainty following his death when his disciples fall into tormenting doubt, and the victory of Resurrection. In the passion of agency, the prospect of slaughtering kin wracks Arjuna, he begs Krishna for guidance, he engages in dialogue with Krishna which gradually allays his hesitations, and finally

Krishna's manifestation of his Divine form brings absolute conviction.

The ontological structure of the passion situation has three moments. In order to grasp them, we must recall the function of a passion situation within a religious tradition. The passion situation presupposes institutionalization of a religious tradition. Any religious tradition posits two points of intersection between the transcendent and the human. The first, the giving of a teaching, may be called the constitutive disclosure of the transcendent; the second, the rendering of transcendent power to those who keep the teaching, may be called the actualizing disclosure of the transcendent. These two points reciprocally involve each other: the purpose of the teaching is showing how to draw upon transcendent power or achieve transcendent illumination, while the transcendent depends upon the teaching for its access route to the mundane.

As we have discussed, the elements of finitude in a religious tradition, its rootage in a particular cultural history, render it vulnerable to attack by the structure of existence. In such a crisis, a faithful adherent to a teaching challenges its adequacy and self-consistency, its capacity to offer comprehensive guidance, hence the strength of its reciprocal connection with the source of transcendent power or illumination. At such a juncture, a new disclosure of the transcendent is needed to reveal the adequacy of the teaching not only to normative experience but to external irruptions which jeopardize the structure of that normative experience—to existential breakdowns. No religion stands secure until it has withstood this extreme challenge, hence this third form of disclosure, which may be called the regulative, is integral to the structure of a great religious tradition ensuring its congruence not only with the structure of a culture but with the structure of being in general.

To be sure, the *raison d'etre* of the passion situation is reception of regulative disclosure of the transcendent. But in doing this, it must review normative religious teaching to demonstrate its apparent failure, on the one hand, and on the other hand must portray the protagonist, his doubts removed by theophany actualizing the transcendent in his life on its renewed basis. Thus the receptacle of the regulative disclosure must embrace the constitutive and actualizing disclosures in order to clarify its relationship with them.

Here emerge the three moments in the ontological structure of the passion situation: first, review of the constitutive disclosure, the normative religious teaching; second, the regulative disclosure, a theophany justifying the constitutive disclosure in the light of existential crisis; third, a presentation of the protagonist actualizing his relation to the transcendent on the new footing given by the regulative disclosure.

In the passion of sufferance, these moments arise in the dialogue of Job with his friends, the voice from the whirlwind, and the final image of Job with his estate and family restored. In the passion of obedience, the protagonist himself has delivered a new constitutive disclosure instituting total faith in the saving power of God which is doubted under pressure of the passion situation, the Resurrection is the regulative disclosure and Jesus' forty days on the earth thereafter display the actualization of his union with God, with the transcendent. With the structure of the passion of agency, we will now deal in detail.

III
The Passion of Agency

The acceptance of a religious teaching rests upon a profound trust in the transcendent source whence it derives. All living demands trust—in self, neighbour, time—of which the highest form is trust in the solidity of the structure of existence as conveyed in a religious tradition. The crisis which provokes a passion situation, by implicating the credibility of religious teaching, undermines trust in its source. Regulative disclosure must restore trust in both, teaching and source. Of the three passions we have mentioned, it is within the passion of agency that the most evident dialectic separation between trust in teaching and trust in source occurs. The drama of the *Bhagavad-Gita* consists in Arjuna's circumspect testing of the plausibility of Krishna's teaching through which he gradually realizes a trust in their source. The progress of the drama winds its way with an Oriental subtlety which apparently has defied the understanding of many Orientals; for it resides not primarily in any superimposed emotional interactions between Arjuna and Krishna, but in the nuances of the dialectic exchange itself, in the changing questions and the shifting level of diction.

Commentators have virtually without exception found the *Gita* a loosely organized philosophical hodgepodge of related discourses. At the same time, all have recognized in a rudimentary way that these discourses appear in a dialogic context; yet all have assumed that discourses and dialogue are only incidentally related, that the dramatic situation supplied a pretext for inserting philosophical ideas without any essential connections obtaining between dramatic form and discursive content of the *Gita*. In truth, close critical reading reveals marked alterations in the philosophical subject matter, delicately correlated with the deepening relationship between the protagonists. This should not come as a great surprise to the modern mind, which psychology has trained to recognize in all ostensibly "rational" disquisition an emotion base: two learned professors engaged in a scholarly dispute may appear to the uninitiated to be considering ideas and nothing more, but the familiar ear can detect the exchange of considerable passion in the overtones of phraseology. The elusiveness of the *Gita* stems from the fact that its philosophy, taken sequentially, is the very vehicle of its dramatic action which, with the single exception of the theophany in chapter eleven, manifests entirely in the overtones of language. In a sense, the *Gita* is a most astonishing tour de force, for it is as serious about its philosophy as about its drama—yet the two indwell each other in the identical language. We are in the West accustomed to philosophical novelists, such as Dostoevsky and Mann, and literary philosophers, such as Nietzsche, but one can always discriminate neatly between the components, for one invariably exploits the other: thus Mann exploits philosophy to create novels of intellectual appeal and Nietzsche exploits literary style and dramatic turns of phrase to embroider his philosophy. The *Gita* uniquely is both real philosophy and real drama, at one and the same time; drama is achieved in the order of discourses, themselves impeccably aloof from obvious deference to their dialogic context.

Dramatically, the *Gita* is a love story. Philosophically, it is a survey of the spiritual life in theory and practice. As the book unfolds, the situational love story converges with the philosophical discussion until both reach a climax simultaneously. The plot of the love story begins with a sensitive depiction of Arjuna's love for his relatives. As the "conqueror of sloth," the incomparable agent, Arjuna has apparently evinced unstinting devotion to his duty also. Now love for relatives and devotion to duty, conflict, and Arjuna in effect denounces his duty to slaughter his relatives. Arjuna has identified himself with his relatives, accords to them his highest love for in killing them he sees an action tantamount to killing himself. In rejecting the duty prescribed by his caste, Arjuna has implicitly rejected the author of the castes. But who is that author? None other than his charioteer and friend, Krishna, incarnation of God. How may Arjuna be induced, given his supreme and loyal love of kin, to join in battle against them? Two conditions are necessary, one positive and one negative. Negatively, Arjuna must be convinced that his relatives will not perish at death but merely exist in another form, moreover that his sword is the instrument of a foreordained destiny for which he is not accountable. But surely this negative conviction is in itself insufficient, providing no antidote to loving loyalty which would find no emotional respite in these cosmological data, would continue to feel in the murderous act a suicidal contradiction. No, only a positive transference of Arjuna's highest love to another object can free his warrior's blade to perform its duty. But any object will not do, for Arjuna would continue to feel great love for his kin and great guilt in attacking them. This new object must itself fulfill two conditions. First of all it must respond to Arjuna with a sublime love that by its nature can contain no malice, so as to gain Arjuna's unswerving trust; second, it must appeal to Arjuna on the basis of this trust to accept assurance of the ultimately benign purpose underlying the apparent viciousness of battle—which it can guarantee because it has ordained the purpose, a fact to which Arjuna gives credence on the basis of the same trust. These conditions fulfilled, Arjuna could take a spiritual leap, inferring from the supernal love he can feel the ultimate benevolence of its purposes, which he cannot understand. This exactly parallels the situation of Job, whose encounter with the

Source of all justice enables him to defer to its mundane purposes, which he cannot understand. As alliance with supreme love permits Arjuna to act without reservation, so conviction that he is disposed by supreme justice permits Job to suffer without reservation.

The soul of the *Gita*, then, is the poignantly dramatic transfer of Arjuna's greatest love and highest loyalty from his kin to God, apprehended in the person of his friend Krishna. This realization casts the philosophical dialogue in an entirely different light, for it becomes none other than the minute depiction of God on trial by man, with Arjuna's faith at stake every instant. Unless Krishna's replies satisfy Arjuna's exacting queries, the uncompromising keenness of agony will repudiate the Divine teaching and its incarnate vehicle. In this tense correlation of dramatic movement and true teaching, the remarkable unity of dramatic form and discursive content is consummated, the origin of the *Gita*'s universal appeal located.

We discover the immediate nexus between form and content in the nature of the negative condition for inducing Arjuna to fight, namely his rational conviction that duty, even in the onerous form he now confronts, aligns with and fulfills cosmic structure and purpose. But such rational conviction has a positive aspect as well, for it vindicates the superior wisdom of the collocutor who convinces and prepares the way for lodging absolute trust in him; the affirmation of reason is prerequisite to the affirmation of love.

IV
Towards Interpretative Analysis

The detailed analysis of the *Gita*, in light of the proposition that its philosophy embodies its drama and its drama embodies its philosophy, represents a task of considerable hermeneutic diligence. A brief paper such as this sufficiently justifies itself in executing with some thoroughness a propaedeutic function. Hence, we cannot intend that the following remarks be exhaustive but we may hope that they suggestively block out the major exegetical labor which ought properly to succeed them.

The *Gita*, divides, then, into three sections. In the first six chapters, Arjuna vanquishes his doubt in the teaching of Krishna, culminating in intellectual acquiescence, belief, in them. In chapters seven through eleven, Arjuna places his trust positively in the person of Krishna, for which a theophany rewards him. The remaining seven chapters depict Arjuna as a man of faith, in communion with and devoted to Krishna as God. This progression from belief through trust to faith follows the three ontological moments of the passion situation; the content and overtone of the discourse varies according to the structure of each moment respectively, with the level of Krishna's responses—both objective content and subjective presentation of himself—in correlation with the quality of Arjuna's querying.

The first section, a re-clarification of the constitutive disclosure in Hindu tradition, subdivides into two parts of three chapters each. Arjuna desperately requires practical guidance, and normative religious precepts seem too pedestrian to address the crisis of his agency, his passion situation. But practical guidance requires in turn theoretical justification, else it can be rejected as rootless and arbitrary. Accordingly the two parts present first the practice and then the theory of the principles of agency.

In Chapter 2, Krishna answers Arjuna's urgent plea to instruct him regarding the slaughter of kinsmen with an initial assurance of the indestructibility of the Atman: "The truly wise mourn neither for the living nor for the dead. There was never a time when I did not exist, nor you, nor any of these." Immediately following this negative assurance comes a positive injunction to caste duty: "... to a warrior, there is nothing nobler than a righteous war." This leads to a characterization of *Karma Yoga* and its goal of union with Brahman, which moves Arjuna to inquire how one may identify a man absorbed in Brahman. Krishna concludes the chapter with a description of the enlightened man. Arjuna's opening question in Chapter 3 shows he has lost the thread of the argument and confused means with ends: "If knowledge of Brahman is superior to action, why tell me to do these terrible deeds?" In the previous chapter, Krishna had consistently demonstrated that proper action leads to enlightenment, and hence these relate as means to end; Arjuna in his confusion asks in effect why employ the means if the end is superior to them, an absurd question. The heart of Arjuna's difficulty is mixing up knowledge of Brahman, goal of all *yoga*, with the *way* of knowledge, one of the means for attaining that ultimate knowledge. Krishna elucidates the distinction, goes on to remind that even the enlightened continue to act, although action is no longer obligatory. As knowledge represents both one means and the general goal, so action represents one means and a concomitant of that general goal. Arjuna, provisionally accepting the ultimacy of the way of action for himself, now asks what makes men act wrongly, deviate from duty into evil. The first part concludes with Krishna's implication of rage and lust as the heinous foes of duty. Throughout this part, Krishna has spoken in a third personal way and his relationship has been that of wise teacher to critical but sincere student.

As the second part of the first section opens, Krishna immediately shifts his ground and presents himself for the first time in his true guise: "I am the birth-less, the deathless, Lord of all that breathes." He continues by posing the issue of the theoretical ground of the principles of agency: "What is action? What is inaction? Even the wise are puzzled by this question. Therefore, I will tell you what action is." After a description of active worship and reaffirmation of enlightenment as the reward of all action, Krishna closes Chapter 4 by detecting a lingering doubt in Arjuna of the truth of the living Atman. This doubt, I suggest, is the pivot of this entire second part. In the light of Krishna's annunciation of himself as the ultimate teacher, lack of confidence in his teaching has an utterly different meaning than Arjuna's Chapter 3 accusation of inconsistency; that discussion was mediated entirely by the laws of logic and reasonability, as is appropriate between a mundane teacher and an eager but critical student, and judicious sparring after the truth—having recourse to reason alone—is completely in good form. Now, however, that Krishna has on the one hand dispensed with Arjuna's reasonable objection and has on the other hand revealed himself as the supreme authority, lingering doubt signifies a direct lack of trust in Krishna, a thinly veiled suspicion of his claim. Only once more does the *Gita* refer to such a gnawing doubt, at the end of Chapter 6 when Arjuna is troubled by the fate of an aspirant who has not exerted himself sufficiently and falls back, perhaps losing both the worldly and the spiritual life. It is in this passage, I believe, that Arjuna summons the courage to articulate the very doubt which had disquieted him since Chapter 4. But, according to the inseparability of philosophy and drama in the *Gita*, the doubt, no mere dramatic decoy, is metaphysically crucial, the turning point of both the philosophical and dramatic progressions. When Arjuna asks at the beginning of Chapter 5 for Krishna's definite commitment either to renunciation of action or action as the superior path, we must in hindsight perceive his struggle for an invincible assurance of the route to salvation. Krishna agreeably clarifies the theoretical issue by acknowledging the superiority of disciplined action over renunciation, but again emphasizes the unity of the goal to which all paths are directed. Proceeding, Krishna dilates upon his Chapter 2 characterization of enlightenment with a more voluminous description of the illumined soul who has pursued action until able to renounce it and live permanently in the peace of the Divine presence. Chapter 6 presents the reciprocal idea, that the *yoga* of action presupposes renunciation of anxiety over results. This initiates a portrayal of *yoga* meditation, to which renunciation is a prelude. Chapters 5 and 6 together define the complex relationship of the ways of knowledge and action, an intricate complementarity. On the one hand, action is superior—but its superiority rests in the fact that it is the easiest approach to genuine renunciation, which may be extended in the practice of meditation. On the other hand, the *yoga* of action cannot be practiced at all without a preliminary attitude of renunciation, for this *yoga* means precisely that action is to be performed for the sake of God rather than for results. Thus the dialectic of enlightenment begins with a volitional commitment to renunciation, a "phenomenal" renunciation, and moves through action to achieve a transforming and pervasive attitude of real renunciation. But this in an important sense removes the priority of action as such, and recognizes the preeminence of the mental disposition from the start for action is vitiated without constant intention of renunciation. In that case, everything depends after all on ability to control the mind. Now, in the Chapter 6 discussion of meditation, Krishna treats most intensively the principle of mental control. This facilitates Arjuna's definition to himself of his fundamental doubt, brought to a head in his complaint that the restlessness of the mind foredooms a smooth and successful voyage to Brahman.

At the bottom of Arjuna's doubt lies a suspicion of the unmanageable recalcitrancy of the mind. But this discloses the precise point at which Arjuna loses confidence in himself; in the mastery of physical disciplines Arjuna, conqueror of sloth, is supremely proficient, but Arjuna implicitly acknowledges in his dubiousness that wresting steady control over the mind is a far more imposing task than conquering action. As a warrior and as an adept in agency, Arjuna has been accustomed to the finality of worldly efforts and the awesome responsibility of one engaged in the risks entailed in acting; a military battle epitomizes the battles of life which all men perpetually encounter, in which there can be only one winner and one loser and no degrees in between. The agent stakes everything upon his prowess, prepared to endure the consequences should his best effort fail. It is natural for one so schooled in the harsh realities of personal responsibility to regard the search for enlightenment as a highest battle, which—as a warrior—one either wins or irrevocably loses. The drama of the three chapters comprising this second part revolves about the conflict between Arjuna's fear that the restless mind can do naught but forfeit this crucial battle, and his incipient trust in Krishna. Where is the solution? It has not occurred to Arjuna that the merits of a seeker for Brahman may redound to his credit even if he falls by the wayside, for the merits of a soldier count for nothing when he is routed. But Krishna, in reply to Arjuna's anxious inquiry, asserts, "No one who seeks Brahman ever comes to an evil end." This remark, like a spring breeze, anticipates the unsuspected graciousness of the Divine, taking a benevolent interest in the devotee. Krishna awakens Arjuna to the strain of grace, present in the law of *karma* itself, which vouchsafes to the religious seeker the ultimate realization of his quest. As the first part of the first section ends discussion of practical principles of agency by warning against the obstructions on the path to enlightenment, emphasizing the necessity for personally responsible wariness, so the second part concludes discussion of the theoretical principles of agency by guaranteeing that all who take the path will eventually overcome the obstructions.

At the onset of Chapter 2, Arjuna asked, "Is this real compassion I feel or only a delusion?" The breakdown of his structure of values caused Arjuna to doubt not only their transcendental source, but his own judgment for vesting his complete trust in them. Faith in God and self crumbled simultaneously. His doubt expressed at the end of Chapter 6 gathered together all the threads of Arjuna's uncertainty, reflecting his loss of confidence in his own spiritual equipment as well as his sense of the benevolence of the universe. Krishna's answer has restored Arjuna's lapsed faith in the wisdom of his tradition, has renewed his belief in Hindu teachings at lest tentatively. But the equilibrium achieved is unstable, and to ground it securely, to make his tradition again a practicable rule for Arjuna, a regulative disclosure of the transcendental in the second section of the *Gita* must establish the magnitude of Krishna's authority incontrovertibly. But, paradoxically, Arjuna has had to merit through a trustful surrender to Krishna's wisdom the theophany which alone can permanently tie down that trust; this accords with the logistics of faith in all great religious traditions, an inverse example of which is the disapprobation evinced towards "doubting Thomas" for whom only seeing the risen Jesus was believing: he whom only miracles can convince is never really convinced, while a free act of faith will earn gratuitous proofs.

In the second section of the *Gita,* Krishna's persona shifts to the most sublime level it achieves in the book; throughout this section, Krishna peals forth oracularly as God incarnate, describing in the first person his cosmic glory. Whereas in the first section, Arjuna took the initiative in interrogating Krishna, now Krishna assumes the lead to carry Arjuna through the burgeoning of his trust on the groundswell of the avatar's own power. It is as though Arjuna has now proven his willingness to trust and may now yield himself to the gratuitous embrace of Krishna who will lead him forward swiftly and surely to the consummate vision of his Divine Form; the grace of regulative disclosure inheres in the dialogic form itself. The section takes its form from the dialogic rhythm, breaking down into two units of dialogue, each consisting of two chapters, plus the eleventh chapter which climaxes the dialogue in theophany.

This dialogic rhythm contrasts markedly with the mono-logic and didactic character of the first section. To be sure, Krishna still does most of the talking. Yet Arjuna has now become vitally engaged, and participates in a sensitive interplay with Krishna in which he actively picks up and responds to his friend's signals. From an attitude of negative and critical dubiousness, he has thrown himself boldly into the framework of relationship delineated by the avatar which rushes straightaway to its numinous conclusion. The two units of dialogue display the same form: in the first chapter, Krishna powerfully solicits the commitment of Arjuna to him both by enjoining it directly, and indirectly through grandly wondrous and vibrantly candid, breathtaking depictions of his power and attributes; in the second chapter, Arjuna responds appropriately in an eager request for additional self-characterization. There is an intense relational exchange here in which the two protagonists become closely bound to one another.

Chapter 7 commences immediately with Krishna reaching out for Arjuna's ultimate loyalty: "Devote your whole mind to me, and practise *yoga*. Take me for your only refuge. I will tell you how, by doing this, you can know me in my total reality without any shadow of doubt." When Chapter 8 opens with Arjuna's response, "Tell me, Krishna, what Brahman is," the inattentive are prone to slough this off as comparable to any of the earlier questions Arjuna has posed. On the contrary, this exemplifies strikingly the way in which overtones convey the emotional byplay within the philosophic discourse. For, at the conclusion of Chapter 7, Krishna has said: "Men take refuge in me, to escape from their fear of old age and death. Thus they come to know Brahman, and the entire nature of the Atman, and the creative energy which is in Brahman." Arjuna's query which follows fastens directly onto these three items. But, according to Krishna, knowledge of these is engendered through direct relation with Krishna. Therefore Arjuna's questioning indirectly petitions deepened relationship with his friend. Both context and connotation distinguish this question profoundly from the abstract and defensive, critical disputation in the first section.

In Chapter 9, Krishna grasps the lead even more forcefully than in Chapter 7: "Since you accept me and do not question, now I shall tell you that innermost secret ...." Krishna announces that the whole universe is pervaded by him in his eternal form, and adjures Arjuna to surrender himself completely to him. In Chapter 10, Arjuna responds with an eloquent tribute to the Divinity of his friend and an outright demand for a full cognitive penetration into him: "Krishna, this is the truth that you tell: my heart bids me believe you.... Therefore teach me now, and hold back no word in the telling, all the sum of your shapes by which the three words are pervaded; tell me how you will make yourself known to my meditation...." No longer can the reader mistake the thrust of this dialogue, which retrospect instructs resided in the more constrained response of Chapter 8. Finally in Chapter 11, seized by an ecstasy of conviction, Arjuna implores an unmediated vision of the universal Form of Krishna. This Krishna instantly grants, and the second section of the *Bhagavad-Gita* terminates in an ejaculatory gusher of language tumbling over itself in fruitless but exquisite endeavor to verbalize the ineffable. At the end of the chapter, Krishna—restored to his temporal form—crystallizes unmistakably the pattern of the second section: "This my Form of fire ... alone of all men, Arjuna, I showed to you because I love you."

The theophany has resulted not, oddly enough, from practice of the *yogas* of action or knowledge but from the devotional yearning of Arjuna and the reciprocation of gracious love from Krishna. Evidently devotion has circumvented necessity for the *yoga* practice so painstakingly outlined earlier. Does this represent a contradiction? Chapter 12 suggests it is not. The third section of the *Gita* begins appropriately enough with Arjuna asking whether love for personal Deity or absorption in the impersonal constitutes the profounder approach to God; Arjuna, after all, has just realized God in all His abysmal depth through love alone. The reply manifests an inner logic which, I think, need not necessarily be read as paradox. The problem is that of discovering the most efficient route to oneness with God, and the most direct approach to unity is through love. It was, in fact, love which brought Arjuna to identify himself so completely with his relatives that he could no more consider killing them than killing himself. For those who can feel love for Him, access to God is immediate. Love betokens a spontaneous polarization of the will towards its object, and supreme love is polarization towards a single object above all. Those who can love God, the *Gita* here implies, are most fortunate; for those whose natures are not endowed with such warmth, other approaches to God exist as well. The power of the devotional path can be apprehended only by treading it, whereas the other paths may be discussed abstractly and methodologically. Unlike the path of love, they all involve elements of coercion, for the refractory mind and will must be subdued, and sophisticated technique.

The glorious paradox of the *Gita* is simply this: as Krishna laid aside Arjuna's objections to *karma yoga*, convincing him of its efficacy and increasing his enthusiasm for it, through this very display of wisdom he gained Arjuna's deepening trust and veneration. At that moment when Arjuna's doubts were surmounted and he stood most ready, it would seem, to dedicate himself to *karma yoga,* his interest transferred decisively to him who had won his trust by true teaching. The development of this trust, an undercurrent in the first section, swelled to predominance in the second—Arjuna slipped unobtrusively into *bhakti* through his very conviction of the power of other approaches to God by attaching his concern to him who had elicited the conviction! Thus Arjuna's *bhakti* simultaneously confirms the value of the ways of knowledge and action, and of intensive meditation, and demonstrates the manner in which they transcend themselves to become devotion; or what is devotion, *bhakti,* if not the self-transcendence of *yoga* itself, the growth of a direct involvement and fascination with the Source of the wisdom that informs the other paths? This *bhakti* of Arjuna and the *Gita,* then, rather than rivaling the other *yogas* becomes their surest validation and at the same time points beyond them. I believe that this interpretation may resolve the difficulty of the *Gita's* lavish superlatives, bestowed on all the forms of *yoga* with what occasionally appears to be indiscriminateness. All are glorified because all are aligned with various dimensions of the Divine Being, and distinctions emerge within this context of general effulgence.

Be that as it may, the mood as we enter Chapter 12, beginning of the third section, has taken another turn. Arjuna's opening inquiry regarding the ultimacy of the devotional path displays in context a post hoc character; having already found himself through his devotional yearning for the Divine Form, Arjuna can have no more than an intellectual interest in the path of absorption in the unmanifest. But what sort of an interest in this precisely? It is the interest of a man in a greatly beloved object, the tranquil wish to know it and penetrate it in every way. This sets the tone for the third section in general. In the first section, Arjuna's questioning had a practical motive, oriented to his existential crisis and the resolution of it—Arjuna had an immediate concern in discovering the principles of agency, in order to determine how to comport himself in the passion situation. The questioning of the second section, in contrast, sought relational knowledge which would bind him to his friend for whom he was conceiving a supreme devotion. Now in the third section, with the relation consummated, interest gravitates to the nature of the beloved for its own sake. Similarly, human love passes through the stages of forming relationship, and maintaining, enhancing, deepening it: in the first stage, there is desperate concern for winning the beloved; in the second stage, with commitment secured and no longer an issue, the lovers settle down to the pleasurable occupation of getting to know each other intimately. But Arjuna's lover is Lord of the universe, his nature the nature of all things; interest in this awesome beloved entails, therefore, an interest in the structure of reality for its own sake—what we normally call metaphysical knowledge, what Spinoza aptly termed the intellectual love of God. This section of the *Gita*, accordingly, is the repository of its cosmology as such, representing Krishna's response to Arjuna's delight in him. Chapter 13 through 15 deals with the nature of knowledge and the known, the next two chapters with good and evil and the varieties of faith, the final chapter with the nature of action. We will, for the sake of brevity, offer only one example of the dramatic contrast between the issues of the three sections, an example which a more extended analysis could multiply many times.

In Chapter 2 Arjuna asks how to identify a man absorbed in Brahman, in Chapter 8 he asks what Brahman is, in Chapter 13 he asks what knowledge is. These questions embody, though related, an unmistakable progression from the external to the internal. They reflect a movement from practical concern through relational concern to metaphysical concern in accordance with the ontological moments of the three sections; Arjuna's interest switches from himself to his friend to the universal nature of his friend. We need not labor this heavily, trusting in the reader to make his own comparisons, but it is of some note that metaphysical discussion as such the *Gita* seems to entrust only to the man who has realized God. The implications seems to be that only sages in communion with the Divine properly have a concern with metaphysics, that such communion indeed is a prerequisite which alone can legitimize a metaphysical interest which to other men is premature, distracting and an evasion of their first task of achieving spiritual perfection. We might infer that the *Gita* would take a dim view of the Western effort to achieve spiritual wholeness through pursuit of philosophical speculation.

The third section portrays Arjuna as a man of faith, wholly committed, prepared to actualize his faith through his life. His mind is firm, he no longer feels constrained by the compunctions of his passion from the execution of his soldierly duty. Through his *bhakti* devotion, he has become the *karma yogi* he was urged to become in the first section; this illustrates the profound mutuality of *bhakti*, *yoga* transcending itself, and the performance of the *yogas* as such. Through a regulative disclosure of the transcendental as the Divine form of his friend Krishna, Arjuna has defeated his anguished hesitation and reestablished his Hindu faith on a new immovable ground; with his highest love now vested in God, he can grapple with the tragic duty of decimating kin whom he also loves, he can exercise an ultimate agency which earlier seemed beyond toleration. This has been accomplished through three separate dispensations of grace; the first was a grace of understanding, clarifying the precepts of faith and duty, the second a grace of theophany, confirming faith and duty, the third a grace of abiding communion, empowering the fulfillment of faith and duty. Krishna ordains, as the *Gita* draws to its conclusion, that any man who meditates on that discourse has worshiped him in spirit. And one must surely feel that, together with the passions of Job and Jesus, in the passion of Arjuna, God has vouchsafed and preserved the way to Him.

Karuna

The Nature of Buddhist Compassion: *Karuna*

Kenneth K. Inada

Immediately after the first A-bomb was dropped on Hiroshima in 1945, Albert Einstein made a prophetic statement: "The bomb has changed everything except the way man thinks." Fifty-one years later, the statement still remains as a reminder and a powerful challenge to humankind. It seems that we have yet to understand the full implications of the statement, nor have we taken drastic visible measures to correct the unbalanced conditions of the world. Our knowledge of fusion and fission in terms of nuclear energy, to be sure, has been a boon for the advancement of science and technology but it remains to be seen whether that knowledge can be gainfully shifted over into the dynamics of social and humanistic realms.

It is time to seriously focus on the issues and reassess our epistemic nature and function. Since prior to and after World War II, many thinkers, including those in post-modern and post-structural movements, have clearly enunciated the problems and pitfalls of our normal perception of things. In brief, our epistemological tools are wholly inadequate to the task of revealing the wholeness or fullness of the nature of things. The problem in the West goes as far back as the Greek tradition, to the so-called Western Axial Age where the Pre-Socratics freely offered solid basic ideas on the cosmological nature of things. They were free thinkers speculating on whether nature is, for example, in a flux, becoming, being, absolute or relative. With this background, it was Plato who crystallized Greek thought by opting for the cosmological nature of being over becoming and by extension firmed up the epistemic nature of things. His theory of knowledge rejected becoming as unreliable and instead promoted being as the very basis of reasoning and knowledge. Undoubtedly, this was a very bold move and insight into the noble grounds of reason, a move that has affected Western civilization in incalculable ways. I have already discussed elsewhere[1] the so-called Platonic legacy in which we live and think, and that we have not changed much in our thinking despite the dawning of the Einsteinian world at the turn of this century and now in mid-century the nuclear age. The mechanics of our thinking is still very simple or relatively primitive in that it still functions within the framework of clearly defined objects, subjects, or elements of being, all of which fire up and refire the generation of dichotomous thinking and static understanding of the nature of things. Such understanding seems nice and indeed is perfect for logical functions but life is not all logic. Something is amiss here.

The missing link is missing because we have gone into extremes in our thinking, i.e., either being or becoming, permanence (staticity) or impermanence (flux). Where Plato opted for being and permanence, as seen earlier, the contemporary mood seems to be moving toward becoming and impermanence. I realize that I have presented a rather simple comparison with resulting differences but a look at the situation today reveals a telling tale of confusion, muddleheadedness, indifference and neglect for human goals and aspirations. What then can be done?

The solution to the problem is to see the epistemological function holistically such that the missing link no longer exists in the scheme of things. This means that, first of all, the contention between being and becoming do not appear at all. Our habits of thinking has split those metaphysical concepts into separate categories of existence without our deep probes into the epistemic nature of things. In other words, a deeper probe would have revealed that being and becoming are not total strangers but really correlative terms insofar as human endeavors are concerned. They require each other, support each other and indeed define each other.

Parenthetically, it should be noted that the historical Buddha's great insight (*nirvana*) into the nature of things (*dharma*), revealed to him the way of the middle (*madhyama-pratipad*). The middle way avoids the extremes —the extremes of something (being) and nothing (not being), or substantialism and nihilism/annihilationism. But avoidance means more precisely detachment (*viraga*) from the passions/desires (*trsna*) which include both empirical and rational elements. Even nihilism/annihilationism is a form of passions/desires and thus elemental in nature. The key point here is that the Buddha discovered the hidden and subtle organic force in the nature of attachment nascent to all passions/desires. Every passion/desire then has this phenomenon of attachment which is the incipient cause for the rise of suffering (*duhkha*). How is this possible?

It is because attachment impedes, indeed brakes though temporarily, the natural flow of dynamic existence. It turns the dynamic flow of existence into samsaric conditions, i.e., into wave-like incongruous flow of existence. This flow is also referred to as the wheel of life because it keeps on turning by virtue of the continued, if not habitual, phenomenon of attachment. It becomes a treadmill, an actual instance of the myth of Sisyphus.

How then do we get out of samsara? The Buddhist answer is this: keep everything in place, both being and becoming except that now the phenomenon of attachment is eradicated. Is it possible? The Buddhist always refers to the nirvanic experience as "seeing things as they are" (*yathabhutam*). But this reference is much more easily said than done because the Buddhist is now focusing on the serious dedication and ultimate mastery of *yoga* to rise above the samsaric conditions. This is not the place to discuss *yoga*, but suffice it to say that *yoga* is the very foundation of most systems of Asia and indeed it is that which distinguishes Eastern thought from Western. Moreover, my presentation on compassion cannot be clarified nor completely understood without certain *yogic* effort at overcoming the ill-nature of samsaric elements. So now we engage in earnest in the discussion of Buddhist compassion.

There is hardly any question at all that the dynamic existence exhibits the fact that we are all instances of flowing ontological complexes, a truly open and moving ontology. It should be carefully noted here that this is not a move back to Platonic ontology of being in any shape or form but a truly dynamic phenomenon that even denies ordinary conception of a self (*atman*) and replaces it with the highly unlikely doctrine of non-self (*anatman*). The Buddhist will go a step further to assert that the ordinary conception of a self is nowhere to be found and that it is instead a mere designation, conventionally speaking, for the organic constitution of an individual (*skandha*).

By extension, we are able to assert that compassion is also a dynamic human phenomenon. But then, what do we exactly mean by the dynamic? Our normal understanding of it has been very weak and superficial for the most part and couched in generalities and vagueness. We must of course examine it with extra care, precision and depth to the best of our ability. This is not easy since its very nature is so intimate with our very activities as human beings. As a human phenomenon, however, I venture to characterize dynamism as marked by:

1. impermanence or momentariness
2. growth or maturation
3. openness or borderlessness
4. extension or reaching out in the existential flow
5. incorporation or absorbing everything in its wake
6. resilience, tenderness or pliability
7. mutuality or co-existentiality
8. reflectiveness or responsiveness
9. unique status of being(s)-in-becoming

Although we do not normally characterize our experiences or activities in such abstract ways, nevertheless, in human relationship we do experience directly or indirectly (i.e., as an aftermath of an experience) some or most of the characteristics. Elsewhere,[2] I have discussed the nature of soft versus hard relationships. Needless to say, compassion as a supreme virtue, falls within the category of soft relationship where the related elements so-called, are present but they do not rear themselves as empirical and rational elements as in hard relationship. In other words, the compassionate nature as a dynamic experience is open, resilient, pliable and tender, and thus it is able to absorb all elements without making and adhering to sharp and rigid distinctions. In this way, it retains the unique status of being(s)-in-becoming. So that we can say that the soft open dynamic nature sustains us as organic creatures, to let us be what we are as human beings in harmony with others or the world at large and to aspire for and project goals in order to responsibly enjoy them. Were it not for soft and open dynamism, our activities would be governed overwhelmingly by the cold and abstract elements within the province of hard relationship, elements that are always so attractive and attachable (*upadana*) but in the final analysis they may become the basis for not only stagnation but determinism, if not fatalism. In brief, the open road to freedom may be snuffed out by attachment to those elements and reduced to mere puffs of existence.

Buddhist meditative discipline is geared precisely for the understanding and implementation of a harmonious human relationship with the total surroundings. In the final stages of meditation, there are the famous brahma-vihara, literally, the house or abode of the ultimate nature of existence. The *Visuddhimagga* (Path of Purification),[3] refers to them as the four boundless states (*appamanna*), namely, loving-kindness (*metta*, in Pali), compassion (*karuna*), altruistic or sympathetic joy (*mudita*) and equanimity (*upekkha*). Their most significant factor lies in their inception and sustenance of the boundless or illimitable dynamic nature of things. Each is marked by openness, borderlessness, extensiveness, tenderness and reflexiveness. Loving-kindness is the beginning, a personal trait that opens up and reaches out to involve another in one's own realm of existence. The same trait can be said of compassion with the proviso that now all beings without exception, including non-sentients, are incorporated. Altruistic or sympathetic joy is quite novel and unique but it depicts yet another dimension, albeit hidden for the most part, of human relationship, i.e., the reflexive, mutual and blissful state in a group setting. This state might be illustrated by parental care and love of children including those of other parents. And finally, equanimity indicates the firmness and stability of all three previous states and the envisionment of all things under the aegis of sameness or equality. Examples of this state might be made by reference to the contents of some proverbial statements, such as, "all men are born equal," or "all men are brothers."

Needless to say, the four boundless states are beyond manipulation and deliberation for they are in the nature of soft relationship and firmed up in solid meditative discipline. They are the stuff that makes and sustains our social life on the highest level; indeed they are the boundless divine states of existence.

The nature of compassion reached its apex in the Mahayana tradition with the concept of *bodhisattva*, literally the enlightened nature of being. The *bodhisattva* is a would-be Buddha who delays entrance into the nirvanic realm of existence but who already manifests traits of enlightenment. Numerous stories and anecdotes dot the Buddhist texts depicting profound pity for all beings and displaying acts of self-sacrifice, all of which ultimately turn out to be the deeds of a *bodhisattva*.

In the human realm, *bodhisattvahood* consists in both compassion (*karuna*) and penetrative insight (*prajna*), two facets of the selfsame dynamic becomingness in the sense that one delineates on the practical aspect and the other the conceptual. Both mutually reflect each other and thus support and define each other. A mother, for example, who loves all children, including her own brood, manifests at once supreme love and wisdom, i.e., deepest concern for all beings and highest form of intelligence. The conduct of *bodhisattvahood* (*bodhisattvacarya*) is a supreme example of the activation (realization) of the principle of mutual penetration and mutual identification. It exhibits at once the nature of total relationship of all beings, sentient and nonsentient, such that every being reflects, penetrates and identifies every other being and, vice versa, every other being singularly or in toto returns the compliment. In popular illustrations, it refers to the hall of mirrors or the jewelled net of Indra where each jewelled knot reflects and contains all other jewelled knots and vice versa. In more philosophical terms, it depicts the status of affairs in our experiences as well as in the extended cosmological (environmental) realm where all is one and one is all; or from another aspect, all in one and one in all. The *bodhisattva's* deed then manifests this total immanent nature in the most intimate and deepest sense.

The compassionate nature is then an intimate portrayal of the whole run of things. But instead of understanding and harmonizing with this status of things, we tend to deviate from it in ways that suit our limited vision of things, being steadfastly oriented in our accustomed realm of passions and desires. In other words, although the locus of compassion is to be found everywhere and can be activated at any time with proper understanding, faith and aspiration, we opt for the easy but ultimately ill-way of attaching to and thriving in the elements of those passions and desires. The compassionate nature also makes it abundantly clear that a living/dynamic being has the rare trait of extending itself as far as it could and at the same time return to its source and enrich itself in the process. The mutuality of existence in terms of this extension and return cannot be expounded easily since it is not accepted as a normal phenomenon in our experiences. Most would probably assign such an activity to a higher being than human but Buddhism cannot tolerate such a huge gap in existence. Buddhism always maintains the possibility of incorporating the greater realm by way of the boundless, illimitable grasp of things as we have already seen in the discussion of the brahma-vihara, the abode of the divine states of existence. Indeed, I sincerely believe that this quest for the boundless had been the principal motive for the development of the Mahayana tradition. The concept of its namesake, *maha* + *yana* (great + vehicle), means exactly that: the vehicle that propels one to grasp the unfettered supreme realm of reality. The *bodhisattva* is then the potential human vehicle for such a venture but it entails the awakening in a sentient creature of the aspiration for enlightenment (*bodhicitta*). Without this initial desire, nothing will come about, just as there will be no progress in learning without a desire to learn.

It was said earlier that the *bodhisattva* has the twin nature of wisdom and compassion. Wisdom of course means the penetrative sweeping vision of things, a macro-vision if you will. Now, the problem is this: How is the penetrative macro-vision possible? The early Mahayanists were challenged by this question but resolved it by the strict ethical yogic vision of things, known technically as *prajnaparamita*. This sharp vision cuts through the mass of ordinary perception of things like a thunderbolt or diamond cutter. Indeed, there is such a sutra by that name, *Vajracchedika_Prajnaparamita Sutra*.[4] The vision allows one to preceive things as empty but at once full. To preceive all, one must perceive without attachment and therefore empty but at the same time the perception has not destroyed anything and therefore the fullness of existence remains. This Sutra goes on to assert the famous equation: form (*rupa*) is empty (*sunya*) and the very emptiness is form. It exhibits the fact that phenomenal existence and enlightened existence are merely two aspects of the selfsame reality. And thus the *bodhisattva* perceives all phenomena (*skandha, dharma*, etc.) under the aegis of emptiness and simultaneously bestows pity and compassion for all beings.[5]

The profundity of the *bodhisattva* ideality of life generated a huge spiritual and humanistic movement in Mahayana Buddhism. It becomes the principal force for the establishment of a tradition as well as its dissemination throughout Asia proper. The highest point on this *bodhisattva* ideal was reached by way of the appearance of Pure Land (*sukhavati*) Buddhism. This school starts with the mythical *Dharmakara Bodhisattva* who made 48 Vows, all of which underwritten with the simple vow that he will delay his entrance into the nirvanic realm until all beings are saved. This is a metaphorical way of asserting that the perfect natural state of existence will always be there awaiting the day when all human imperfections are resolved or removed. In consequence, the Pure Land School projects an intimate but infinite realm personified by Amida Buddha, another mythical figure, who constantly bestows pity on all beings and is the source of salvific energy to all aspirants with pure faith. The school follows all the basic doctrines of Buddhism but in its subsequent developments in the Far East, particularly China and Japan, it has taken on all the trappings of a bonafide religion, such as, observing meticulous ceremonies, prayers, chants and icons of worship. Because of this, some scholars have interpreted the school as a deviation from orthodox Buddhism but this is decidedly not the case. The school has only presented a cosmologically rounded out nature of the total nature of things in which lowly samsaric creatures can still find a home and aspire for the highest.

The school, in brief, is another profound exemplification of the principle of mutual penetration and mutual identification of our lives at large, an intermingled display of wisdom and compassion where every member is a vital component in the harmonious actualization of the pure realm of existence in the here and now. To take an active role in the implementation of the principle may well be said to be a novel way of thinking and living. Can we measure up to this challenge?

Notes

1. "The Buddhist Aesthetic Nature: a Challenge to Rationalism and Empiricism," in *Asian Philosophy*, Vol. 4, No. 2, 1994. Pp. 139-50.

2. "A Buddhist Response to Human Rights," in Claude E. Welch

and Virginia Leary, eds., *Asian Perspectives on Human Rights*. Boulder: Westview Press, 1990.

3. Bhikkhu Nanamoli, tr. *The Path of Purification* (Visuddhimagga). Colombo, Sri Lanka: R. Semage, 1956. See especially Chapter IX, Description of Concentration—The Divine Abidings. Pp. 321-353.

4. See Edward Conze, tr., *Buddhist Wisdom Books*, containing the Diamond Sutra (Vajracchedika Prajnaparamita Sutra) and the Heart Sutra (Prajnaparamita Hrdaya Sutra). London: George Allen & Unwin Ltd., 1975.

5. The Mahayanist credited for crystallizing the doctrines into a coherent whole and thereby giving directions to the Mahayana movement is none other than the great thinker, Nagarjuna (c. 150-250). See especially his major work, *Verses on the Fundamental Doctrine of the Middle* (Mulamadhyamakakarika) in various English translations.

Karuna and the Theandric Experience: A Hermeneutic of the Transition from *Theravada* to *Mahayana*

John R. A. Mayer

Although the Judeao-Christian tradition understands itself as monotheistic, even in the context of an emphasis on the doctrine of the Trinity, ever since Pascal we have become accustomed to contrast the God of Abraham and Moses from the God of the philosophers. How are we to understand this contrast? Are there two gods? Is the God of the philosophers an idolatrous notion, that the jealous God of Abraham and Moses would want us to turn from? A few years ago a conference on the theme of *God – a Contemporary Conversation*, organized by the Unification Church devoted a thematic section to "God: Speculation or Experience?," and the papers were later published in a book by the same title. It is regrettable that Dr. Panikkar was not among the participants, but I am certain that he would have been a key spokesperson for the claim that all our speculative theologies are founded on and based in experience. This does not mean that every speculative theologian or philosopher is the individual who would claim a vivid theophany; one can carry on a speculative-inferential process based on the reception of a theological tradition, which, however, is based on the experience of another.

One might ask whether there is only one experience of the Divine which is repeated in the individual experiences of the many mystics and founders of religious traditions, or whether there are quite diverse experiences which in turn lead to quite diverse approaches to expressing the onto-theological implications of these. It is not easy to answer this question abstractly. After all experience is always subjective, and therefore unique and distinctive. And yet a variety of unique experiences are capable of being characterized collectively. This is why the classical philosophical formulation of the problem is the problem of the "One *and* the Many" rather than the "One *or* the Many."

From the evidence of the persuasive study by Rudolph Otto published as the classic *The Idea of the Holy* one is lead to believe that the experience of the Divine includes simultaneously elements that are described as fascinating, awesome, mysterious, joy-evoking, and filling the individual with dread. Clearly such a catalogue of diversity asserted all together implies the probability that in some cases some of these reactions and feelings predominate; in others, different ones. Thus the answer to the question of whether all theophanies are fundamentally the same is more plausibly negative rather than affirmative. Another important contrast in my view has to do with the intensity of the experience of the Divine. In such cases as that of Saul on the road to Damascus, or the account of the mystics would lead us to believe that the experience is intense and clearly identifiable as to is temporal occurrence. Its impact on the experiencer is such as to redirect his or her life, ground the writings of the individual. In contrast, I believe there is a much milder kind of experience of the Divine, which is more akin to the Platonic notion of forgotten, hidden knowledge. Such may be the case with all those individuals who "have ears to hear" the writings of the mystics, who respond with a sympathetic resonance to the theological claims of the traditions, to whom the notion of transcendence is not totally foreign, but "makes sense." This kind of mild mysticism is just as important socially and historically as the more intense and more conventionally recognized one, since it is this milder form that enables the writings of the mystics and theologians to be sympathetically received, transmitted and culturally valued. Our conviction, then, is that the ground of reflection or thinking about the nature and character of the Divine is a meeting, an experience, a disclosure which provides a criterion for asserting whatever one asserts, be it categorically or tentatively.

If this analysis is correct, then it becomes clear that the God of Abraham and Moses is not a different God from the god of the philosophers, but that the philosophical-speculative tradition, which, of course is considerable and multiform, is dependent on an experience disclosure, whose importance and validity is prior to the ascription of importance and validity to the claims and assertions. From this it also follows that diverse and logically non-coherent claims can each be appreciated as stemming from particular experiences, in combination with the cultural and linguistic contexts familiar to those who respond to their encounter. Thus, for example, whether the encounter is characterized as a meeting with a Person, to whom a male gender is attributed, who is the loving and just Creator of the Universe, or characterized as the rapture laden absorption into the Absolute in which we live, move and have our being, or yet again, as the disclosure of the abyss of Nothingness on which the contingency of all being floats, but which cannot be known since knowing implies an object of knowledge, a being, are but diverse human responses and characterizations of the grace-laden source of human religiosity. Our task, then, is not to choose from among these, but to receive what each description has to offer to our adumbrations, our own degree of spiritual memory. Love of our own tradition, and loyalty to it should not shut us off from traditions in the plural sense, for ultimately all traditions are but our own, once we cease to be chauvinists valuing the more narrow identities excessively, forgetting the fact that we are humans, heirs to the human heritage in all its richness and diversity.

And yet, a different tack may also be taken to illuminate and underscore the *contrast* between the God of Abraham and the God of the philosophers and theologians, rather than disclosing their identity.

Martin Buber is to be recognized for this insight. In his famous account of the relationships of "I-Thou" and "I-It," he points out that the former is immediate, present, and not conceptual. It is lived, and it is formative of the"I." However, because human consciousness is not only awareness but also memory, when a meeting, an "I-Thou" relation is recalled and reflected on, it becomes transformed through articulation, thought, analysis and interpretation. The "Thou" of the encounter is reduced and objectified into a conceptually accessible and defined "It." Thus, by the time a meeting is presented to consciousness not as an immediacy, a complex whole, but as something capable of being thought and named, it has become transformed from being "I-Thou" to being "I-It." This transformation is simultaneously the preservation of the truth of the meeting, and its distortion and alteration into the more definite, more limited, more determinate characteristics of thought and language. Indeed, depending on the way one thinks about the puzzlesome nature of "truth," one might either say that the "truth" of the meeting is created through its articulation into descriptive and inferred propositions, since it is these that are either true or false; or one might argue, as Buber would, that such reflection always at least partially falsifies the reality of the meeting.

It is this latter claim that leads Pascal into the disclaimer about the God of the philosophers. For what is given in the meeting is not only that which therewith becomes disclosed; what is also given is that which remains essentially hidden, a mystery, a Thou who addresses and invites, who creates and calls the I into self-transformation, but is not the object of knowledge, though is, becomes and remains the object of love and desire. The disclosure of hiddenness is what we call "mysterious," and Otto describes the experience as characterizable by the expression "*mysterium tremendum.*"

Thus while we are empowered to retain and transform "I-Thou"s into "I-It"s, we must be vigilant in remembering that such a transformation is also a reduction, an interpretation, a subjective speaking of the meaning of the experience. Thus, ultimately every theology is but a phenomenology; and this means that opposite, contrasting and incompatible claims are not genuine contradictions between which or among which one must rationally choose in a disjunctive manner, rather, one can see that even what appear to be superficially explicit contradictions not cotenable, are in effect warranted assertions about encounters; and can be co-entertained in the same manner as one can co-entertain two people asserting: "spinach is delicious" and "spinach is awful," recognizing the respective validity of each of the claims without denying the other.

Thus we can understand Panikkar's approach to the study of different religious traditions as based on the recognition that these traditions gain their diverse and particular expressions as the reflective articulation of a not fully articulable immediacy, which he calls "cosmotheandric experience." He maintains that sound and fundamentally coequally respectable religious traditions, are all rooted in the divine "cosmotheandric experience," and indeed, that one need not reject or repudiate one's own narrower tradition in valuing, interpreting and recognizing traditions that are culturally different. This is the underlying thrust of his study, *The Hidden Christ of Hinduism*. Unlike those who think that this is but an attempt to Christianize Hinduism (as occasionally Christianity has been Indianized by them) Panikkar is really recognizing that both Christianity and Hinduism are the transformations of immediate experience into religion, lifestyle, *praxis* and doctrine, responsive to the creative call of the Divine.

But what about Buddhism? Can one say the same of this tradition, when it has been characterized by scholars as atheistic? Did not the Buddha respond to Malunkyaputta's and Vaccha's questions about speculative metaphysics in a way that denies the importance of theism? The Enlightened One reminds his questioners that he has not promised to solve the intellectual problems arising from concerns about the mortality or continuation of souls, about the origin or eternity of the world, etc.; that he is about is to help sentient beings to overcome *dukkha,* and the solutions to speculative problems do not contribute to this. (Majjhima Nikaya *Sutras* 63 and 72) The well-known American Buddhist scholar Dwight Goddard has said: "No teacher was so godless as Lord Buddha, yet none so godlike." (Dwight Goddard *A Buddhist Bible,* Beacon Press, Boston, 1970 p. 20.) So, perhaps it is easy to think of the great monotheistic traditions as diverse expressions of God's self-disclosure, God's encounter with humans as all having a common root, and it is not difficult to show how in the Indian forms of spirituality there is a functional analogue to the God of the West be it in Brahman of Vedanta, be it in the characterizations of Lord Vishnu or Lord Shiva in the Vaishnavite and Shaivite traditions. Dr. Panikkar has done this admirably. But how can Buddhism, with its apparent indifference to theism be also included in this great integrating envisionment? Answering affirmatively to that query is the objective of the rest of this paper.

We shall accomplish the task set in two stages. The first one is to show how it is consistent with the cosmotheandric experience not only to issue in theologies and metaphysical theory founded in a theistic envisionment, but in cautioning against all theologies and metaphysical claims. That will establish the *possibility* for Buddhism too to be a religious response to the self-disclosure of the divine in a human experience, not fundamentally incompatible with the theistic and theological affirmations characterizing the other traditions.

But establishing this possibility is insufficient for showing Buddhism to also in fact be a consequence of the cosmotheandric experience. This can be accomplished by focusing on the centrality of *karuna*, compassion, in the Buddhist tradition. We must show how Buddhism, especially as it evolves from Theravada to Mahayana, is a growing awareness of the importance of love in the spiritual life of the person. And love is necessarily more than either a mere vertical relationship between the lover and some abstract beloved, such as truth or justice; nor is it a merely horizontal relationship of loving preferentially this or that particular person or thing. Love in its full-blown characterization has to incorporate a lived relation to transcendence, and an awareness of the belonging together of all sentiency, which will bridge the gap between subject, me, and object.

Thus the emphasis on the primacy of a vivial love is the Buddhist response to the cosmotheandric experience; in recognition of the possibility of a multiplicity of potentially divisive objectifications. Thus the Buddhist invites one to focus on the preparation for the reception of the cosmotheandric experience, rather than on previous historical objectifications thereof. For it is recognized by the wise that the transmission of these objectifications can be both a blessing and a curse. The blessing is the birth of a tradition that can be and often is a reliable guide to those on the path; the curse is the danger of mistaking the objectifications as the only matter owes primary importance, considering them as sufficient and final. In other words, the dogmatic and intolerant appropriation of any tradition is what causes strife and suffering, and is thus fundamentally inconsistent with the centrality of love and compassion that is the heart and nature of the cosmotheandric experience. Thus, when Buddhism shuts itself off from theological speculation, it is in fact repeating the Pascalian claim of the fundamentality of the God of Abraham and Moses in place of the God of the philosophers, identifying the Enlightenment experience with the encounter, and speculation with the consequent speculative intellection of it, that is the "I-It" trace of the original "I-Thou," which is the empowering, transforming event that happened under the Bodhi tree for Gautama Shakyamuni, and to whose repetition he invites all those who would gain the tranquility and blessedness of the well lived life.

At first this has lead his followers to be "lamps unto themselves," seeking to discover the presence of the hidden truth that must be the essence of any consciousness whatever. However, as the search for Enlightenment and Liberation, which was first apprehended as self-perfection, the development of those personal characteristics which would make one into an *arhant*, a fully perfected individual, begins to bear fruit, the character does begin to develop to the insight that the search for that kind of salvation, that kind of liberation is essentially selfish, and hence inconsistent with the very character that one sought. That "character" is not a private property, or a set of characteristics belonging to an ego, but is integrally involved with ones relations to others, not just particular, significant others, but all others, especially those who suffer, is the direct consequence of the incipient success on the way toward *arhanthood.* That is therefore but a required prelude to the realization that there is no substantial self; that Enlightenment is a two-stage development, the first of which is a "personal" accomplishment, but that is incomplete and insufficient; the second and final fulfillment is not individual, but is achieved only when all sentiency overcomes its suffering, which is none other but its separation from and forgetfulness of the cosmotheandric experience in which love heals all separation. Thus the ideal of the *arhant* comes to be replaced with the ideal of *Bodhisattva,* the being who declines personal liberation and "sets it on the back burner" so to say, until all sentiency is liberated. The *Bodhisattva* is prepared to forego all the merit accruing to his or her own deeds, since there is no independence; and is thus ready to participate in helping all who need help— be they human or at any other level of sentiency, since compassion is to encompass all. Surely this practice is but an exemplification of what it means to love God with all thy heart and mind and soul, and thy neighbour as thyself. Hence we can conclude that Buddhism is also responsive to the cosmotheandric experience, and that its response is exactly one of focusing on the primacy of the experience as an "I-Thou," rather than valuing the transformation of it into an "I-It" through reflection; and recognizing that the essence of the experience has to do with evoking compassion, and providing tranquility through the assurance of the appropriateness of transiency both as a remedy for pain, and as a condition for novelty and change.

We thus conclude that Buddhism is indeed a very powerful and insightful member of the great traditions of humankind, disclosing verities about the way to resolve the tension between the demands of truth and the demands of community, in favour of the latter. For our predilection for truth tends to make all of us intolerant of those who refuse to follow our paths into it, even if we know that we should be loving to our fellow beings. In the realization of the centrality of compassion, the Buddhist heritage discloses itself as a member of the religious traditions which have responded to the cosmotheandric experience with some kind of monotheism that also stresses the centrality of be it *bhakti* be it *agape*. For in the end though we all speculate, even as Buddhists, what is the goal of speculation is to reveal not knowledge but love as the primary source of creative power.

The Mahayana Buddhist Pantheon: A Phenomenology of Divine Love

Richard A. Berg

Mahayana Buddhism may be described in a variety of ways. Denominationally this kind of Buddhism styles itself the *maha-yana* or great vehicle of salvation from suffering, a title implicitly contrasted with the Buddhism of southeast Asia which it demeaningly refers to as Hinayana, the small vehicle by means of which only a few may be saved.

Geographically it is the Buddhism of central and east Asia including Tibet and Mongolia, China, Korea, Japan, Taiwan, and of one southeast Asian country, Vietnam. Theologically it is the Buddhism of *Bodhisattvas* (literally "Enlightenment Beings") or divine savior figures who collectively constitute the great vehicle of salvation named in the denomination's title.

Iconographically Mahayana Buddhism is distinguished by the sculpted and painted likenesses of these *Bodhisattvas* in the temples and home shrines of its devotees and believers. Ethically the defining feature of the Mahayana is the *maha-karuna* or great compassionate love of its pantheon of *Bodhisattvas* for all other sentient beings.

It is the aim of the investigation which follows to elucidate the meaning of the Mahayanist pantheon of *Bodhisattvas* as a whole ultimately in terms of the ideal of its *maha-karuna* kind of love.

The method of investigation, the phenomenological method invented by Edmund Husserl, has positive and negative aspects intended to mutually elucidate the meaning of the phenomenon being investigated as a whole. On the one hand, its negative aspect named after the mathematical operation called bracketing requires that questions, assumptions and assertions about the objective reality or existence of the phenomenon be deferred at least temporarily in order to pursue questions about its meaning or essence. On the other hand, the positive aspect of Husserl's method is a step-by-step description of the bracketed phenomenon, in this case the Mahayanist pantheon of *Bodhisattvas*, in order ultimately to elucidate its meaning. The first step, a preliminary description to achieve what Husserl calls a free imaginative variation on the phenomenon, is based on several visits to five different Canadian Mahayana Buddhist temples. Since Husserl's method regards those aspects of the phenomenon which turn out to be invariable as the *logos* essential to its meaning, the next step is to find out exactly which aspects of the pantheon are invariable. A negative outcome on this point is that none of the pantheon's finite features is discovered to belong to its invariable essence. However, the ensemble of these failures of finitude does in the end add up to something positive insofar as bracketing them all advances the enquiry to the concluding insight that it is only the infinite *maha-karuna* kind of love which encompasses the Mahayanist pantheon's invariable essence, its ultimate meaning as a whole, rather than the latter being captured in any of its partial finite aspects.

I

In view of the obvious possibilities for cross-cultural misunderstanding of religious phenomena like the Mahayanist pantheon, the negative aspect of phenomenological enquiry had best be called into play first, guided by Husserl's slogan "To the things themselves!." For in this instance it is by no means clear just what the things themselves, the *Bodhisattvas*, are. One way of addressing the problem is to approach the Cham Shan Temple in suburban Thornhill on the north side of Toronto, since it has the helpful Chinese inscription over the front entrance to its Main Hall: "Welcome to the Happy Land." On entering a Mahayanist temple then we are spiritually entering a Happy Land, not merely physically entering a building. Moreover, once inside we not only stand before the temple's sculpted and painted images breathing incense-scented air, but are also thereby sensually transported into the presence of its Buddhas and *Bodhisattvas*, each welcoming us into his or her own Happy Land. Thus we do not on this view encounter the *Bodhisattvas*, the things themselves, at all merely by looking at their sculpted and painted figures in the temple. At this point it should be clear that to say of the *Bodhisattvas* that they are only un-living objects of wood and stone, and that adherents' devotion to them is nothing more than idol worship is to conflate Husserl's two types of question about essence and existence in a way that is perhaps best illustrated by comparing the temple's sculptures and paintings with photographs of the investigator's own beloved family. Mahayanists do not worship un-living objects of wood and stone any more than we love the glossy photographs of our loved ones instead of loving the actual people whose likenesses they present.

Methodologically then Husserl's initial bracketing of questions about reality and existence tells us that it is always wrong-headed for the enquirer to begin by declaring any phenomenon, religious or otherwise, existent or non-existent, true or untrue in its representation of reality without first trying to understand just what the phenomenon essentially is or what it means. This wrong-headed type of misunderstanding Husserl regarded as a distinctive feature of what he called "the natural attitude." However, I believe that such a typical Western mistake has more specific roots in the three great monotheistic religions that have shaped the thought and culture of enquiry in the West. For example, the Roman destruction of the second Jerusalem temple in 70 C.E. ultimately transformed Judaism from a ritualistic sacrificial religion into a logocentric or word-centered religion based on the widely distributed *Talmud* text rather than being localized in a physical building that could ever again be destroyed. In Christianity the inspiring logocentrism of Western culture reached new heights with the Divinization of the Word in the gospel of *John*: "In the beginning was the *Logos,* and the *Logos* was with God and the *Logos* was God ... and the *Logos* was made flesh and dwelt among us ..." on *John's* account in the person of Jesus Christ. Finally the Islamic understanding of the received and recited text of the *Qur'an* as an earthly copy of a heavenly original, and Mohamed as the seal or last of the prophets, closed the book as it were on the adventure of encounter with the picture-image thinking of iconographic Eastern religious cultures. In sum the three great monotheistic religions of Judaism, Christianity and Islam have each in its own way collectively contributed much to the now secular tendency of logocentric thinking that pervades Western culture, including its intellectual style of enquiry. When such a word-centered culture encounters icono-graphic traditions of Eastern religious thought, its "natural attitude," to use Husserl's term, is the iconoclasm willfully expressed in the deliberately obtuse notion that the Mahayanist pantheon consists of idols of wood and stone and that Mahayanist love and devotion are nothing more than idol worship.

Because such erroneous thinking is so pervasive and persistent, so deeply rooted in the religious ground of Western culture, Husserl's negative method of bracketing will have to be invoked as an ongoing task which the iconoclastic Western enquirer undertakes to sustain while naturally attempting to describe the religious phenomena of the iconographic-thinking East as though they were essentially word-centered like those of a typical Western religion.

II

With this negative methodological preamble completed, let us now turn to the things themselves, the *Bodhisattvas* of the Mahayanist pantheon. Having at least partly elucidated what it means to say that it is questions of essence and not questions of existence that are the subject of this enquiry now makes possible a preliminary description of the *Bodhisattva* pantheon as it appears in five different Canadian Mahayanist temples: three ethnic Chinese Buddhist temples, starting with the Cham Shan Temple in suburban Thornhill, then the Tai Bay and Hong Fa Temples in Toronto; and finally two Vietnamese Buddhist Temples, the Hua Nghiem Temple in Toronto, and the Tam Bao Temple in Montreal. A preliminary description of the *Bodhisattva* pantheon in these five temples accomplishes what Husserl would call a free imaginative variation on the phenomenon, the outcome of which suggests what features may belong to its invariable essence.

The Cham Shan Temple complex on the west side of Bayview Avenue just north of Toronto consists of three separate buildings: a Main Hall flanked by Guan Yin Hall on the north, and Di Tsang Hall to the south. Just inside the door of the Main Hall is Weito, traditional guardian of Buddhist temples and protector of the faith, standing with his sword of protection. Beyond him is the Main Hall's *Bodhisattva* pantheon with the central figure of Siddhartha Gautama Sakhyamuni, (the historical Buddha); flanked to the south by Mi Lao (Maitreya), the Buddha of the future; and further south again by Ti Tsang, the crowned and scepter-wielding *Bodhisattva* of the present age which spans the time between the departure of Sakhyamuni and the arrival of Maitreya. On the other hand, to the north of the central Sakhyamuni is Kuan Yin (Avalokitesvara), the feminine-looking *Bodhisattva* of compassion and mercy.

Although the Cham Shan Temple's three-hall complex and trinitarian arrangement of glass-cased Happy Lands in its Main Hall emphasize Ti Tsang, Sakhyamuni, and Kuan Yin, even a partial description of the Main Hall's pantheon would be incomplete without at least mentioning that the three *Mahasattvas* (Great Beings) stand out from a background of innumerable small unnamed *Bodhisattvas* on the shelved western wall behind them; and moreover that the central Sakhyamuni is flanked in front on either side by a head-high conical *Bodhisattva* heaven rising from the floor with shelves of even smaller more innumerable unnamed *Bodhisattvas*, each in his or her own place in the heavenly hierarchy. In sum, the overall impression of the pantheon tends to the sublime as the sheer number of *Bodhisattvas* surpasses the ability to apprehend them all individually. Inside the Di Tsang Hall's main entrance is a chanting table running lengthwise towards the western wall at the back of the building. At the far end of the table is a large Amitabha (Amida Buddha) standing on the main altar; while on the three walls away from the main entrance are rows of small portrait photos of departed loved ones, by now hopefully reborn in Amitabha's Western Paradise. Although it is Ti Tsang's Hall, there are but two small crowned Ti Tsang's seated on the two side wall altars. Finally, there is one more small Amida seated on the back wall altar behind the main altar devoted to the large standing Amida. Moreover the Hall's only chant written before these figures "Namo A Mi Tu Fo" is devoted to Amida and not to Ti Tsang. Thus Ti Tsang is not featured as prominently as Amida, even in his own Hall.

In front of Guan Yin Hall, standing under a protective roof beside the temple bell, is the *Bodhisattva* herself, represented in two sculpted glass-cased figures, one holding a child and the other pouring out her mercy; while inside, at the top of the stairs leading to the second floor dedicated to her worship, she appears once more, again glass-cased. Finally, behind the Hall's main altar a massive Kuan Yin towers, rising up two stories to a ceiling window radiating light down upon her myriad helping hands, arms cloaked in a vast translucent red shawl, flanked on the north side by a Sakhyamuni altar, and on the south by Avalokitesvara. The last figure to call attention to itself is a tiny seated medicine Buddha on the north side wall, celebrated in a written chant giving thanks for averting calamity and prolonging life.

In retrospect, the impression of Cham Shan Temple that lingers is that of Kuan Yin looming large over all the other Buddhas and *Bodhisattvas* in the pantheon, and of her myriad helping hands, like the innumerable shelved *Bodhisattvas*, tending towards sublimity as they exceed the ability to apprehend them all individually. Immanuel Kant would have called this overall impression an apprehension of the mathematical sublime, here evoked in a religious experience whose deeper significance as yet eludes us.

The first impressions of the Tai Bay Temple on the west side of Bathurst Street in downtown Toronto are quite different. Its pantheon on a raised stage against the temple's western wall features Amitabha (Amida Buddha) as the central figure with two Kuan Yins on either side, another Kuan Yin in front of him and Sakhyamuni, the historical Buddha, in front of her. Thus the Tai Bay Temple pantheon creates the impression of Amida as the central Buddha with the various *Bodhisattvas*, including the historical Buddha, radiating outward from him like the rays of the sun, somewhat like the arrangement in the Cham Shan Di Tsang Hall where Amida again is central. Subsequent visits to the refurbished temple, now renamed Ching Kwok Temple, reveal a more magnificent pantheon, though with the centrality of Amida remaining unchanged, since it remains an Amidist temple.

The three-storey Hong Fa Temple on the north side of Bloor Street in downtown Toronto also has a pantheon similar to the Tai Bay Temple's, but only on its second floor. At the back of the first floor hall, a glass-cased Sakhyamuni sits facing south, an altar before him. On the second floor a smaller porcelain Sakhyamuni again appears seated in a similar position, though this time not alone. For behind him in a tall glass case stand three large golden figures: Amitabha in the center, with *Bodhisattva* Mahasthamprapta on his right hand side (west) and Kuan Yin to the left, the same kind of arrangement observed at the Tai Bay Temple. Finally in the temple's third floor library Sakhyamuni once again sits alone facing south, an altar before him, this time with the Chinese inscription overhead: "Three-World Guiding Teacher."

Hence, although the Hong Fa Temple's second floor pantheon shows the same radiating pattern of *Bodhisattvas* with Amida at the center, the match between the temple's three floors and the three-world concept, the vertical pattern of the three Sakhyamunis, and the crowning words above the highest Sakhyamuni all tend to confirm his status as the highest Buddha in the pantheon.

Yet another version of the Mahayanist pantheon appears in the Hua Nghiem Vietnamese Buddhist Temple on the north side of Gerrard Street in Toronto. A glance through the street entrance brings Vi Da Ho Phap (Weito), the temple guardian *Bodhisattva,* into view standing guard over religious texts against the temple's eastern wall; while at the north end of the temple farthest away from the street, the main pantheon features Thich Ca Mau Ni (Sakhya-muni), the historical Buddha, at the center, seated in the familiar pose on a lotus; with Dia Tang (Ti Tsang) on his right hand side (west of him); and Quan Am (Kuan Yin) to the right. An arched doorway on either side of this trinitarian pantheon opens into a smaller room where a painting of Bo De Dat Ma (Bodhidharma), flanked by two altars with small portrait photos of deceased parishioners over offerings of fruit and flowers, hangs on the back side of the wall behind the central pantheon. Finally an even smaller room in the north eastern corner of the temple is devoted to a small crowned and sceptered Dia Tang.

Not surprisingly, the *Bodhisattva* pantheon in the Tam Bao Temple on Van Horne Street in Montreal is quite similar to the Hua Nghiem arrangement since the Montreal temple is in effect its mother church. As the visitor emerges from a basement stairwell into the temple, he is confronted first by Vi Da Ho Phap, the temple guardian *Bodhisattva,* standing against the temple's eastern wall holding his book of wisdom and sword of protection; while at the far northern end of the hall the same trinitarian pantheon is seen, with Thich Ca Mau Ni at the center behind the main altar, Dia Tang on his right hand (west), and Quan Am to the left. On the temple's western wall a painting of A Di Da Phat (Amida Buddha) is surrounded by photos of the deceased now hoped to be with him in his Western Paradise, all over a side altar of flower and fruit offerings

Since these last two Vietnamese Buddhist temples feature what I have termed the trinitarian pantheon, and since the Chinese Buddhist Cham Shan Temple's Main Hall pantheon and also its three-hall arrangement of buildings are dedicated to the same three *Bodhisattvas*, all in the same type of arrangement and in the same direction, together they suggest a way of explaining the Mahayanist pantheon in term of these three Great Beings.

III

However, there are in fact several different explanations of the Mahayanist pantheon of *Bodhisattvas*, the others no less plausible than the one just cited. The pantheon may be viewed not only literally in terms of a kind of trinitarian theology, but alternatively as nothing more than a kind of moral metaphor of the virtues valued in Mahayana Buddhism. It may also be viewed by Mahayanist devotees as a way of locating themselves in space and time, giving them a powerful sense of spiritual place in the world. It can as well be represented as a sort of cosmology describing the world as conceived in the Mahayanist tradition. Finally the meaning of the *Bodhisattva* pantheon may be sought in at least three different kinds of rational monism, three different ways of saying that all its *Bodhisattvas* or perhaps even all that is, is one.

What all the above explanations share in common is the rational attempt to impose some kind of order on the pantheon's multifarious *Bodhisattvas*, and that in the attempt they all reduce it to something less than the full meaning of the religious phenomenon worshipfully encountered in our five temple venues. That is why each in turn, after receiving a critical exegesis of its initial plausibility and ultimate shortcomings, will be individually bracketed and set aside in order to elucidate the *Bodhisattva* pantheon's meaning ultimately in terms of the *maha-karuna*, great religious love, that is unique to Mahayana Buddhism.

The Pantheon as Trinitarian Theology

In three of the five temples Siddhartha Gautama Sakhyamuni, the historical Buddha, occupies the central position in the temple's main pantheon, with Ti Tsang at his right hand and Kuan Yin on the left. Although it is tempting to view this arrangement as suggesting a kind of trinitarian theology, this suggestion would define the pantheon too narrowly in at least three different ways. For it would fail to include versions of the pantheon such as those of the Tai Bay and second floor Hong Fa temples which have some other Buddha such as Amida at the center. Secondly it would exclude pantheons like that of the Tai Bay Temple again, this time for having no Ti Tsang, at least not on my first visit in 1990 to the temple. Even more importantly, the trinitarian theology is too narrow for excluding Amida who appears in all five temple venues even if he is not central, or not even a part of the temple's main pantheon at all.

In sum a trinitarian theology, though it may hold appeal for the literal-minded, remains highly problematic since it is unnecessarily exclusive. Moreover, since it specifies no common denominator among those *Bodhisattvas* it does include, the pantheon is in the end imperfectly rationalized on this model.

The Pantheon as Moral Metaphor

It is exactly to escape this kind of literal-minded ness that it has been suggested the *Bodhisattvas* are nothing more than metaphorical representations of the virtues valued in the Mahayanist tradition. The moral metaphor interpretation of the pantheon is most successful in the case of Maitreya whose name obviously derives from *metta*, the Pali term for the loving kindness toward all sentient beings which would make this world his Happy Land. Then there is Manjushri holding the book of *prajna* wisdom which associates him with his virtue. Indeed it is the advent of the *prajnaparamita* (perfection of wisdom) literature which is one of the marks of the rise of the Mahayana.

However, beyond this point the moral metaphor theory of the pantheon begins to break down. For it encounters increasing difficulty beginning with the problem of having not one but many *Bodhisattvas*, Kuan Yin, Avalokitesvara and Ti Tsang, for example, all associated with *karuna*, the virtue of compassionate merciful love. On the other hand, one and the same Amida Buddha is associated with both wisdom and compassion rather than one or the other. Even worse, *Bodhisattva* Mahasthamprapta expresses the wisdom of compassion. At this point the dualism of wisdom and compassion as separate and distinct virtues is revealed as a *shunya* (empty) notion, as is the notion of a one-to-one correspondence of *Bodhisattvas* with virtues. Because the Buddhist virtues are thought to arise interdependently, each one interwoven with the others, their non-duality is ultimately incompatible with the idea of a *Bodhisattva* for each of them. Hence another approach to interpreting the *Bodhisattva* pantheon is needed.

The Pantheon as Temporal Locator

When we ponder the Tai Bay and second floor Hong Fa pantheons which displace Sakhyamuni, the historical Buddha, from the central position, one way of making sense of this displacement is in terms of time. From a temporal viewpoint, Sakhyamuni is the Buddha of the past even if his enlightenment is seen as the pivot of history; Ti Tsang is the Buddha of the present, and Maitreya the Buddha of the future. The present age of Ti Tsang has on this view lasted over 2500 years since Sakhyamuni's Great Awakening as 1996 CE, for example, is 2539 AGA. Moreover, Mahayanists view the present not only as a middle age but also as a period of decline from Sakhyamuni's golden age when many people were quickly and easily enlightened to the present day where only a few achieve it and with great difficulty. This age will end only when the nadir is reached and Maitreya arrives to inaugurate his future age of *metta*, loving kindness among children, as only they will know how to respond to the Buddhist teaching which will by then have been lost and forgotten among adults. Thus the *Bodhisattva* pantheon may be said to give Mahayanists a powerful sense of their place in time. Nevertheless, there is good reason to believe that a temporal account of the pantheon in terms of these three *Bodhisattvas* hardly exhausts its meaning. Firstly, it fails to include Kuan Yin, easily the most popular *Bodhisattva* in east Asia. Nor, looking more deeply, does it give a complete account even of the pantheon's temporal dimension which includes a strong sense of temporal dislocation. When we scan Kuan Yin's innumerable helping hands and the other innumerable unnamed Buddhas and *Bodhisattvas* on display in the background of the Cham Shan Main Hall and the various other Mahayanist temples, our apprehension of them tends to prevent us from fixing our attention on Sakhyamuni, Di Tsang and Maitreya in the temporal foreground.

This visual sense of temporal dislocation is perhaps best verbally expressed in the *Lotus Sutra*. As the sutra begins, Sakhyamuni emits an illuminating ray from between his eyebrows. Maitreya asks Manjushri why, and is told that he remembers how countless aeons ago another Buddha just like this one, and between them a succession of innumerable *kotis* of other Buddhas just like them, emitted such a ray of light immediately before expounding the *Lotus Sutra*. Indeed that is what this Sakhyamuni does, it is said, for the length of sixty intermediate *kalpas* of time, after which he pauses for some fifty such *kalpas* during which time miraculously no one gets tired, and so on. Thus the sutra narrative hardly begins before the reader's sense of time is thoroughly dislocated from the familiar foreground of finite human temporal consciousness. In sum the *Lotus Sutra's* succession of *Bodhisattvas* through countless *kalpas* and *kotis* of time "like the grains of the Ganges (sand)" corresponds verbally to what we apprehend visually when viewing Kuan Yin's innumerable helping hands and the other innumerable unnamed *Bodhisattvas* in the various temple pantheons. Finally, there is more to our sense of place than just the sense of place in time, and the same may be said of our apprehension of the *Bodhisattva* pantheon.

The Pantheon as Spatial Locator

The meaning of the pantheon then requires being more completely described in terms of its sense of direction or place. If Sakhyamuni, the historical Buddha, is at the spiritual center of things, then all other places may be located by the four cardinal points north and south, east and west of him, with a *Bodhisattva* in each of these directions. The most prominent of these locators is surely Amida Buddha in his Western Paradise. Much less known and worshiped is his mirror image, the *Bodhisattva* of an eastern paradise who is variously denominated; while *Bodhisattvas* of the north and south, though not at all popular objects of devotion, are placed there as rationally required to complete the spiritual geography of the four quarters, giving Mahayanists a religious sense of place.

Difficulties in explaining the pantheon's meaning in terms of spatial location involve confusion and uncertainty in its spatial sense. For example, Amida Buddha's Western Paradise is a spiritual location; while Avalokitesvara, it is suggested, originated in the geographical northwest of India. Moreover, from the viewpoint of China and points eastward, Sakhyamuni also has a western location, as is noted in the Chinese *koan* asking why Bodhidharma brought the Buddha's *dharma* teaching from the west. The problem then is how to think coherently about the different Happy Lands, and the spatial relationships among the various spiritual and geographical, fixed and variable directions and locations.

Most disconcerting of all, the Mahayanist pantheon exhibits a spatial dislocation that corresponds with the one already noted in time. Once more the innumerable unnamed *Bodhisattvas* in the background of the various temple pantheons correspond visually with *The Lotus Sutra's* verbal descriptions of "the Tathagata, & etc ... in countless innumerable spheres in all directions"; or again, "In all directions ... Buddhas, like sand of the Ganges." With Buddhas in every direction like grains of sand, there are now far too many of them to frame our sense of spatial location. The pantheon's sense of religious place thus requires some other type of location described along different lines.

The Pantheon as Cosmology

Recalling the three-storey Hong Fa Temple with its three Sakhyamunis and over its highest Sakhyamuni the words "three-World Guiding Teacher" suggests that the pantheon frames the triple world itself as its meaning. One such version of the triple world has Amida Buddha on high in his *Sukhavati* (Land of Bliss), Sakhyamuni the historical Buddha on the earthly plane, and Ti Tsang as the *Bodhisattva* whose special mission it is to rescue those in hell below.

Difficulties in this cosmological interpretation of the pantheon include similar sorts of questions about the cosmic relationships among the various Happy Lands, earthly locations and hellish places. Even more importantly, all the same questions about the spatio-temporal sense of the pantheon dissolving into the mystical sublimity of its myriad *Bodhisattvas* remain without rational answers as well.

The Pantheon as Rational Monism

Since it has by now become evident that all the foregoing explanations of the Mahayanist pantheon ultimately attempt to impose some kind of rational order on its plenitude of *Bodhisattvas,* the issue of rationality is best addressed more directly. There are at least three traditional ways of rationally representing the many *Bodhisattvas* as in some sense one. These are the ways of personal monism, somatic monism and finally the impersonal monism of the one Buddha-nature view.

The implicit personal monism of the Tai Bay and second floor Hong Fa pantheons suggest that behind the many *Bodhisattvas* is just one Buddha. In this version that one Buddha is Amida, even though, just like all the other Buddhas and *Bodhisattvas,* he has his own special mission, that of welcoming into his Happy Land all those who in their dying distress call upon him: "Namo Amida Butsu." For this reason other versions of personal monism posit a cosmic Buddha who has no other function than that of rationally organizing the pantheon, though even here just how it is that ultimately all *Bodhisattvas* are only one person remains a mystery.

With this mystery now conceived as a rational problem, one traditional solution is the somatic monism of the *trikaya* (triple body) doctrine. According to this doctrine all the different *Bodhisattvas* are expressions of one and the same cosmic body. What makes Sakhyamuni the historical Buddha is his *nirmanakaya* (physical body). Other earthly Buddhas have an earthly body too. But celestial Buddhas like Amida in his Happy Land have a glorious *sambhogakaya* (blissful body) seen in visions, etc. Both the foregoing are more or less emanations from the Buddha's *dharmakaya* (cosmic body) which is the source of the other two types of body, and hence of all the many *Bodhisattvas* in the entire pantheon.

Although the *trikaya* (triple body) way of rationalizing the pantheon somatically represents an intellectual advance over the personal monism of just one ultimate Buddha, the idea of the physical and blissful bodies of the multitudinous Buddhas and *Bodhisattvas* emanating from the *dharmakaya* of this one cosmic Buddha like rays from the sun is still only a metaphor based on solar imagery. Just how it is that a multitude of bodies can emanate from one body like rays from the sun, or whether such an idea even makes sense is not at all clear without a rational explanation of what they all share in common.

It would seem to be exactly to satisfy such a rational requirement that the doctrine is formulated of all Buddhas and *Bodhisattvas*, indeed all human beings and everything else that exists, all sharing one and the same Buddha nature. As Hui Neng, the future sixth patriarch of the southern Ch'an (Zen) school, said when asked in *The Platform Scripture* how he as a barbarian from the south could aspire to become a Buddha: "there is no north and south in the Buddha nature ... what difference is there in our Buddha nature?" With this one Buddha-nature doctrine, the high point of rationalizing the Mahayana Buddhist pantheon has been reached.

There are, however, problems with the doctrine of the Buddha nature conceived as the ultimate attempt at rationalizing the pantheon. In the first place it is impersonal, as characterized in D. T. Suzuki's description of *satori* (sudden enlightenment) experience, while the *Bodhisattvas* are personal. Additionally, its characteristic impersonality reflects more the solitary practice of *zazen* (meditation) than it does the interpersonal experience of temple worship mutually implying the *karuna* (compassion) of the pantheon of *Bodhisattvas* and in return the gratitude and devotional love of Mahayanist adherents.

Finally there is the problem of the courage and consistency of intellectual convictions similar to the one faced by the young Socrates in Plato's *Parmenides* when he is asked whether he believes there are eternal ideas not only of the highest virtues but also of terrestrial things like human beings, fire and water, and even of undignified things like hair, mud and dirt. The Mahayanist version of the problem is posed in terms of Zen *koans* like: "Does a dog," or in other formulations a shit stick, "have the Buddha nature?"; along with the commentary: "If you say yes or no, you lose your own Buddha nature." At this point the limit of rational attempts at explanation of the pantheon has been reached as a rational explanation is exactly what is not wanted here.

If all the foregoing attempts at elucidating the *Bodhisattva* pantheon have come to this end, that is because they all try to explain its meaning by reducing it to one or another of its rational functions as though "the meaning is the use." It is precisely because the theological, moralistic, cosmological and other uses of the pantheon are each a facet of its overall meaning that they are all individually partial, one-sided, reductive explanations.

What is needed at this point is an overall interpretation of the pantheon that restores its wholeness of meaning. Thus while not denying the foregoing and other partial meanings of the pantheon, they are now bracketed or set aside in favour of a grander vision of all the temple Buddhas and *Bodhisattvas* including the unnamed myriad that typically line the temple walls.

IV

The one all-inclusive trait shared by all *Bodhisattvas* that makes them *Bodhisattvas* is the shared *maha-karuna,* compassionate love, expressed in their common vow not to enter *nirvana* until all sentient beings have been saved from suffering.

Elucidating the Mahayanist pantheon's meaning in terms of its *Bodhisattvas' maha-karuna* kind of love requires first explaining that by suffering Mahayanists mean the same as all other Buddhists, namely enduring the human condition of sickness, old age and death pictured in the first three passing sights seen by the naive young Sakhyamuni early in his life story. But while most of us pass through the drama of human suffering only by necessity and much against our will, the Mahayanist *Bodhisattvas* do so voluntarily. Out of compassion for suffering humanity, they vow not to enter *nirvana* until all sentient beings have been saved from suffering. It is the act of volition expressed in the *Bodhisattva* vow and not any rational distinction like that between Creator and creature that distinguishes the pantheon of *Bodhisattvas* from the rest of suffering humanity. By undertaking this vow and steadfastly pursuing its achievement, some metaphysically envisioned through repeated voluntary incarnations, the *Bodhisattvas* accumulate the meritorious *karma* that makes them the Great Beings who collectively compose the *Mahayana* (Great Vehicle) of salvation for all.

The grand dynamic of the *Bodhisattvas'* compassionate activity moves on two directions which tend to diminish the distinction between, on the one hand, celestial Buddhas such as Amida and Maitreya, and on the other, earthly incarnate Buddhas like Sakhyamuni. Tibetan Buddhists, for example, regard *Bodhisattva* Avalokitesvara and Amida Buddha as repeatedly incarnating themselves as successive Dali Lamas and Panchen Lamas respectively; while, moving in the opposite direction, Chinese Buddhists tell how a monk, Darmakara, and a nun, the third daughter of a northern Chou ruler, took *Bodhisattva* vows to save their parents, the mother of the first from hell for meat-eating and the father of the second from fatal illness, so that in the end the former became *Bodhisattva* Ti Tsang and the latter much beloved Kuan Yin.

In this broadest perspective on the pantheon, its essential aspect is not the claimed historical reality of individual *Bodhisattvas*, nor its metaphysical aspect with supporting concepts of meritorious *karma*, accumulation and transference of merit, voluntary incarnation etc., since all such notions must be suspended or bracketed at least temporarily in order first to apprehend the vast panorama of a love so expansive that it quite surpasses on all sides the time and space of the world historical drama of suffering humanity, a panorama which ultimately reaches out to embrace its observers since the same volitional dynamic observed in the pantheon as object of devotion in the Mahayana is reflected in devotional practice itself. For the limitless love envisioned in terms of *Bodhisattvas* on all sides like grains of Ganges' sand is reflected and returned by the devotee's limitless gratitude for such love. The ultimate expression of this gratitude is, of course, to undertake the *Bodhisattva* vow oneself; so that you and I and all other sentient beings who are, were, or ever will be, undertake to follow the *Bodhisattva* path of *maha-karuna*, limitless compassionate love.

The ultimate meaning of the *Bodhisattva* pantheon is then envisioned when all sentient beings have finally heard Sakhyamuni's *dharma* teaching and taken refuge in the *sangha* or ideal Buddhist community; when Kuan Yin has rescued the last victim of disaster and illness; when Ti Tsang has made his last trip to hell to save the last suffering sentient being from its flames, and safely delivered him to Amida; when Amida has welcomed the last of the deceased into *Sukavati*, his Happy Land; indeed then the religious drama of human suffering pictured on the wheel of *samsara* will thereby have been completely absorbed into the greater compassionate picture of the Mahayanist pantheon of *Bodhisattvas*: horrific hell will then have been changed into blissful heaven; *samsara* will have been transformed into *nirvana*.

While the Mahayanist transformation of *samsara* into *nirvana* fails to make logical sense when thought dualistically in terms of suffering and bliss conceived as mutually exclusive categories, when looked at volitionally Mahayanist *maha-karuna*, conceived as non-dualistic love, reaches out to overcome the rational distinction between self and other, sufferer and savior.

This is not to say that the conditions of suffering, sickness, old age and death, no longer obtain; but rather that Mahayanist all-embracing love and the compassionate activity it inspires transforms the meaning of these events from that of an involuntary, passive and egoistic experience into a life-experience that is voluntary, active and altruistic. When this vision is pursued beyond the limits of self concern, it reaches ultimately toward the nameless unknown *Bodhisattvas* of everyday life, *Bodhisattvas* nonetheless even when we know them not. Beyond the limits of everyday life, the *Bodhisattva* pantheon is a picture of the conviction that no matter how great is human suffering, the greater love of those who, out of compassion, voluntarily share the human condition to ameliorate it is infinitely greater.

Looking from the samsaric side of life, John Milton's Satan says in his epic poem *Paradise Lost*: "The mind is its own place and in itself can make a heaven of hell (and) a hell of heaven," having in his case just lost the latter. It is the unique feature and ultimate meaning of the Mahayana Buddhist pantheon of *Bodhisattvas* that it presents a picture, not of the individual mind trapped in its own personal hell, but rather of the collectivity of all the sentient beings who are, were or ever will be together expressing *maha-karuna,* the infinite compassionate will to make the hell of human suffering into a heaven or Happy Land.

Compassion at the Crossroads: Schopenhauer on the Basis of Morality

Timothy J. Madigan

"Poor Schopenhauer had this secret guilt, too, in his heart, the guilt of cherishing his philosophy more than his fellow men." So wrote Friedrich Nietzsche, in his incisive essay from *Thoughts Out Of Season,* "Schopenhauer as Educator." Nietzsche goes on to say: "He often chose falsely in his desire to find real trust and compassion in men, only to return with a heavy heart to his faithful dog again. He was absolutely alone, with no single friend of his own kind to comfort him...."[1] In the following paper, I will argue that this friendless and bad-tempered philosopher still has much to teach us about the nature of love. I will further argue that he can provide a bridge between the three dominant traditions of the Western World: Buddhism, Christianity and humanism.

In his recent book *The Silence of God,* Raimundo Panikkar discusses the modern phenomenon of atheism. Many of the functions traditionally ascribed to God are now achieved by humans, through science and technology. "It is increasingly difficult," Panikkar writes, "to find someone who will turn to God rather than the doctor for healing, or who does not bother to have an emergency water supply in case the seasons fail."[2] This is a new type of atheism, unlike the anti-clerical movements of the past, which combated obscurantism and churchly abuses and which strongly influenced Schopenhauer and Nietzsche in their own polemics. "Strictly speaking," Panikkar writes, "the new atheism rises up neither to combat nor to deny God unequivocally." Rather, more and more people seem to live without a transcendent grounding for their lives. It is perhaps not coincidental that many in the Western secular world are pursuing an interest in Buddhist studies, for, he notes, "Both cultures, the modern, of Western stamp, and the Buddhist, are atheistic."[3] *The Silence of God,* subtitled *The Answer of the Buddha,* gives a masterful exploration of the differing meanings of the term "atheistic." In it, Panikkar cautions that it may be unwise to attempt a complete break with the long-prevailing Christian tradition which had for centuries furnished a large part of humanity with an effective framework of support. And yet the silence of God may provide a common ground, or what Panikkar calls "The Crossing of the Ways," for the three major human traditions of Christianity, Buddhism and atheistic humanism. In his book *The Intra-Religious Dialogue,* he quite rightly cautions us against the tendency to conflate all three into one amorphous lump – the teachings, practices and even the languages of all three traditions are not amenable to such a shallow interpretation, and "nothing is more harmful than hurried syntheses or superficial parallelisms."[4] Rather, he advocates what he calls "the notion of homology," examining the correlating points of differing systems. This method does not imply that one system is superior to another, nor that the systems are interchangeable. It seeks points of commonalty, which can serve to broaden an appreciation of the systems and allow for the opportunity for real discussion amongst all participants. One such homologous notion, common to all three traditions, is the subject of this 10 year symposium: love. "By *love,*" Panikkar writes, "I mean that impulse, that force impelling us to our fellow-beings and leading us to discover in them what is lacking in us. To be sure, real love does not aim for victory in the encounter. It longs for common recognition of the truth, without blotting out the differences or muting the various melodies in the single polyphonic symphony."[5] I would like to propose that Arthur Schopenhauer's philosophy—in particular his discussion of compassion as the basis of morality—can further this homologous project.

At first glance, Schopenhauer would seem a poor bridge-builder between traditions. He occupies an anomalous position in the history of philosophy. His writings are a peculiar mixture of rigorous analysis of concepts, idiosyncratic interpretations of previous systems, and biting attacks on his enemies. For much of his life he was ignored, and most of the copies of his masterwork *The World as Will and Representation,* in Nietzsche's words "had to be turned into wastepaper...."

> The imminent risk that his great work would be undone, merely by neglect, bred in him a state of unrest—perilous and uncontrollable—for no single adherent of any note presented himself. It is tragic to watch his search for any evidence of recognition, and his piercing cry of triumph at last, that he would now really be read *(legor et legar)*, touches us with a thrill of pain. All the traits in which we do not see the great philosopher show us the suffering man, anxious for his noble possessions: he was tortured by the fear of losing his little property, and perhaps of no longer being able to maintain in its purity his truly antique attitude toward philosophy.[6]

Yet, unlike Nietzsche, Schopenhauer did receive recognition before his death. There is a note of childish glee in his reaction to this late-found fame. Blaming his long-standing obscurity on professional academics who had denied him his proper due, he compared himself to Caspar Hauser, the mysterious young man who was said to have spent his first sixteen years in total isolation.[7] In the preface to his work *On the Will in Nature* he crows that "I have to convey a sad piece of news to the professors of philosophy. Their Caspar Hauser ... whom they so carefully secluded and so securely walled in from light and air for nearly forty years that not a sound could betray his existence to the world – their Caspar Hauser, I say, has escaped! He has escaped and is running around the world; some even imagine he is a prince."[8] It is here that he offers the cry that so pained Nietzsche's delicate ears: "What I mean is that people have begun to read my works and will not again refrain from so doing. *Legor et legar* ('people read me and will read me'): and it cannot be altered."[9] For the remaining six years of his life, and for decades thereafter, his work was indeed much discussed, not only by professors of philosophy (at least those who did not take offense at being referred to as "the most miserable compilers of compendia"), but also musicians like Wagner, and novelists like Thomas Hardy, Thomas Mann, Leo Tolstoy and Marcel Proust.[10] Yet his influence has waned in recent years. There remains something rather *outré* about the man and his writings – neither the analytic nor the continental schools of philosophy have embraced him to their bosoms, a fact he no doubt would have appreciated.

One should not dismiss him too quickly, however, for while his writings are certainly *sui generis* (the heavy use of Latin phrases is quite in keeping with his style), Schopenhauer was the meeting ground for several philosophical traditions. He himself gave credit to three main sources of inspiration: Plato, Kant and the *Upanishads*. Certainly he was unique in admitting Eastern thought—Hinduism and Buddhism—into his writings, at a time when few Western writers took such traditions seriously, or paid them much heed. He read the *Upanishads* every night before retiring, and makes frequent references to them. In addition, he was well-steeped in English empiricism, being particularly fond of Hume, whose writings on religion he once hoped to translate into German. Patrick Bridgewater, in his book *Arthur Schopenhauer's English Schooling*, ascribes Schopenhauer's blistering attacks on Christianity to the grueling three months he spent at the age of fifteen in a stereotypical English boarding school, run by a man he referred to as a "parson terrorist."[11] Bridgewater's claim that "the intemperate nature of the philosopher's language is readily—and only—explicable in terms of having Dr. (Samuel) Johnson's example rammed down his throat"[12] by Thomas Lancaster, the "parson terrorist," strikes me as implausible and overly reductive. It smacks too much of *Jane Eyre*. Schopenhauer, through his father's influence, had already been steeped in the anti-clerical writings of Voltaire, and inherited some of the latter's caustic wit. He didn't need three months of pedantic schooling in a narrow-minded Christian setting to make him re-echo the cry "crush the infamous thing." His hatred of dogmatism, mummery and obscurantism was an ingrained part of his character. Still, Bridgewater ably shows the roots of Schopenhauer's lifelong love for England. It is not surprising that his writings are sprinkled with examples he had culled from his daily reading of *The London Times*.

For all of his fire-breathing comments, Schopenhauer did not despise Christianity. As Brian Magee notes, in his book *The Philosophy of Schopenhauer:*

> Although in no sense whatsoever a religious believer, indeed a declared atheist, he had the profoundest respect for Hinduism, Buddhism and Christianity.... He thought that Christianity, rightly understood, was much closer to Buddhism than is generally recognized. He regarded the history of the Church, and indeed of Christendom, with a good deal of contempt, but this was because the teachings of the founder to whom lip service was paid had been so monstrously perverted or disregarded.... Schopenhauer regarded Jesus the man as being almost a sort of natural Buddhist....[13]

What was it that Christ and the Buddha had in common? They both preached the virtue of compassion. And it is the notion of "compassion" which, Schopenhauer argued, was the foundation for all systems of morality, whatever claims to the contrary they might make.

It might seem strange that a man who demonstrated little fellow-feeling in his own encounters with others should place such a high value on compassion. As John Atwell notes in his recent book *Schopenhauer: The Human Character*: "The things he prized most highly—celibacy, compassion, disregard for acclaim—he did not practice."[14] But Schopenhauer was well aware of this seeming contradiction, commenting in *The World as Will and Representation* that "It is just as little necessary for the saint to be a philosopher as for the philosopher to be a saint; just as it is not necessary for a perfectly beautiful person to be a great sculptor, or for a great sculptor to be himself a beautiful person. In general, it is a strange demand on a moralist that he should commend no other virtue than that which military as a "pre-emptive strike.") As a philosopher, his job was to describe and analyze compassion—there was no compunction to actually practice it.

Schopenhauer's most detailed examination of compassion is found in his essay *On the Basis of Morality,* written in 1839. It has a peculiar history. In that same year, at the age of fifty, he received his first public notice when his *On the Freedom of the Human Will* was awarded the prize for best essay in a contest sponsored by the Norwegian Scientific Society. Flushed with success, he submitted an essay to the Royal Danish Society of Scientific Studies, which had posed the following question: "Are the source and foundation of morals to be looked for in an idea of morality lying immediately in consciousness (or conscience) and in the analysis of the other fundamental moral concepts springing from that idea, or are they to be looked for in a different ground of knowledge?" Answering in the negative, Schopenhauer propounded the theory that the source and foundation of morals had nothing at all to do with knowledge, but rather in what he called "the great mystery of ethics"—compassion. Fully expecting to win this second Scandinavian academic contest, he arranged for both essays to be published together in a work entitled *The Two Fundamental Problems of Ethics.* He was outraged to discover that the Royal Danish Society did not award him the prize. To add insult to injury, the Society's published rejection made it known that his had been the *only* entry. Schopenhauer had his two essays published together, in 1841, but the title page for the second essay proudly read: "*On the Basis of Morality*: *not* awarded a prize by the Royal Danish Society of Scientific Studies, at Copenhagen, on 30 January 1840." The introduction consisted of a lengthy diatribe against the Society's failure to understand or appreciate his argument, coupled with a scathing attack on the Society's admiration for Hegel, "the *summus philoso-*

phus, who always had 'the thought' only in his mouth, just as public houses have on their signboards a portrait of the prince who never frequents them."[16] Schopenhauer scholar David Cartwright adds: "Indeed, Schopenhauer's sense of being wronged was so great that in the preface to the second edition of *The Two Fundamental Problems of Ethics* (1860), he was still spitting fire."[17] And this just months before his death. No one could hold a grudge like Schopenhauer could.

On the Basis of Morality asks the question: what can motivate individuals to overcome their egoistic tendencies? Surely not adherence to theistic commandments or the categorical imperative. Morality is not grounded in rationality. Empirical investigation shows that there are only three fundamental incentives which motivate human actions:

a) Egoism: the desire for one's own well-being.
b) Malice: the desire for another's woe.
c) Compassion: the desire for another's well-being.

"Man's three fundamental ethical incentives, egoism, malice, and compassion," according to Schopenhauer, "are present in everyone in different and incredibly unequal proportions. In accordance with them, motives will operate on man and actions will ensue."[18] One can see the Platonic influence in this threefold categorization. He adds that people will be stirred to actions by the motives to which they are primarily susceptible. For instance, should you wish to induce an egoist to perform an act of loving-kindness, you must dupe him into believing the act will somehow benefit himself. But unlike the egoist, who tends to make a great distinction between himself and all other humans—and indeed all other living things—and who lives by the maxim *pereat mundus, dum ego salvus sim* ("may the world perish, provided I am safe"), a man of compassionate character makes no such sharp distinction. Instead, he sees himself as fundamentally a part of and involved with the suffering world. For the egoist, Schopenhauer says, humanity is the non-ego, but to the compassionate man, it is "myself, once more."

> Every purely beneficent act, every instance of wholly and truly disinterested help, which as such has another's distress as its motive, is, if we probe the matter to the bottom, really a mysterious action. It is practical mysticism insofar as it ultimately springs from the same knowledge that constitutes the essence of all mysticism proper. In no other way can it be truly explained. That a man gives alms without having, even remotely, any other object than that of lessening the want that oppresses another, is possible only insofar as he recognizes that it is his own self which now appears before him in that doleful and dejected form, and hence that he recognizes against his own inner being-in-itself in the phenomenal appearance of another.[19]

It is no wonder, then, that he calls compassion "the great mystery" of ethics, nor that he was intrigued by the examples and the discussions of this found within the Christian, Hindu and Buddhist traditions. In his view, the only means of explaining ethics is through metaphysics, and he adds

> On account of this undeniable ethical metaphysical tendency of life, no religion in the

> world could gain a footing without an explanation of life on these lines. For by means of its ethical side, every religion has its fixed points in our minds. It makes its dogma the basis of the moral incentive which everyone can feel, but for that reason does not yet understand, so closely connecting dogma and moral incentive that the two appear to be inseparable. Indeed, priests try to proclaim that unbelief and immortality are one and the same thing. This is the reason why the believer considers the unbeliever to be identical with the morally bad, as seen in the fact that expressions such as godless, atheistic, unchristian, heretic, and the like, are used as synonyms for moral depravity.[20]

He also makes the point, in his book *On the Fourfold Root of the Principle of Sufficient Reason,* that it is a mistake to relate religion to theism as the genus to a single species. As Panikkar notes, Schopenhauer considered Buddhism to be unambiguously atheistic[21], and included Taoism and Confucianism as equally atheistic world-views. "Incidentally," Schopenhauer writes, "it should be observed that the word atheism contains a surreptitious assumption, in that it assumes in advance that theism is self-evident."[22]

We see here a meeting place for dialogue. In *The Silence of God,* Panikkar provides a rich description of various types of atheism and their connection with Buddhism. Like Schopenhauer, he points out that what has been called "atheism" is not, or need not be, a reaction against a series of propositions proving the existence of a Supreme Being. "It is not a kind of corrective for theism."[23] Instead, it represents a new stage in the development of humanity. Schopenhauer's life and writings perhaps mark the turning-point in this development in the Western World. In his preface to *On the Will in Nature,* he discusses what he calls "the steady growth of unbelief," which goes hand-in-hand with the expanding empirical and historical knowledge science has provided (a notion Nietzsche would return to with his famous statement "God is dead and we have killed Him"). But Schopenhauer, in discussing the clash between atheists and theists, places a curse on both their houses. The former, obsessed with accumulating new information and unconcerned about the past, "calmly throwing out of the window the intellectual labor of two thousand years," are mere scoffers of religion. "Either catechism or materialism" is their battle cry. They reject not only the form, but the spirit and sense of Christianity. The theists, though, fan the flames of this growing unbelief by their adherence to Tartuffian hypocrisy, and their preoccupation with gratuities and churchly privileges. In *The Fourfold Root,* he adds that the Church is tottering. "The number of those rendered unfit for belief by a certain degree and extent of knowledge has become considerable. This is testified by the general dissemination of that shallow rationalism which is showing ever more openly its bulldog face."[24] How does one escape from this impasse, with dogmatic belief on one side and shallow materialism on the other? Perhaps not surprisingly, Schopenhauer presents himself as the means of escape. Like the cavalry coming to the rescue, he declares "There is a boiling-point on the scale of culture where all faith, revelation, and authorities evaporate; where man desires to judge for himself, and wishes to be not only instructed but also convinced.... Hollow verbiage and the impotent efforts of intellectual eunuchs then no longer suffice. On the contrary, there is need for a philosophy seriously meant, in other words, one that is directed to truth and not to salaries and fees. Such a philosophy, therefore, does not ask whether it has to please ministers or councillors, or serve this or that religious cause for the time being."[25] In other words, read *The World as Will and Representation* and all its corollaries. Schopenhauer will lead the way.

For all his bombast, there is much wisdom in this advice – perhaps more so for our own time than when it was written. Schopenhauer deserves credit for appreciating the insights of Eastern thought. He recognized that the philosophy of his own day was rapidly becoming desiccated and self-referential, with little to say about the issues most pertinent to people's lives, while at the same time the age-old religious structures were tottering from the accumulated blows of scientific, cultural and historical reevaluations. He was one of the first people to propose a true dialogue between traditions, and his own manner of living demonstrated this cosmopolitanism. His study contained a gilt-bronze Buddha on a marble stand, a bust of Kant, an oil portrait of Goethe, and – attesting to his love of animals – sixteen portraits of canines.[26] Schopenhauer also owned a succession of poodles, naming his favorite "Atma" and commenting upon its remarkable intelligence.[27]

A study of Schopenhauer's work, examined from the standpoint of the various traditions he critiqued, would be a fruitful endeavor. As John Atwell puts it:

> In my judgment, Schopenhauer stands both historically and doctrinally at the crossroads between 'modern philosophy' (say Descartes through Kant) and its aftermath (or if one pleases, 'postmodern thought,' from say, Nietzsche through Michel Foucault. In philosophy proper, Schopenhauer annihilated every form of metaphysics not

> thoroughly 'grounded' in experience; he introduced into intellectual, cultural, and literary circles the terrible, awesome power of reasonless will along with the often uncontrollable sexual drive; he acknowledged and tried to explain, instead of trying to explain away, vastly different sorts of persons, from the diabolical villain to the money-grubbing professor of philosophy to the true scholar; he suggested a metaphysical framework of moral virtue that owes virtually nothing to reason or intellect (and which, I think, has not even today been adequately considered).[28]

Our task, then, is to consider in further detail Schopenhauer's examination of compassion. It will be made easier by what I perceive as a renaissance in interest in Schopenhauer in the English-speaking world. In recent years, new editions of *On the Will in Nature* (1992), The Germany Library edition *Arthur Schopenhauer: Philosophical Writings* (1994),[29] *The World as Will and Idea* (1995),[30] *On the Basis of Morality* (1995), and *The Wisdom of Life and Counsels and Maxims,*[31] as well as such examinations of his work as Rüdiger Safranski's *Schopenhauer and the Wild Years of Philosophy* (1990)'[32] Christopher Janaway's Past Masters Series volume (1994),[33] and John E. Atwell's two studies, *Schopenhauer: The Human Character* (1990) and *Schopenhauer on the Character of the World: The Metaphysics of Will* (1995). Perhaps Caspar Hauser has escaped again.

Notes

1. Friedrich Nietzsche, *The Philosophy of Nietzsche,* edited by Geoffrey Clive (New York: Signet Classics, 1965), p. 338. This description – aside from the dog – is more appropriate to Nietzsche himself than to Schopenhauer.

2. Raimundo Panikkar, *The Silence of God* (Maryknoll, NY: Orbis Books, 1989), p. 95.

3. *Ibid.*, p. 102.

4. Raimundo Panikkar, *The Intrareligious Dialogue* (New York: Paulist Press, 1978), p. 31.

5. *Ibid.,* p. 35.

6. Nietzsche, Ibid.

7. Werner Herzog's 1976 film biography of Hauser has an appropriately Schopenhauerian title: *Every Man for Himself and God Against All.*

8. Arthur Schopenhauer, *On the Will in Nature,* translated by E.F.J. Payne (New York: Berg Publishers, Inc., 1992), p. 5.

9. *Ibid.*

10. In his book *The Philosophy of Schopenhauer* (Oxford: Clarendon Press, 1991), Brian Magee devotes two chapters to discussing Schopenhauer's influence on several noted creative artists.

11. He had been placed there by his mother, in the middle of a European tour the family was taking. Finding Arthur to be an impediment to her own enjoyment of the tour, she decided to leave him in England while she and her husband continued their excursions. No doubt this had an effect on the future complete break between mother and son.

12. Patrick Bridgewater, *Arthur Schopenhauer's English Schooling* (New York: Routledge, 1988), p. 358.

13. Bryan Magee, *The Philosophy of Schopenhauer* (Oxford: Clarendon Press, 1991), pp. 320-21.

14. John E. Atwell, *Schopenhauer: The Human Character* (Philadelphia: Temple University Press, 1990), p. 255.

15. Arthur Schopenhauer, *The World as Will and Representation*, Vol. I, translated by E.F.J. Payne (New York: Dover Publications, Inc., 1969), p. 383.

16. Arthur Schopenhauer, *On the Basis of Morality*, translated by E.F.J. Payne (Providence, RI: Berghahn Books, 1995), p. 18. His animosity toward Hegel was longstanding. As an instructor at the University of Berlin, he deliberately scheduled his own lectures at the same time as Hegel's, only to give up teaching in disgust when no students came to hear him.

17. *Ibid.*, p. x.

18. *Ibid.*, p. 192.

19. *Ibid.*, p. 212.

20. *Ibid.*, pp. 201-02.

21. Panikkar, *The Silence of God*, p. 179.

22. Arthur Schopenhauer, *On the Fourfold Root of the Principle of Sufficient Reason*, translated by E.F.J. Payne (La Salle, IL: Open Court, 1992), p. 188.

23. Panikkar, *The Silence of God*, pp. 96-97.

24. Schopenhauer, *On the Fourfold Root*, p. 179.

25. *Ibid.*, p. 180.

26. Bridgewater, p. 347.

27. My friend Jill Lenz, a professional dog trainer, has given me independent verification regarding the intelligence of poodles. She writes that "the breed is immensely popular here and abroad. It is consistently in the AKC's top ten by registration numbers, and we recognize 140 breeds. I think it is because of their intelligence and splendid temperaments that they enjoy such popularity. Even as a fancier of herding breeds, I must agree with Schopenhauer—they are one of the most intelligent and personal. In his book *The Intelligence of Dogs,* Stanley Coren ranks the poodle second only to the border collie in Obedience and Working Intelligence" (personal communication).

28. John E. Atwell, *Schopenhauer on the Character of the World: The Metaphysics of Will* (Berkeley, CA: University of California Press, 1995), p. 183.

29. Arthur Schopenhauer, *Philosophical Writings,* edited by Wolfgang Schirmacher, translated by E.F.J. Payne (New York: Continuum, 1994).

30. Arthur Schopenhauer, *The World as Will and Idea,* edited by David Berman, translated by Jill Berman (London: The Everyman Library, 1995).

31. Arthur Schopenhauer, *The Wisdom of Life and Counsels and Maxims,* translated by T. Bailey Saunders (Amherst, NY: Prometheus Books, 1995).

32. Rüdiger Safranski, *Schopenhauer and the Wild Years of Philosophy* (Cambridge, MA: Harvard University Press, 1990).

33. Christopher Janaway, *Schopenhauer* (New York: Oxford University Press, 1994).

Satisfaction

Stephen Frost

It might be a universal human sensibility to believe that *satisfaction* with one's life is possible. People want to be satisfied, often are not, but still believe that it is possible. Even despair suggests the possibility of an absent *satisfaction.*

Satisfaction might imply *satisfaction* in the things of God or Gods or Absolute Realization. Ultimate *satisfaction* might imply the integration of perception or the unity of knowledge. *Satisfaction* might imply meaning, or purpose in life, or justice, justification, or *making satisfaction* in the sense of making up for something, atonement, or doing penance.

I use this word, *satisfaction,* to commence a discussion about an important, but elusive phenomenon. Terms like *composition* or *form* might serve as well to open this analysis. But these seem too literary, not quite universal enough for my interest. There are other such options but for the purpose of this essay *satisfaction* will do.

I am not primarily interested in what are considered here secondary or tertiary levels of *satisfaction* such as sexual *satisfaction,* or the *satisfaction* gained from accomplishment, intellectual discovery, or winning at cards, for example. Although any of these might play a part as one intuits the possibility of complete *satisfaction.*

Methodology

The *methodology* that developed along with the intuition that complete *satisfaction* is a viable topic for analysis, is unique to this subject and includes elements unusual in critical evaluation. For instance, because this study is not a physical-chemical experiment, but an investigation into discursive and non-discursive perception, a certain amount of autobiographical information is justified, even necessary.

This is not only so that the reader may know my bias or understand better the angle from which I approach this topic, but because this subject matter can only be comprehended as it is situated within the context of human personality and culture. This phenomenon itself alters with culture and personality while still remaining, I believe, a universal phenomenon in human perception. My practice of the religio-cultural traditions and techniques to be commented upon here, have both formed my personality and influenced the conclusions I deduce.

What I have done to understand the content and impact of this intuition is to "study" religion and art. Within this context, I also studied for and am ordained a priest in an ancient and rigorous dispensation. I remain a practicing artist and poet—my B.A. is in Art and English Literature. For my Masters and Ph.D. studies in theology, comparative religion and aesthetics, I "read" under one of the great contemporary masters in the History of Religion and the Philosophy of Science, Raimundo Panikkar. I am familiar from my youth with some of the inner workings of shamanism. I have lived in the cultures that I study and am now on intimate terms with the history of mysticism and its techniques.

The nature of *satisfaction* results in a complex of elements that required such training. I intend in this essay to describe this complex of elements and how they have been and still are important for the formation of culture and definition of personality.

Art: The Shift of Consciousness, Myth, Science

A complex of approaches is used to examine this topic. Art, in certain religions such as Buddhist Tantra and the Christian Hesychasm, is one of the vehicles used to explore this complex of topics. The ability to shift into *other* states of consciousness is also an element explored here. Myth and history cut revealing facets on the face of this gem. Literature, science and world philosophies: Critical method is employed as well as ancient practices traditionally used to transform reality or one's perception of it. These, within an interdisciplinary context, are engaged to comment upon the perception and means of ultimate *satisfaction.*

Time

Consideration of the nature of time is pertinent here as well. Temporal and atemporal categories are compared. Temporal rule opposed to atemporal consciousness is contained in the contrast between the more primordial Animistic Shamanism of hunter-gatherer societies and civilization, for example. How we view time and structure life styles as the result is at the heart of our issue. It is a collective shift *of consciousness* in history that leads away from nature toward technocratic civilization, changing the quality or even the possibility of *satisfaction*. An example of Christian techniques for such altering of consciousness to a more atemporal realization would be 1700 years of Christian monasticism or the archetype of the monk generally.

The Energies

Any examination of ancient world philosophies reveals a secondary strata of cosmological and physiological belief developed from a world wide experience of psychic, physical-mystical "energies." A description and evaluation of these is a necessary element in this complex of issues related to *satisfaction* and perception.

Erring

In a similar way, concepts and practices associated with the practice of *erring* are an important consideration here. The medieval knight errant wandered the realm doing good and heroic deeds, waiting for and seeking to do God's will in a manner dependent upon the shift of consciousness—to find the Holy Grail, for instance. One abandons oneself to the mercy of God. The *Hesychast* or Tantric monk uses specific practices to accomplish similar goals—ultimate realization of absolute reality. The Vedic *sunyasin* takes to the roads and depends upon the divine spirit for sustenance. Is this *satisfaction?*

The shift of consciousness between linear, logical, analytical thought, to non rational states of consciousness as found in some forms of prayer, art, or Zen, for example, suggests an underlying world of primary importance in the construct of human identity and culture. One example of this shift comes from *Zen and the Art of Archery*. The Zen archer stands with bow drawn and arrow cocked. The archer aims, then waits awhile. As the archer waits, consciousness shifts so that the target and archer identify as one, letting the arrow fly to its target. It is the *shift of consciousness* that (re)defines humanity and its capacities.

The shift is a capacity that people have exercised since the dawn of human consciousness. It is a natural but specialized experience for which the religious practitioner ardently prepares, yet it remains an essential human trait. While the shift is a specific phenomenon, it is also a reference to and implicit in the more general, yet fundamentally significant temporal/non temporal considerations about human perception.

The shift of consciousness is an essential thread that weaves itself through most religious traditions. That the shift occurs is an anthropological fact. For the shaman, it is at once a spiritual and a technical process at once. It gives access to the *sacred* as it engages the *realm of Power* (of the gods or archetypes) that enables the shaman to resolve the problems of his/her concern.

For the Buddhist, the shift overcomes the object-subject dichotomy of identification, having abandoned a solely sensate-based perception. This makes possible all the great Buddhist accomplishments, especially compassion, detachment and the Bliss-wisdom of the Void.

For the Christian, the shift accompanies a more general *metanoia* and the emptying of self in *kenosis.* The superficial self, the egotistical self is over come or re integrated, the ineffable, original self is revealed—the Go[o]d News! By such self abandonment, the rhythms of the Divine Spirit might be known.

The shift is, by its very nature expressive, not only in the lives of individuals as well as cultures but is as well, the foundation of various archaic cosmologies. Panikkar, relates this telling anecdote about the Native American peoples' objection to the construction of a new atomic site. To the natives, the intrusion of the atomic site would cut their common relationship with their ancestors. The engineers, however, could not understand their position.

In fact, ancestors, spirits, etc., are all absolute nonsense unless one is ready to undergo that emptying of self, to enter into that *kenosis* about which we have spoken. Otherwise, we are not ready for dialogue. Dialogue does not consist in offering hospitality. It may perhaps consist in asking hospitality, and asking it without sandals, without money, without preconceived ideas, allowing the right hand not to know what the left is doing. Not thinking beforehand what one will say, but receiving it with one's whole heart. This research about the nature of *satisfaction* reviews three religious traditions and one sub-topic which is pertinent to all three religions: (a) Shamanism, (b) Buddhism, (c) the Christian Hesychasm, and (d) the Energies. When comparing our contemporary situation with problems of the past, we have to take into account the different horizons of intelligibility; in other words, we have to consider the different myths which underlie the cultures we are discussing—our culture not excluded.

Art and Religious Aesthetics

Icons, *mandalas*, and Abstract Expressionism contain elements important to this discussion; i.e., such art *bridges* opposite realities as temporal non temporal worlds. In fact such art can be an active, animate agent to make these connections necessary for *satisfaction*. Panikkar, who is both traditional and progressive, stands together beneath this aesthetic valence with the more traditional Hans Urs von Balthasar, a Catholic apologist of eloquence. Both are masters of influence in reference to the arts operative in religious culture. Von Balthasar's theology of aesthetics is founded upon a *self-justifying, inner-radiance* of the divine in-dwelling that expresses itself in the image, and images, of God, i.e., in art and sacramental religious perception. Most simply, art, by its physical nature and gestalt content, can make the connection between spirit and matter, between the non-temporal and the temporal.

Panikkar, appreciating both traditional and contemporary world-views, proposes a schema that allows human culture to maintain the threads of tradition while addressing the concerns and realizations of modernity. From a literary perspective, according to Panikkar's "response" to Paul Ricoeur, the subject-object epistemology fails to provide a valid tool for understanding the central, hermeneutic problem of human knowledge. According to Panikkar, "a text is only a text when it is interwoven with the texture in which we live and understand." An integration of perception is necessary in many areas of analysis in order to appreciate the meaning of a text, or those who produced the text.

Such an cross-disciplinary approach is also commented upon in George Landow's book, *Hypertext* as it describes the function of such thinking in: (1) a Shamanistic milieu; (2) with certain modern artists such as James Joyce; (3) in computer and media-generated approaches that have resulted in a revolution in critical theory. *Hypertext* compares Shamanistic thinking with computer-generated approaches to the processing of knowledge in that both use similar methods of association as the connecting function that accesses/uses knowledge in a network of associative relationships to produce understanding. This is opposed to solely, linear, scientific logic. Thus, my eventual conclusions, as well as the process that produces them, should properly reflect such a network of reasonable, interdisciplinary relationships to present its point of view. Otherwise, we are asking the wind to keep the flag from flapping by trying to fit these particular patterns of human knowing associated with the *shift of consciousness* into a solely discursive format. In other words, I use this approach because I believe that this is the only reasonable way to approach this topic.

This perspective reflects how religious histories in the past have expressed themselves about this intricate connection between temporal matters and eternity. For instance, for thousands of years there has been a tendency to interpret the co-incidence of natural phenomena—earthquakes, storms, etc., as spiritually significant to a particular person or people. History becomes folktale, fiction mixes with fact, to become sacred scripture. An example would be the plagues in Egypt that preceded the Exodus of the Hebrews.

There is substantial evidence indicating more than one exodus of Hebrews from Egypt over a period of time during which Egypt was subject to various natural disasters. Yet, this overall experience has been poetically and mythically reinterpreted since ancient times in a way typical of religious literature/histories that try to come to terms with the interaction between time and non-time, the world and God.

Whatever the motivations of various peoples who might use or abuse such literature, this artistic format is a most effective vehicle for evoking certain invaluable states of consciousness when such literature is not expected to perform in a literal manner.

One can find the same format in much Shamanistic experience. A ritual is performed or asceticism practiced and a storm happens. Therefore, the gods are thought to have responded. Nature is not merely mechanical. The universe does not have to respond only according to scientific precepts. Science must respond according to the realities of the world. For example, what to some might rightfully just be a breeze, or a gust of wind, to another might be a valid form of communication from an ineffable quarter of reality. That scenario has been expressed in various ways according to the means available in any given culture. Both the scientific and the mystical interpretation must be important for the evaluation of any perceptible phenomenon.

The myth making function in the intellect and imagination of human culture is a vital issue within the operation of perception. For instance, it is important for me to be a priest to understand this consciousness from within.

The priest functions as a living symbol, a person ontologically changed to mediate in service, the mercies of God. This maintains a necessary *mythos* that is by its very nature, symbolic. Being what it is, ultimate reality is unknowable in the sense that it precedes anything conceptual. This might be experientially perceived according to religious or philosophical intuition, but can only be referenced metaphorically. Yet, it is necessary to do so since it is reality along side our more mundane considerations.

Art is the intuition of the whole. Religion is reconnecting to the original and eternal "moment" of consciousness. Mythic thinking creates a visionary consciousness more open to the color and negentropic meaning important in both worlds. Symbol or sacrament is the bridge between different things or worlds.

The *satisfactions* associated with ancient symbolic traditions that seek integration of consciousness—discursive and non discursive—are described in terms of bliss, ecstacy and love.

Such a symbolic lifestyle as lead by the shaman, priest or monk, for example, encourages a shift in cultural attitude, evidenced in the re-structuring of reality, of time itself, into a sacred reference. In this, one is living the myth in which the whole culture participates. This might be found also in the seasonal feasts and calendar observances of cultures like the Zuni of New Mexico or the Highland Guatemalan Mayas; observances that also make the connection with the sacred. This might be further exemplified by the seasonal cycles found in the festive and ordinary cycle of Masses and the Divine Office of the Church.

More Art

If I may speculate freely for a moment, perhaps Abstract Expressionism is at one end in a spectrum of possibilities for spiritual art, including the artistic development through the Renaissance to the classical and primordial worlds.

Existentialists felt it necessary for human society to somehow start over. The Western world and therefore the entire world, is quickly becoming a technocracy and has, since the end of the medieval period in Europe, increasingly rejected a theocratic/centric social and cosmological model for society and the universe.

I have re-explored the beginnings of art and religion—shamanism, yogic *mandala,* fetish, icon—given obvious limitations—from the personal experience of practice and study, so that I can know what we have done now that the Renaissance has run its course. Now that the high *satisfaction* possible in symbolic systems of practice, understanding and expression in world cultures such as those of Tibet or medieval Europe, fades more and more rapidly.

The Nude

Attitudes towards the human body as primary symbol of the person is of pivotal concern here. The Tantric operation, if practiced in full, would involve a whole cosmology of associations in which the body is the central symbolic model. In particular, it involves the circulation through the whole body and personality of a system of vital, psychic energies, analogous to the system of the universe.

Raising these energies from the psychic center at the base of the genitals or perineum (*Muladhara*) up through the psychic central nervous system to the crown chakra (*Sahasrara*) at the top of the head is the action that re unites heaven and earth, (*Kundalini* and *Shiva*) female and male, all dualities in fact, to produce the Nirvanic condition of *Enlightenment.*

In the Hesychasm, something comparable is in progress when the Great Robe Monk, or the *thaumaturge,* draws the sexual energies up, and pushes the intellectual energies down, into the heart, the symbolic center of the personality, to experience a spiritual Eucharist of the divine indwelling. Panikkar proposes something similar, on a universal level of human consciousness, when he tries to draw together the elements of time: past-present-future, into one moment of trans-temporal, eternal consciousness.

Disrepute

There are also certain *disreputable* elements in spiritual lore that are important to our topic as well. Among these are: Psychoactive substances such as peyote, San Pedro cactus, alcohol, etc.; torture motifs such as found in the Plains Indian Sun Dance; and others that involve extreme physical, emotional, or psychic exertion, including transsexual trauma; and various other asceticism and yogas. Extraordinary as these might seem to some, they are secure in the anthropological inheritance of serious religious practice.

An adjacent understanding that lends a cohesive effect to our study of *satisfaction* refers to a state of consciousness that sees all reality as a body of connections. At one end of a spectrum this might be represented by the sublime Buddhist teachings of subject/object unification, with detachment at the heart of one's practice, or by the highly exalted Body of Christ that extends into both temporal and non temporal worlds.

At the other end, the unitive body might be seen in the more pragmatic effects of the *thaumaturge*, for example, who travels the full range on this spectrum between Christ and the Magi. A model for this is, of course, the Gospel miracle stories that provide evidence for the people that Jesus, as human paradigm and icon, had "other world" powers. (Some thought them Satanic then, and labeled him as a drunk and a glutton as well. *Matt. 11:19*) In some cases, perhaps because of the disreputable and inhibition-quelling qualities of inebriation, for example—Jesus' first miracle was to turn water into wine—combined with deep-seated, often subconscious intentions and belief patterns, one's conventions are circumvented and new realms open up.

Substance abuse is not the issue under discussion here. Beginning with the cultural and individual phenomenon of Shamanism, rooted in the early Stone Age, we can see a complex of insight, practice and techniques for achieving insight and power. Inebriation is one from a group of radical techniques not uncommon in Shamanism and many subsequent religions: Transsexual trauma, terror, torture, alcoholic inebriation, use of sacred (psychedelic) substances, humiliation and sickness. All are "ingested" in combination with mythological belief patterns and perhaps used in combination with more moderate practices such as meditation, pilgrimage, and other traditional practices. The danger is initiation of psychological unbalance or even death. Some young Eskimo shaman novices, when forced into a transsexual experience, commit suicide, others adjust (Eliade, *Shamanism,* p. 258).

The positive effect, with certain individuals, is to disorient one enough, or to separate one enough from one's personal or cultural context to discover access to fundamental elements from the sub-strata of consciousness, the instinctual "stuff" of personality; i.e. Knowledge, Powers, and Transcendence arise. Jung might refer to this as "figures" or "powers" that arise even spontaneously from the Unconscious.

One can discover the use of such techniques simply by reading Casteneda, or by more laboriously doing comparative religious study and experience. For an example of radical personality adjustment, a male might be exposed to the archetypal feminine and thus display in one's life transsexual behavior in such a way that loosens the vice-like grip of ordinary consciousness that might allow for the extraordinary archetypal experiences.

Through experience of extreme alcoholic inebriation's, for another instance, one does not just come to understand perceptive faculties that are not apparent when one is "in control" but one experiences these faculties in such a way that integrates and empowers both in the extraordinary world of the psyche and the ordinary world of "daytime" consciousness. This is not to claim that simply getting drunk or getting high or having unusual sex will do this for you, but in certain circumstances with certain individuals, unusual phenomena evocative of the satisfaction pertinent to this study sometimes might occur.

An archetypal shadow of Dionysian ritual hovers about all this, with the female *maenads* pausing in their dance just before the orgiastic dismemberment of their male sacrificial victim. But the high altruism of many religious traditions mediates the fury of being, as in Tantra.

Let us conclude this erring introduction with a final note about just that, *erring.* An oft berated and sometimes exalted role in human society is that of the *pilgrim.* This is one who has given up on society and the domestic scene, goes out on the roads of the world to abandon *self.* As mentioned previously, in India this would be the *sunyasin.* From Orthodox countries, accounts found in books such as the *Philokalia,* or even *The Way of the Pilgrim,* tell revealing and charming stories about being "On The Road...." This is also called "serpentine wandering," or "sauntering."

From Mark Taylor's book *Erring,* we have in the first selection below a passage from Henry David Thoreau:

> *Sauntering:* which word is beautifully derived from idle people who roved about the country, in the Middle Ages, and asked charity, under pretense of going *a la Sainte Terre,* to the Holy Land, until the children exclaimed, 'There goes a *Sainte-terrer,' a Saunterer,* a Holy-Lander. They who never go to the Holy Land in their walks, as they pretend, are indeed mere idlers and vagabonds; but they who do go there are saunterers in the good sense, such as I mean.

Taylor continues:

> The time and space of graceful erring are opened by the death of God, the loss of self, and end of history. In uncertain, insecure and vertiginous postmodern worlds, wanderers repeatedly ask: 'Whither are we moving? ... Are we continually? Backward,

> sideward, forward, in all directions? Is there still any up or down? Are we erring as through an infinite nothing?' While the death of God is realized in the play of the divine milieu and the disappearance of the self is inscribed in markings and traces, history 'ends' when erring 'begins,' and erring 'begins' when history 'ends.'

The actual experience that has produced this essay is a mixture of elements. But I hope the mix to be dynamic, pacific and not deadly—in either the awesome, often terrible energies of the twentieth century or the convalescent wisdoms that have guided our survival for forty thousand years of *Homo Sapiens Sapiens* until this, our own volatile era.

Agape

Love's Centrality in Early Christianity: An Appreciative Footnote to the Writings of Raimundo Panikkar

William Klassen

My intention is to look at the centrality of love in the literature of the earliest Christian communities and to do so in dialogue with Raimundo Panikkar, who has engaged in a lifetime of interfaith discussions long before it became popular. He has moreover done so with a grace and integrity not always found in such discussions.

It is therefore a special privilege for me to be here today and engage in dialogue with all of you, but especially with Raimundo whom I first met in 1985 in the library of the Ecumenical Institute, Tantur in Jerusalem. I share Panikkar's conviction that "any problem today which is not put in a universal context is, at least methodologically wrongly posed," (1971, 247)[1] although at the same time neither of us can avoid what has been called, "the scandal of particularity" which, baffling as it may seem, has been an important factor in western religious thought at least. As he himself notes, when we read the gospels we wonder "whether the presence and significance of the outside world was ever felt at all" (ibid, 248). It has often jarred me when I stand at Arbela on the horns of Hittin looking from Gadara to Sepphoris and wonder that Jesus could have lived on such a very limited plot of ground, been so insulated if not isolated from the larger world around him and still have such profound insights and construct such a powerful, unconventional kingdom. How indeed, one asks, can Jesus leave his executioners with the words: "Father forgive them for they don't know what they are doing" (Luke 23:34), thus expressing affinity with Socrates and setting a precedent for Mahatma Ghandi, Martin Luther King and Nelson Mandela on how power can be expressed through the resolve of finding a better way than through revenge and kingdoms of love and justice can be built? Those radical tears, weeping over Jerusalem are not matched by the irony with which Socrates addressed those who held his fate in their hands. One cannot imagine Socrates weeping over Athens and certainly Jesus' Stoic contemporaries would despise such a shocking display of weakness, indeed lack of manliness.

To be sure, Panikkar sees the Gospels "condemning time and again the works of the devil, false spiritualities, and selfish behavior." This I find baffling. Do they not rather depict Jesus as releasing people from the power of the devil? Is it not rather true that the condemnations are hurled only at the professionally religious? To all, rich and poor, male and female, is extended an invitation to take on the easy yoke, the light burden, in order to learn from a teacher noted for his gentleness and meekness. Mark seems to portray Jesus as one who has come to make all things right (7:37), and the description Jesus gives John the Baptizer about what is happening strikes a quite different note. Jesus announces good news, not the harsh judgment of John the Baptizer; he is the messenger of peace and joy so central to the message of 2 *Isaiah*. He recognizes accurately that "damnation of anything which does not belong to the existing status quo as a well-known Christian attitude" is not drawn from the gospels and both Raimundo and I would recognize that today such a reading of the gospels is rather seen as a misreading. These are fine points and cannot detain us here.

I shall attempt to do three things:

1. Describe briefly the way in which the early Christians saw love (Klassen,1992). Last year we looked at the continuity those views of love, especially in the Johannine writings, formed with Jewish views of love. I then spoke of the flawed legacy of John's view of love, but especially of his treatment of his fellow disciple, Judas. (Klassen, 1996:137-59). Today we look at it simply in terms of the windows that are provided to that community through the literature they left us.

2. Secondly I seek to establish some historical framework from which to view the relationship between early Christian views of love and those from the wider world around them. Here I share Panikkar's concern that the early Christian literature must be viewed through the eyes of the east as well as the west. The eye glasses of Aquinas and of Aristotle are not the only ones through which one must view this evidence. Is not Paul's famous reference to self-immolation (1 Cor 13:3) his attempt to relate to India? Professor Panikkar's response is welcome, for to him it is no secret that I have only one oar with which to row my boat.

3. Finally I test the question of self-love. It is a possible although certainly not the only topic under which we view the question. It is the urgent question precisely because Panikkar and others raise the issue of the meaning of "love your neighbour as yourself." Can this really be understood other than by exclusion: "Love your neighbour as your own Self?" (Ibid. 254).

I
The Earliest Christian Writings

a. The Usage of ἀγαπάω and ἀγαπή.

It is well known that in the earliest Christian sources the word for love is ἀγαπή and ἀγαπάω. It occurs as a verb 142 times in every book of the NT except Acts, as a noun 116 times and as an adjective 62 times. By comparison it occurs in Josephus 75 times in a much larger body of literature and the noun never appears in his writings, the adjective about four times. According to Bauer's Lexicon it appears in the following ways:

1. Love as a life-affirming action flowing from people to people, wives, neighbours, enemies, et al (Perkins, 1982).
2. Love as a life-affirming action directed to heavenly beings; Jesus 1 Pet 1:8, especially in John. Christianity took from the Hebrews, the command to love God: Mt. 22:37; Mk 12:30.33.
3. God's love for the people: (cf. Dio Chrys. 3,60) 3x in pagan sources. Rom 8:37;9:13; (Mal 1:2), 2 Cor. 9:7. 2 Th 2:16; Heb 12:6 (Prov. 3:12); John 14:21; 1 John 4:10.19.
4. Jesus' love for people: Mark 10:21; Gal 2:20, Eph 5:2; John 11:5; 15:9. The word becomes crucial to describe the relation between Master and disciple and the one question on which the relationship rests is: "Do you love me?" asked by Jesus of Peter (John 21:7.20). There is also a reference to the "beloved" disciple (13:23; 19:26) but Jesus also loved all of his disciples, including Judas and as a token of that love washed their feet,

loved them ἐις τέλος, completely and without interruption to the end (John 13:1).

5. The word can also be used to describe a concrete action: John 13:1.34. (Feet-washing). 1 John 3:18, cf. TGad 6:1.
6. It can also be used to describe attachment to things, Luke 11:43; 2 Pet 2:15. κοσμος: 1 John 2:15, 2 Tim 4:10, opinions of people, John 12:43, one's life 1 Pet 3:10.

The word is attested in pagan sources as early as the 3rd cent B.C.E. and also 2nd century B.C.E. so it is not new but the centrality of place in the earliest sources is striking and unusual. Recall that it is used for all important relationships and that for John it is clearly stated that God is ἀγαπῄ (1 John 4:9,16) and that God "loved the world so much that God sent the Son into the world" (John 3:16) to spell out that love, which he did by dying for humankind. That death was a result of his solidarity with people who amounted to nothing in that society: women, children, tax collectors and sinners. That solidarity was expressed in such a manner as to invoke upon himself the wrath of the power structures under which he lived and so religious authorities in concert with Roman concern for peace and security killed him. He died out of love and he died for those above all who killed him. No need to try to apportion blame for the death of Jesus. He voluntarily gave up his life. No one took it from him. A heinous death was viewed by the earliest Christians as a sacrifice of love with eternal consequences. To the early Christians came the task of viewing the death of Jesus as bringing forth good consequences just as their contemporaries knew that the death of the innocent Socrates continued to reap a rich moral harvest for their society.

Hard as that is for us to understand, we see it daily and have experienced it in the death of Martin Luther King, John F. Kennedy, and most recently in the death of Itzak Rabin, killed by a devout Jew acting, as he said, at God's command.

Every writer in the early church stressed that view of love and each one made it central to the ethos they were promoting. In the post-Lutheran era it has been common to describe justification through faith alone as the center of the Gospel and Luther with great passion defended this insight he had gained, as he said, "directly from the Holy Spirit." A careful study of the sources indicates however, that it is love and love alone which is the central reality of the early Christians. They were convinced that God was primarily a God of Love and that what Jesus communicated more than anything else was that love. They also believed that they were now constrained by the love of God to love the neighbour. The simple division between eros and agape drawn in Nygren's motif research in which Luther becomes the redeemer of the New Testament's view is now generally rejected because of the disembodied view of love it represents and the picture of God which lies behind it (Klassen, 1992).

Moreover, according to Tertullian, "It is our care for the helpless, our practice of loving kindness, that brands us in the eyes of many of our opponents. 'Only look,' they say, 'look how they love one another' " (*Apology*, 39). The body of Christ, as Paul so eloquently affirmed has no greater priority than love (1 Corinthians 13). In the fruits of the spirit love ranks first (Gal 5:22). A brief excursion into Paul's view may be useful. As for its literary genre, at least eleven have been proposed and recently two scholars have suggested that it belongs in the rhetorical category of an encomium (Sogountos, 1994; J. Smit, 1991).

II
St. Paul and I Corinthians 13

This part of one of Paul's letters deserves a special place for it is the highest tribute paid to love in any literature, certainly in Christian literature. The quality of its literary style and the problems in relating it to its context, but above all its lack of theology or Christology and the attention to parallels ranges from the poet Tyrtaeus (ca 640 B.C.E.) whose praise of virtue focused on warlike strength, which (ἀρετη) prowess "is the noblest prize and the fairest for a lad to win in the world" (fragment 12) attainable only through participating in bloody slaughter and reaching forth to strike the foe (Conzelmann, 1975:220). Other examples are cited by Conzelmann from Plato but most interpreters would see the closest analogy in 4 Esdras and the contest described there on what is the most powerful thing in the world and the encomium to truth there presented.

When Paul promises to show a "better way" he is availing himself of a rhetorical term much used in Judaism, but also commonly used by Epictetus (Weiss, 1910). His better way is to reject the passion for charismatic gifts and concentrate on ἀγαπῄ instead, which he does not see as a charismatic gift but as the most important element to being in Christ.

The chapter divides into three clearly distinguishable parts:

Part 1: 1-3: a) Speaking in tongues of men or angels without Love is to be a clashing cymbal or noisy brass; perhaps reminiscent of the clashing cymbals of Cybele's procession conducted by priests who were, along with poets dubbed "drums and cymbals of self-advertisement" (DeWitt, 1954:146).

b) The gift of prophesy; knowing all mysteries and all knowledge; "Paul takes a specifically Christian factor—Spirit-inspired utterance in community—and transposes it into the universal style of wisdom teaching" (Conzelmann, *ad loc*). Even if I have in addition to knowledge, faith to move a mountain; without love, I am nothing.

c)If I give all I own, even deliver my body to be burned, without love, that profits nothing. This series moves from unusual speech to self-sacrifice. It highlights what can be done with the mind and what can be done by faith. By putting them all together in this way he covers all that is generally seen as religion: liturgy, articulate prophecy, and acts of charity.

The case of self-immolation had numerous antecedents and was a standard illustration of the time (Weiss, 1910:315). Paul stresses even in the act of self-immolation, the highest point one can reach, in the Christian community, one thing is essential: love.

Part 2: a)The Nature of love is here described (4-7). The structure of this sentence is divided into four parts. First, verse 4a has two positive assertions: Love is patient, it is gentle. Then there follow seven negative affirmations about love (4b-5): love is not envious, boastful, conceited, rude, selfish, touchy, keeps no score of wrongs. The third part has a contrasting antithesis: Love does not gloat over other peoples' sins but rather delights in the truth.

There is nothing love cannot face. There are no limits to its faith, its hope, its steadfastness.

b) The gift of prophesy; knowing all mysteries and all knowledge; "Paul takes a specifically Christian factor—Spirit-inspired utterance in community—and transposes it into the universal style of wisdom teaching."

(Conzelmann, *ad loc*) and having in addition to knowledge, faith to move a mountain; without love, I am nothing.

c) If I give all I own, even deliver my body to be burned, without love, that profits nothing. This series moves from unusual speech to self-sacrifice. It highlights what can be done with the mind and what can be done by faith. By putting them all together in this way he covers all that is generally seen as religion: liturgy, articulate prophecy, and acts of charity. The case of self-immolation had numerous antecedents and was a standard illustration of the time (Weiss, 1910:315). Paul stresses that in the Christian community, one thing is essential: love.

> Whatever you do,
> I may speak in human or angelic tongues-
> without love
> I am a sounding gong or a clanging cymbal
> I may have the gift of prophecy-
> know every hidden truth
> I may have faith strong enough to move mountains
> without love, I am nothing.
> I may dole out all that I possess,
> or even give my body to be burned, without love
> I am none the better.

In this striking section in which thought moves in three waves top to bottom (J Weiss) a work of faith which moves mountains Which leads us to the second point. 2. Even self-immolation is futile if not done out of love.

1 Corinthians 13:3
"Give my body to be burned"

According to Strabo (15:1,73), born about 64 B.C.E. describing India and specifically the Ganges River he continues:

> one might add to the accounts here given that of Nicolaüs Damascenus. 73. He says that at Antioch, near Daphnê, he chanced to meet the Indian ambassadors who had been despatched to Caesar Augustus; that the letter plainly indicated more than three hundred ambassadors, but that only three had survived (whom he says he saw), but the rest, mostly by reason of the long journeys, had died; and that the letters was written in Greek on a skin; and that it plainly showed that Porus was the writer, and that, although he was ruler of six hundred kings, still he was anxious to be a friend to Caesar, and was ready, not only to allow him a passage through his country, wherever he wished to go, but also to co-operate with him in anything that was honorable. Nicolaüs says that this was the content of the letter to Caesar, and that the gifts carried to Caesar were presented by eight naked servants, who were clad only in loincloths besprinkled with sweet-smelling odors; and that the gifts consisted of the Hermes, a man who was born without arms, whom I myself have seen, and large vipers, and a serpent ten cubits in length, and a river tortoise three cubits in length,

> and a partridge larger than a vulture; and they were accompanied also, according to him, by the man who burned himself up (*katakausas heauton*) at Athens; and that whereas some commit suicide when they encounter adversity seeking release from the ills at hand others do so when their lot is happy, as was the case with that man; for, he adds, although that man had fared as he wished up to that time, he thought it necessary then to depart this life, lest something untoward might happen to him if he tarried here; and that therefore he leaped upon the pyre with a laugh, his naked body anointed, wearing only a loin cloth; and that the following words were inscribed on his tomb: Here lies Zarmanochegas, an Indian from Bargosa, who immortalised himself in accordance with the ancestral custom (kata ta patria) of Indians. (Loeb Classical Library Translation, H. L. Jones, 1930)

Strabo wrote in the years after 64 B.C. but Nicaläus of Damascus lived in the 1st B.C.E. Dio Cassius born a hundred years after Strabo, 54:9 wrote as follows:

> Many embassies came to Caesar and the people of India, who had already made overtures, now made a treaty of friendship, sending among other gifts tigers, which were then for the first time seen by the Romans, as also I think, by the Greeks. They also gave him a boy who had no shoulders or arms, like our statues of Hermes. And yet, defective as he was, he could

> use his feet for everything, as if they were hands: with them he would stretch a bow, shoot missiles, and put a trumpet to his lips. How he did this I do not know; I merely state what is recorded. One of the Indians, Zarmarus, for some reason wished to die,—either because, being of the caste of sages, he was on this account moved by ambition, or, in accordance with traditional custom (*patrian nomon*) of the Indians, because of old age, or because he wished to make a display (*epideixis*) for the benefit of Augustus and the Athenians for Augustus had reached Athens—he was therefore initiated into the mysteries of the two goddesses (translated by Ernest Cary, Loeb, 1917).

What is strikingly relevant for our discussion of Paul is that here is an event recorded by two Greek historians prior to the time of Paul and self-immolation is seen as the highest form of allegiance they could show to Caesar. It is also described as the according to the traditions of the Indians.

What is noteworthy is that every major issue dealing with love is here articulated by Paul. What is perhaps the most noteworthy is that the contemporary questions of self-love, an action which ventures all too quickly into narcissism, is here addressed. Paul's position is well expressed by the contemporary feminist writer Elisabeth Moltmann-Wendel "By love I mean that impulse, that force impelling us to our fellow-beings and leading us to discover in them what is lacking in us. To be sure, real love does not aim for victory in this encounter. It longs for common recognition for the truth, without blotting out the differences or muting the various melodies in the single polyphonic symphony."[2]

Summary

What Panikkar has done is to show how very close Christian views of love and identity; *advaita* and *Bhakti* come to each other when they are in dialogue with each other. When we are drawn to our religious places or persons because we see that "the very structure of the only One is love and that love is only another name for the experience of the Absolute" (1970b, 301) then we would appear to be very close both in meaning and in experience. Surely here as we reach out towards each we recognize most strongly that we see only in part, in a glass darkly, and yet we also know that the earnest seeker will in the quest for love, for the other will find infinitely more than the seeker who gazes mesmerized into pool admiring his\her own reflection.

Notes

1. "The Relation of the Gospels to Hindu Culture and Religion" p. 247, (1971).

2. "Self-love and Self-acceptance," *Pacifica* 5 (1992): 288-300.

Works Cited

Elliott, J. K. 1971 "In favour of καυθησομαι at 1 Cor. 13:3." *ZNW*, 62: 297.

Gerhardsson, B. 1978. "I Kor 13—Zur Frage von Paulus' rabbinischem Hintergrund." *Donum Gentilicum. NT Studies in Honour of David Daube*, eds. C. K. Barrett, E. Bammel and W. D. Davies.Oxford University Press: 185-209.

Harnack, Adolf. 1911. " Das Hohe Lied des Apostel Paulus von der Liebe (I Kor 13) und seine religionsgeschichtliche Bedeutung," *SPAW*,1: 132-63.

Holladay, Carl R. 1990 "1 Corinthians 13. Paul as Apostolic Paradigm." David Balch, et al., eds. *Greeks, Romans, and Christians, Essays in Honor of Abraham J. Malherbe*. Minneapolis, Fortress Press, 80-98.

Klassen, William 1996 – *Judas: Betrayer or Friend of Jesus*? Fortress Press.

——. 1993 "The Kiss as Sacred Act in the New Testament: An example of Social Boundary Lines." *New Testament Studies* 39 (1993): 122-35.

——. "'Love Your Enemies': Some Reflections on the Current Status of Research." W. Swartley, *The Love of Enemy and Nonretaliation in the New Testament*. (Louisville: Westminster, 1992): 1-31.

——. In the Doubleday *Anchor Bible Dictionary* 1992:

- "Judas Iscariot," 3:1091-96.
- "Love, (NT)," 4:381-96.
- "Kiss," 4:89-92.
- "Peace, (NT)," 5:207-12;

——. "The Authenticity of the Command: 'Love Your enemies,'" B. Chilton and C. A. Evans, *Authenticating the Words of Jesus*. Leiden, Brill, 1999: 385-407.

Moffatt, James, 1914. "I Cor 13:3 Exegetica," *Expositor*, 190-91.

Moltmann-Wendel, Elisabeth, "Self-love and Self-acceptance," Pacifica 5 (1992): 288-300.

Panikkar, Raimond. 1963. *Die vielen Götter und der eine Herr. Beiträge zum ökumenischen Gespräch der Weltreligionen* Weilheim: OW Barth.

——. 1964. *The Unknown Christ of Hinduism*. London: Darton Longman & Todd.

——. 1967a. *Offenbarung und Verkündigung. Indische Briefe*. Freiburg:Herder.

——. 1967b. *Kerygma und Indien. Zur heilsgeschichtlichen Problematik der christliche Begegnung mit Indien*. Kerygma und Mythos, V Hamburg, English Version.

——. 1968. "Hermeneutique de la libertè de la religion. La religion comme libertè." *L'Herméneutique de la Liberté Religieuse*. Paris: Aubier, Editions Montaigne: 58-101.

——. 1970a. *The Trinity and World Religions*. Madras: The Christian Literary Society.

——. 1970b. Advaita and Bhakti: Love and Identity in a Hindu-Christian Dialogue. *Journal of Ecumenical Studies* 7:299-309.

——. 1971. "The Relation of the Gospels to Hindu Culture and Religion." D. G. Miller and D. Y. Hadidian, eds. *Jesus and Man's Hope,* Pittsburgh: Pittsburgh Theological Seminary 2:247-61.

——. 1987 "The Jordan, the Tiber, and the Ganges," in *The Myth of Christian Uniqueness,* ed. by Paul Knitter and John Hick. Maryknoll, Orbis, 1987: 89-116.

——. 1972. *Salvation in Christ: Concreteness and Universality of the Supername*. Santa Barbara, CA.

——. 1973 *Worship and Secular Man*, London: Longman and Todd.

——. 1978 *The Intrareligious Dialogue*, New York: Paulist Press.

——. 1982. *Blessed Simplicity. The Monk as Universal Archetype.* New York: Seabury Press.

——. 1993a. *The Cosmotheandric Experience*. Maryknoll: Orbis.

——. 1993b *A Dwelling Place for Wisdom*. Louisville, Kentucky: Westminister, John Knox.

——. 1995. *Invisible Harmony. Essays in Human Responsibility* Minneapolis: Fortress.

——. Majumdar, R.R. 1981 *The Classical Accounts of India*, Calcutta, Firma KLM Private.

——. Singh, Ravindra Raj, 1991. "The Pivotal Role of Bhakti in Indian World Views," *Diogenes* 156: 65-81.

Pedersen, Siegfried,1980. "Agape-Der eschatologische Hauptbegriff bei Paulus, in Die paulinische Literatur und Theologie," 159-86.

Preuschen, Erich. 1915. "Und liesse meinen Leib brennen," 1 Kor 13:3. *ZNW* 16: 127-38.

Riesenfeld, H. 1978. "Vorbildliches Martyrium. Zur Frage der Lesarten in I Kor 13,3." *Donum Gentilicum*, 210-14. Considers it a quote from Daniel 3:96 Paul therefore thought about the three men in the oven and only about them (213).

Völkl, Richard. 1956 *Die Selbstliebe in der heiligen Schrift und bei Thomas von Aquin.* Münchener Theologische Studien. II Systematische Abteilung. #12 München: Karl Zink.

Wischmeyer, Oda.1981. *Der höchste Weg. Das 13. Kapitel des 1. Korintherbriefes.* (StNT #13) Gerd Mohn: Gütersloher Verlagshaus, 1981.

——. 1978. "Vorkommen und Bedeutung von Agape in der ausserchristlichen Antike," *ZNW* 69(1978): 212-38.

Sigountos, J. G. 1994. "The Genre of 1 Corinthians 13," *NTS* 40: 246-60.

Smit, J. "The Genre of I Corinthians 13 in the Light of Ancient Rhetoric,"*NovT* 33, 193-216.

The Spirit and the Bride say "*Come*": Continuing a Hindu-Christian Dialogue

Katherine K. Young

Raimundo Panikkar, in his article "Advaita and Bhakti: Love and Identity in a Hindu-Christian Dialogue,"[1] compares Christian and Hindu approaches to "love." This provides both reciprocal illumination and theological inspiration:

> In the dialogue between Christians and Hindus, non-duality seems to exclude love as inherently dualistic. An attempt is made here from a Christian point of view to show that love is possible for an advaitin (non-dualist) who otherwise loses a great deal by minimizing its importance. It is true that the traditional advaita position cannot give ultimate value to the special I—thou relationship which is basic in love. He can love the particular not for itself but only as symbolic of the absolute. But if the absolute is itself Love, every part of it may love any other part of it with that same divine love. God 'comes out of himself' in his loving expression in the very being of another person—which is true of 'me' as well. So my love for that other person is at the same

> time God's love. And it is a love for a particular person, if we see that person's essence rather than [sic] his limited, historical situation. There is thus no antagonism between the love of God and the love of the creature: in this way we protect the advaitin's fear of dualism. It may be a valid distinction to say that Advaita love is not individual but may be personal. This love is the highest life of man for it is divine; in fact the Trinity of Christian doctrine may be explained in terms of Advaita if the personal emphasis of love is preserved.[2]

In this article, I will extend Panikkar's discussion to my study of the 9th century C.E. Hindu female saint Antal (Kotai), a young maiden from Tamil Nadu, South India, who belonged to the *bhakti* (devotional) movement associated with Lord Krsna. She composed two major poems, the *Tiruppavai* and the *Nacciyartirumoli*.[3] There are many commentaries on these two works by the *acaryas* (theologian-teachers) who integrated the Tamil devotional poetry into the philosophical system of Visistadvaita (also known as Srivaisnavism) under the rubric of *ubhayavedanta* (both Vedantas: those composed in Tamil and Sanskrit languages). Antal's own poems describe how she wants to be the Bride of Krsna but this desire puts her into direct conflict with her father whose parental obligation is to arrange her marriage to a human man. By reading between the lines of her poems and those of her father, I detect not only a family drama but also a spiritual journey that transforms the lives of the immediate parties and that of the whole community. Antal as the bride invites others "to come." This becomes a spiritual invitation to the genuine religious life.

I am struck by the fact that the phrase "the Spirit of the Bride says 'Come!'" from the *Book of Revelation* in the Christian Bible (a key proof text for Panikkar's article under consideration) is virtually identical to a phrase in another book of revelation: the Hindu Tamil Veda. Before turning to Panikkar's commentary on this idea, it is of some interest to enquire whether the similarity of this phrase is because of diffusion of ideas from one religion to another. The answer would seem to be "no," for diffusion theories have long been in disrepute as reasons for the similarities between Christianity and *bhakti* Hinduism (including early Syrian Christianity in Kerala as a possible point of diffusion, for there are antecedents within Hinduism itself that would make a diffusion thesis less probable). On the contrary, I will approach this similarity as an example of synchronicity, and yet of value to explore further some of the insights generated by Panikkar's approach to the theology of love in the two religions.

Divine Love And Human Love: The Views of Panikkar and Antal

An initial comparison of Christian and Visistadvaita theology reveals a basic difference: the former has the Father/Son relationship as core to its theology (which Panikkar extends to Lover-Beloved on the human plane) whereas Visistadvaita has the Lover-Beloved relationship as core to its theology[4] (which I will extend to the Father/Daughter relationship on the human plane). Panikkar suggests that in the experience of human love, we experience divine love, for human love (such as the unconditional love for one's mother or love for one's husband) is linked to the very center of the Absolute. Its corollary is that divine love supports and legitimates one human's love for another. By contrast, Antal seemingly rejects human love declaring that she will love only Lord Krsna. She says: "see, I could not live if men enjoy my breasts that grow [as I grow up] mediating on the Supreme Person with discus and conch. It would be like a jungle-roaming jackal who, touching the havis with foot or nose, pollutes oblations for celestial gods fed into sacrificial fire by forest sages."[5] In other words, Antal suggests that men's attraction to her breasts pollutes them just as a jackal pollutes the sacrificial oblations made by ascetics.

Antal also chides her father (Vittucittan, otherwise known as Periyalvar) for his hypocrisy in desiring to arrange her marriage. "The impartial [Lord] Tiruvarankar declared a great statement that is true. Vittucittan has heard it: 'Those who love Him [alone], He himself loves them.' If this statement is shown to be untrue in their case [i.e. God himself because he won't marry her and his devotee Vittucittan because her refused to acknowledge that real love of God makes human marriage impossible], who will stand up and reveal their false pretenses?"[6] In this stanza, Antal refers to *Bhagavadgita* 7:17: "Of these, the one of wisdom, always integrated, who loves the Lord *alone*, is pre-eminent." In other words, the person of wisdom should renounce marriage and family. Is this Antal's intention? She declares, after all, that her sole intent is to love only Lord Krsna and marry *only* Him, not a human husband. In this context she chastises her father Vittucittan, a brahmin and therefore a man of brahmanical learning who presumably knows the *Gita* well and who should be able to understand his daughter's desire to marry Krsna alone. In short, how could he be hypocritical? From Vittucittan's perspective, however, he is obliged, according to the rules of proper behavior (*dharma*) also found in scripture of the *smrti* type, to ensure his daughter's marriage to a suitable person. Here, of course, a *human* person is presumed, moreover one belonging to the community of devotees to Lord Krsna (and ideally one belonging to an "ancient," i.e., long standing, family of such devotees).[7]

A clue to Vittucittan's thinking may be found in several of his own stanzas. These have an autobiographical dimension to them, for they go beyond the dictates of genre to individuality of detail,[8] which fits the autobiographical scenario barely disguised in Antal's own poems. Vittucittan, for example, explores several scenarios created by his daughter's refusal to marry the Lord. "We thought of celebrating, with affection and on a grand scale the marriage in our home and keeping her in our home itself. But this girl was thinking of something else"[9] and "having spent the wealth that we have in our hand and having celebrated the marriage, what benefit will we obtain by keeping her with us? On the contrary, it will affect our reputation."[10] In short, it seems that the father is worried that his daughter will run away if she is going to be forced into marriage (Antal herself alludes to this, saying "having told all, if I go on my way alone affronting father, mother, and relatives, it will be difficult to remove the gossip and slander that ensure."[11] Vittucittan is also concerned that if Antal is married, she will refuse to live with her husband, thereby embarrassing Vittucittan and his family. Therefore he suggests that it would be better to allow her to grow near the Lord (that is, to let her live in the temple unmarried, though whether this was an established tradition for women—perhaps with the exception of young widows or abandoned women—is improbable, especially because there are no references to formal ascetic orders for women in the Vaisnavism of this time).

Panikkar too recognizes that divine love is more than human love: "this love is divine, cosmic, full of personality but devoid of individuality, selfishness, caprice and concupiscence."[12] He goes on to say: "it is the deepest and strongest love and also the most human because it reaches the core of the human being, its personality, its ontic relationship with God and with another being like itself. It is not a love of the qualities of the individual, but of the heart of a person, the integral person: body, soul and spirit."[13] It could be, then, that Antal is rejecting that human love which loves merely the qualities of, and not the integral nature of, the person (though that is expected to develop over time). In this contest, she rejects arranged marriage based initially on choice of superficial qualities and not real knowledge and of love the integral person. She also rejects her father's insistence on her marriage, which makes him an accomplice in this sacrilegious act. Arranged marriage, one suspects, has often been a difficult rite of passage for young Hindu girls. The pomp of ceremony and the ideology of mandatory marriage for women was not always sufficient to facilitate the dramatic change at a young age from parental security and love to life in a new household with strangers.

Marriage to Lord Krsna: A Young Girl's Dream

Antal plays with various marriage motifs in her *Nacciyartirumoli*. According to Dennis Hudson,[14] the *Nacciyartirumoli* itself is structured with fourteen decades to correspond to fourteen of the fifteen days of a traditional vow (*nompu*) performed by women to gain marriage and a good husband. It begins on the first day of the month of Tai (associated with Kama and the festival of Holi) and ends on the fourteenth day of Pankuni, just before the full moon on the fifteenth day. The latter is the transition between the cool and hot seasons and the unspoken focus of the entire work, for it is the day the marriage of the deities (especially Kama, the god of love, but also Vishnu and Siva) is reenacted. Antal solicits Kama's help in her quest to marry Krsna and tells him (stanza 4) that since her youth (puberty?) she has dedicated through a solemn vow (*cankarpi*; Skt, *samkalpa*)[15] her growing breasts to God alone. In 5.8 she mentions a binding (*Kaccankam*) agreement for elopement with Krsna, an allusion to the ancient Tamil custom of *kalavu*, secret embrace, which by the code of honor must be understood as marriage, later to be publicly recognized in ceremony (*karpu*), or, if the parents are unwilling, by elopement.

Despite her desire to love only God, Antal accuses even God of selfishness, caprice, and concupiscence because he does not "come" and take her as bride, which he had promised to do. In fact, she rebukes him for ignoring her and her great love. The intense pain of separation fuels her desire for the Lord, but also her contempt for his indifference and hypocrisy.

In the sixth decade of her *Nacciyartirumoli*, Antal dreams of her marriage to Lord Krsna, King of Dvaraka. Curiously, the major reference to marriage occurs in the middle of the work and not at the end, which would be logical given the fact that the vow of fourteen days (represented by the fourteen decades of hymns) should culminate in marriage. Moreover, it is curious that the fifteenth day, the day of marriage for Tamil deities, is not represented in the poem but is only the "unspoken" focus, occurring as it does on the day after the work ostensibly concludes. How is this to be explained? Would it not have made more sense for the *Nacciyartirumoli* to culminate in a ritual marriage to Krsna or at least the dream of marriage to him on the auspicious fifteenth?

Be that as it may, by the fourteenth decade Antal does not mention marriage to Krsna. Instead, she plaintively addresses her female relatives (*ammane, ammane*), asking them whether they have seen the Lord ...?, and they reply, "yes, we have seen him at Vrndavana coming on our way ... yes, he is coming."[16] The full impact of this ending cannot be understood, I suggest, without careful examination of Antal's moods and language throughout the *Nacciyartirumoli*.

In the very first line Antal says: "I worshiped you and your younger brother [Balarama] wondering whether I will live ... ; thus, you must unite me to the Lord...." Throughout the work, she describes her "lips ... pale and trembling ... tresses tangled ... body spotted" (1:8). The fifth decade, just prior to her dream of marriage, is striking, for she speaks of how her "life escapes daily," how she faces debilitation by not sleeping and "whirling about," suggestive of delirium (5:4). She implies in 5:5, the next verse, that she cannot go to see the Lord in his temple, located nearby her home, which implies that she is now bed-ridden. In fact, it is when she is ravaged by fever and hallucinations that she has her dream of her marriage to the Lord. Again, in the eighth decade, she portrays herself as languishing and scorched, asking whether she "will live" (8:2); how she can safeguard ... [her] breath" (8:3); that she has a "disease" and is "suffering" (8:6) and that she is being "tormented to death" (8:9).

Is it not possible that Antal is dying at the end of her work? And when she plaintively asks whether the "Lord is coming," she is bed-ridden and surrounded by her female relatives who are nursing her? Now, it is true that dying is a motif of the Tamil *bhakti* poems. But Antal's use of this has a particular insistence and graphic quality. I suspect that her death may have been related to the extreme fast that she was undertaking as part of her vow, in other words, it was self-consciously a fast to death. There are several other pieces of evidence that help me to substantiate the idea of Antal's fast to death. (1) Vittucittan, her father, after mentioning that he has only one daughter, says that the Lord himself *has taken her away* (*Periyalvartirumolil* 3;8;4). This is a euphemism for death in the Tamil tradition, and no doubt alludes to his daughter's joining Krsna. (2) The title of this work, the *Nacciyartirumoli,* means the sacred word of our lady/goddess. It seems to be contributed by someone other than Antal and therefore could be posthumous. (3) Moreover, there are not more works by Antal (assuming that the Tiruppavai was written first, which has been suggested by some scholars). (4) There is an inscription dated to 973 C.E. at Antal's shrine in her home town of Villiputur, which mentions details for morning worship. Scholars think that Antal and her father probably belong to the 9th century. It is conceivable that because of her love of the Lord and her extraordinary death that she was quickly deified and a temple built to her, for building shrines to commemorate extraordinary deaths was a common folk tradition. (5) Although composed much later, the account of the sacred history of this place (*sthalapurana*) mentions how it was Antal's father who built the temple dedicated to her, endowed all his property to it, and was its first trustee; this is reenacted in temple festivals still today. It is conceivable that Vittucittan's actions were preserved in oral traditions or local myths until later written down. The name Antal ("she who rules"), was probably originally a posthumous epithet (she herself uses the name Kotai in her poems). This epithet may allude to her death and the fact that she had her way, for she married the Lord.

Opening to the Mystical Body

If Antal indeed died as a result of her arduous fast,[17] it is implied that this happened on the fifteenth, the traditional day to celebrate marriages in Tamilnadu. As an actual *sitz im leben* this would be even more extraordinary, for according to Vaishnava theology salvation is often spoken of as marriage to God in heaven. Salvation, in other words, is posthumous. If Antal did die on the fifteenth, or shortly thereafter, inspiring others to adjust the date to fit the drama that took place, then this can be understood in salvific terms to be none other than her marriage with God. Just as Lord Krsna "came" and took his bride to heaven, so her death became an invitation to others to come sincerely, not just superficially, to the Lord. When Panikkar quotes the last words of the book of Revelation: "the Spirit and the Bride say, Come!," he comments: "the Bride [assumes and symbolizes] ... the Universal transformed into and transparent to Love which is precisely the Spirit. 'Come' is the call to the Ultimate through Love, to Advaita through Bhakti."[18] Such a love, suggests Panikkar, both "discovers and effects the identity of lover and beloved"[19] and leads to "worshiping together in an unitive adoration,"[20] a sacramental awareness of the divine identity. Is this not true for Antal as well?

Vittucittan had come to understand how his daughter had assumed and then symbolized the Universal transformed into and transparent to Love. Her non-comprising love of Lord Krsna, therefore, had affected both daughter *and father*. She was no longer the head-strong daughter, chastising her father as hypocritical and her relatives as sinners,[21] but the plenitude of love signifying the oneness of Bride and Groom. (This has been expressed by a later myth of how, when married to the Lord, she merged into his image in the temple at Srirangam.) As in Christianity, the "object of the beatific vision is spiritual and therefore requires an increasing spiritualization of even human love of one's neighbour as one moves in faith from earthly contemplation toward the higher states illumined by supernatural charity."[22] For example, I Cor. 13 says: "Love ... [is] the greatest gift of the Spirt."[23] And Vittucittan was no longer a man of pride, concerned more about his social standing in the community than his love of God. As Antal matures, the divine personal and direct love passes through her to her father and other relatives, making them "to be." Vittucittan finds in Antal's "mature and purified" love, the love of God. I can hear him saying, in Panikkar's words: "the same current that sweeps me into the love of the Absolute makes me love my beloved [here I add the word daughter] as that spark of the Absolute which she truly is."[24] Put otherwise, the love of the advaitin [here I understand Vittucittan] for his beloved [daughter] is indeed the Love of God for both daughter and father. I can also hear Vittucittan saying: "in you I discover the Absolute—though not as an object, of course, but as the very subject loving in me."[25] Likewise, Vittucittan finds in Antal's love the love of God and shares in the constitutive relation of God's love to the beloved.

If a temple was built to Antal shortly after her death, it may have inspired others to worship together in an unitive adoration, a sacramental awareness of the divine identity. If it is said in Christianity that "those who are spontaneously recognized by the people's love to be 'saints' in a special sense are confidently believed to be nearer to God and the earthly church is joined with them in a fellowship of praise and prayer,[26] then does not the fact that Antal's marriage is reenacted in annual festivals all over South India even today suggest the extension of sacramental awareness of divine identity to a larger community? Is this not a Hindu opening to the mystical body? As Panikkar might say: God generates—his Beloved (Antal) as His Thou, manifesting and reflecting Her, and the Spirit is not only the Love personified of the Lover

(God) and the Beloved (Antal), a reciprocal self-gift but also the non-duality (advaita) of Lover and Beloved.

Moreover, young girls even today memorize the stanzas of Antal's Tiruppavai and perform the same vow that Antal describes in this work to attain a husband. Unlike Antal, however, they want a human husband. Her example of love only for the Lord is not their model. This apparent conflict between Antal's refusal to marry any ordinary person and their own desire to do so is resolved by seeing Antal not as human like them but as divine, the Goddess, who has incarnated on earth or as the first among the souls. Their performance of the vow is in remembrance of Antal, who as the goddess or first among the souls, marries Lord Krsna.

The Ontic Status of the Paradigmatic Love: Is Antal the Saint, the Jesus, or the Mary of Hinduism?

Antal is often called a saint by scholars and Srivaisnavas. This label seems to me to do injustice to her status and role in Srivaisnavism, as so, in this section, I wish to compare her to the Christian figures of Jesus and Mary since dialogue between Hinduism and Christianity is the topic at hand and some reciprocal illumination may be forthcoming from his academic exercise. Now, in what way are Jesus and Antal alike? In Christianity, followers participate sacramentally in Christ's dying and rising again (Rom. 6; Col. 2:12-13; 3:1-17), Srivaisnavas do not view Antal's life as dying and rising, though they might if they focused on her own words in the *Nacciyartirumoli* (which alludes to her dying and rising to the supreme heaven, as I have argued) and the subsequent hagiographies that speak of her merger into the image of God at the time of her marriage to him in the Srirangam temple. Jesus, although a "being in flesh," does not reveal the precise nature of union between divinity and humanity that is his.[27] With Antal, however, we can see her spiritual growth and struggle: therefore, she seems on first appraisal, more human, albeit saint-like, than Jesus.

Jesus was viewed as a mediator, for he "reveals God to people and reconciles people to God."[28] In Visistadvaita, there is the doctrine of *purusakara* (mediator). In the theology the goddess Sri came to take on this role. Eventually, when Antal was identified with Sri, she too became a mediator. Let us examine this point in more detail.

As Pillan says [of Sri]: "O you on whose breast resided the lady of the flower who says, I cannot move away from him even for a second ... 'I, your servant, who am without shelter, sat at your feet and entered' [your safe heaven]."[29] This is the first reference to the goddess Sri as the mediator. "Full of compassion and motherly affection, Sri might be expected to win for the suppliant the favor of the Lord in whose nature paternal love is balanced by the resolve to do justice. Because the need for such a mediator, who reinforces father love with mother love, is not made explicit until two generations after Pillan, his use of the term *purusakara* is significant."[30] Sri has been described as eternally inseparable from God (*niryanapetam sriyam*).[31] There is also a reversal of relationship, for the Lord is the sri (glory, auspiciousness) of Sri.[32] Sri traditionally has been associated with royal power and dominion.[33] She is called "mother of the worlds" (*jaganmata*) by Ramanuja who takes the phrase from the Vishnu Purana.[34] Ramanuja's disciple Bhattar says that the devotees may approach Hari (the Lord) because of His relationship with Sri (*Sriguna-ratnakos* v. 51); he repeatedly refers to her as "mother," assigning qualities to her such as compassion and patience (Vishnu himself being assigned autonomy, control of the enemy, constancy, and justice),[35] Bhattar also expresses the erotic relationship between the Vishnu and Sri, speaking of Sri's "flower-cluster raised breast" or how she provides "enjoyments (*bhoga*) replete with sentiments deep and thick caused by the state of [her] ... complete union with the One who is worthy of being [her] ... Lover" or how she indulged in "pleasurable love-sports ... with [her] ... lover who struck the vessels of enjoyment by touching her secret vital places [of her body]...."[36] In such manner, Sri distracts Vishnu from the faults of the devotees. Sri is also said to be eternally youthful and innocent, with breasts not fully developed, a soft, tender body that is between that of a woman and a child.

The 13th century acarya Periyavaccanpillai defines "the verb *srn*, which means 'to serve' in the active and passive voices, and argues that Sri worships the Lord (active voice: *srayaze*), but that "Sri [herself] is worshiped by the world (passive voice: *sriyate*).... He derives a second meaning for Sri by taking the verb *sru*, which means 'to listen.' Relating the active and causative meanings to Sri, he says that she listens (*srunoti*) to the *cetanas* (souls) while a the same time she causes the Lord to listen (*sravayari*) to her words spoken in favour of the *cetanas*...."[37] Periyavaccanpillai further states that although the *cetana* has the same relationship with both the Lord and Piratti, the Lord happens to be a supreme man (*purusottama*) and has the quality of harshness (*kathinya*); in His role as father. He has power for the welfare of the *cetana* while as the ruler (*nirvahaka*) of the entire creation He can also be severe and strict. To balance these qualities, Piratti, who is a woman, has the quality of softness. Because she is the mother of the entire creation, she has affection (*vatsalya*), and because she does not have the responsibility of ruling the universe, she is always sweet. Consequently, she can be a *purusakara* and balance the contrary qualities in the Lord.[38]

With the division of the Srivaisnava tradition into two sects, the figure of Sri was interpreted in two different ways. The Tenkalais sect came to view Sri as first among all the souls (the *jivas*) whereas the Vatakalai sect came to view her as "fully Godhead ... a personification of Vishnu's mercy [who] shares in his ontological status expressed under the categories of all-pervasiveness and lordliness, and is herself regarded as an *upaya*."[39] By the time of the *Guruparamparaprabhavam* (15th century C.E.?), Antal was identified with Sri. Perhaps the author had in mind Antal's erotic relationship with the Lord, perhaps her aspect of ruling over others (Antal, as mentioned previously, literally means she who rules), or perhaps it is her age: young with a body between that of child and woman.

Unlike Christianity, Srivaisnavism does not speak of the Holy Spirit and a "third person," but it may be argued that it does have an analogous concept. If "love is the greatest gift of the Spirit" in Christianity, certainly Antal's story suggests the same. Similarly, if it is said that "the Holy Spirit is God's self-communication as love," which has the same divine essence as Father and the Son and yet is distinct from them both, or if it is said that the "Spirit proceeds from the Father *through* the Son," then something similar may be said of Srivaisnavism. For God out of his grace expresses himself as *vatsalya* (tender affection), *saulabhya* (easy accessibility), and *sausilya* (compassion). Furthermore, according to Christianity, "when God's love is poured into believers' hearts by the Holy Spirit (Rom. 5:1-5), the fruit of the Spirit is produced in their lives: love, joy, peace, patience, kindness, goodness, faithfulness, gentleness, self-control (Gal. 5:16-26). They are thus being changed into the likeness of the Lord Jesus (2 Cor. 3:18; cf. Col. 3:10). The Holy Spirit inspires psalms and hymns and spiritual songs; a melody making unto God (Eph. 5:18-20)."[40] In a similar way, is not God's love poured into Antal's heart which comes to fruition in her final peace?

Why do we not see Jesus' spiritual growth in the same way that we see Antal's? I suggest that this because Antal left two texts written by her. These first hand sources enable us to detect more aspects of her personality between the lines of the genre of *bhakti* poetry. (Nevertheless, by the time of the hagiographies about her, the spunk and ego have been removed). By contrast, we can only view Jesus through the eyes of genre and sacred biography, which were quickly at work officially telling "his story." Although human elements—such as Jesus' birth and death, his anger at the money changers in the temple, and his feelings of being forsaken by God in Gethsamene and betrayed by Judas—there is very little that reveals Jesus' personality.[41] This, of course, has not stopped scholars such as Ernest Renan, Adolf von Harnack, and Albert Schweitzer at the turn of the century[42] and more recent historical Jesus scholars from sketching his historical portrait an describing his personality.

If Jesus died because his message was threatening to political authorities who crucified him (even though he knew what was likely to transpire if he continued to follow his course of action), could not Antal have died because her message was threatening to family authorities (in her case, her death being self-willed through extreme fasting (leading to debilitation and eventually death) rather than other-willed? In Christianity, "the crucifixion was the will of God in the sense that God wills the personal fulfillment of every man and woman, and specifically God willed that Jesus should confront and challenge the network of sin in human society even though such a confrontation and challenge would surely polarize all the forces of sin against him."[43] Could not the death of Antal be the will of God because he also willed that she confront and challenge the network of sin (in the sense of complete love) in human society? Both Jesus and Antal knew, therefore, that they would die. Jesus died for the sins of humans and thereby saved the world. Antal called her relatives "sinners" because they did not recognize real love, but Jesus demonstrated that love and freedom are more powerful than apathy and fear,[44] cannot the same be said for Antal too? Jesus was resurrected; Antal, we are told, left her mortal body, obtained a new eternal one, and rose to the supreme heaven. The death of Jesus allowed for the salvation of all subsequent people. So did the death of Antal.

But it could also be argues that Antal is more like Mary in the Tenkalai (sectarian) sense as the first among the souls. Mary is considered not to be coequal with Christ but rather the chief among saints (God is especially present in her and "our unity with her is an expression of our unity in and with Christ."[45] As with some Christian saints, Antal has "so grown in this sanctifying grace that [she has] become widely revered."[46] Just as Antal is the mediatrix, in a similar way, Mary is called the "mediatrix of all graces (i.e., by the will of Christ, all the grace he earned for us is channeled through her), or co-Redemptrix (i.e., she shares somehow in the redemptive work of her Son, without prejudice to the supreme saving power of his own death and resurrection)."[47] In other words, according to this view, Mary is not a Goddess or a rival. According to the dogma of Assumption (1950), she was "taken up bodily into heaven after her death."[48] So too was Antal. One major difference between Mary and Antal is that Mary is viewed as mother, Antal is viewed first as lover[49] and only through the eyes of the later acaryas is she viewed as a mother. Mary is a secondary figure (the Christian story is focused on the Jesus). And so is Antal according to the Tenkalai sect. According to the Vatakalai sect, however, Antal is the deity herself. As such, she is not ontologically separate from God, but rather his own ontic externalization for the sake of his enjoyment. In this sense, she is more like Jesus. Moreover, Mary did not die for the "sins" of others but Antal, like Christ, did.

As this discussion makes clear, there are significant overlaps when the image of Antal is compared to that of both Jesus and Mary. This is due in part to the sectarian differences found in Srivaisnavism itself. In other words, she is the Jesus or Mary of Hinduism, metaphorically speaking, depending on whether one is viewing her from a Vatakalai or Tenkalai perspective.

Placing Love in its Metaphysical Perspective: The Case of Qualified Non-Dualism

Panikkar observes that "monism cannot be ultimate ... in a pure monism there is no room even for factors like illusion, falsehood, time, a lower level of truth and speech."[50] In India the Advaitin (one belonging to the philosophical school of non-dualism) describes *maya* as the eternal superimposition of illusion of *Brahman* as ground. Thus, *maya* is neither real (*sat*) nor unreal (*asat*). In the Indian philosophical system called Visistadvita—which developed in part out of the theology implicit in the poems of the Tamil Vaisnava poets such as Antal and Vittucittan and in part out of criticism of Advaita—*cit* (souls) and *acit* (world) are said to be eternal categories that cannot exist apart from *Brahman* in what is known as the *aprthaksiddhi* relation. But whereas *maya* is said to be neither real (*sat*) nor unreal (*asat*), *cit* and *acit* are said to be real. Indeed, two metaphysical systems of Advaita (non-dualism) and Visistadvaita (qualified non-dualism) are not that far apart, for both posit a non-dual reality and account for ignorance as in some way outside of but related to *Brahman* by cosmic superimposition or inseparable connection respectively. Yet, ignorance can be removed by the individual to experience non-dual reality ever after. In short, *Brahman*, although qualified by some other eternal principle (external in the Advaitin case, internal in the Visistadvaita case) remains in some way distinct from qualifications.

However, Visistadvaita, like some Christian theologies, sees distinctions within the Absolute. These are understood as God's creative self-movement. As Panikkar says, the "I loves itself and discovers its non-duality (which is in the Spirit) in the Thou (the Son)."[51] Love is "the inner movement of the One without a second" (*ekam evadvitiyam*).[52] The etymology of the word *brahman* is, in fact, the power of growth. As Panikkar says: "The Knower has come out of himself, as it were, has 'loved' that which, by loving, he knows to be his (own) knowledge.... He could not know even himself were he not driven out, or did not despoil himself, only to recover himself immediately in the 'object' (person), in which he has fully invested himself. This element, this total gift of himself, is Love."[53] This is akin to the Visistadvaita idea that *Brahman*, the (knower), comes out of himself in his sport (*lila*) and experience the sheer enjoyment of his own self-actualization and creative exploration in various types of incarnations (*avatara*, *arca*, and *antaryamin*, especially the latter in which he recovers himself in the 'object' (person).

The Visistadvaitin would once again feel a kindred theology in Panikkar's observation that "if a thing is not sheer nothingness it cannot but be the 'recipient' of the unique loving act of the absolute I. Now, because that act is constitutive of that very thing, the integral thing, i.e., perceived with reference to its individual Love; but seen with reference to itself alone, i.e., the 'thing' in 'itself,' is a limited image of the boundless love, just as the whole sun is, though not completely, in each of the broken pieces of a mirror reflecting its rays."[54]

Postscript

Others have long noted that Christianity and Vaisnavism share many theological features.[55] The commonalities increase when the topic is Christianity and Srivaisnavism. To my mind, nowhere has the similarity been so striking as with Panikkar's imaginary dialogue between a Christian and Hindu culminating with the words "The Spirit and the Bride say 'come.'"

I began this paper with an observation of synchronicity. I end it with a new insight that came in an unexpected way and showed that something more than synchronicity has been involved. When I first presented this paper at a symposium at Brock University,[56] Panikkar was in the audience. Afterwards he revealed to me that his father had been a Srivaisnava. (Remember, this is the same community to which Antal belonged many centuries earlier. In fact, her poems are commonly memorized even today by many Srivasisnavas and, as mentioned, her marriage is reenacted annually in Srivaisnava temples).

The creative integration of Hindu concepts of *bhakti* and advaita to Christian concepts of love by emotional closeness of Panikkar's thought to that of Antal, which was so striking to me as I worked on this article, need not be explained by either diffusion or synchronicity but rather the permeable boundaries that occur in an interfaith marriage and the creative hermeneutics of a son, the love-child, if this is not too presumptuous, of two religions.

Notes

1. Raymond Panikkar, "Advaita and Bhakti: Love and Identity in a Hindu-Christian Dialogue" (Journal of Ecumenical Studies vol. 7, no. 2 (Spring 1970), pp. 299-309.

2. Panikkar, p. 299.

3. All translations of stanzas by Antal and Vittucittan in this paper are by the author from the following published edition of the Tamal text of the hymns of the alvars: *Nalayirativyappirapantam* edited by K. Venkatacami Reddiar (Madras: Tiruvenkatatian Tirurumanram, 1973). Commentaries consulted were Antal, *Nacciyartirumoli* with commentary by Periyavaccanpillai (Kancheepuram: Srivaisnava Grantah Mudrapaka Sabba, 1913) and Antal, *Tiruppavai* with commentary by Periyavaccanppilai, edited by Kranamacarya (Madras: Commercial Press, n.d.). Henceforth the *Nacciyartirumoli* is cited as *NTM* and the *Tiruppavai* as TP.

4. The relationship between God and the devotee is described in multiple ways in Srivaisnavism: parent and child; friend and friend; ruler and subject; and so forth but the lover and beloved is one of the most popular.

5. *NTM* 1:5.

6. *NTM* 11:10.

7. Because this is a brahmin family we cannot rule out the possibility of marriage into proper casts despite the fact that this was ostensibly taboo in a community which publicly stressed the equality of all devotees and took great pains in this Tamil environment of the 9th century to disguise any castism.

8. For example, he refers to having only one daughter (*Pertyalvartirumoli* 3:7:10) and Antal mentions having five brothers (*NTM* 6:10).

9. *Periyalvartirumoli* 3:7:10.

10. *Periyalvartirumoli* 3:7:9.

11. *NTM* 12:3.

12. Panikkar 308.

13. Panikkar 308.

14. Dennis Hudson [manuscript].

15. *Sankaipa* is a term associated with the formal beginning of a ritual or vow.

16. *NTM* 14:6.

17. Antal's love may have begun as a spiritual insight of how true love is single-minded love of God. But it was initially also an egoistic love, for she sought her own fulfilment and self-assurance, criticizing her father and by extension her elders in the process. Antal has first to learn how to exercise her own "will power" in an ordinary human way. In this sense, Antal is like those women throughout history who experiment with power through defiance within the family circle as part of their growth in individuality, a growth so often restricted because of confinement to the domestic sphere. Because of their domestic orientation and often their control by men, their bodies were the area of spiritual experimentation and food their only possession to reject. Antal, for example, learns to exercise her will in this manner. By contrast, Panikkar's Advaitin *sadhu* (ascetic) has the *choice* to renounce all his possessions, an experience that makes him overwhelmed with love and joy. But precisely because of these spiritual experiments with renunciation and separation within the home, we see a growth in Antal leading to maturity, transparency, and real love. There is a change from her desire of power over her parents (especially her father) and her elders to boundless and transparent love.

18. Panikkar 309.

19. Panikkar 308.

20. Panikkar 308.

21. *NTM* 12:8.

22. Ileana Marcolulesco, "Mystical Union," in Mircea Eliada, ed. *The Encyclopedia of Religion* (New York: Macmillan, 1987) 10:242. (This encyclopedia is henceforth referred to as Eliade ed.)

23. Geoffrey Wainwright, "Christian Spirituality" in Eliade ed. 3:456.

24. Panikkar 306.

25. Panikkar 306.

26. Wainwright, in Eliade ed. 3:458.

27. There were a number of debates on the nature of Jesus: Arianism said that Christ was only a creature; although he was greater than other humans he was still less than God. Apollinarianism argued that Christ had no human soul but this was denied by the First Council of Constantinople (381); and Monophysitism denied that Christ's human nature was completely absorbed by the one divine person but this was denied by the Council of Chalcedon (451). (Eliade ed. 12:432). Similarly, docetism denied the reality of Christ's physical incarnation and argued that he left the physical body before crucifixion. The emergent Christian tradition finally decided that Jesus was both human and divine but just how remained a mystery. According to Heb. 4:15 Jesus "is like us in all things save sin (Richard P. McBrien, "Roman Catholicism" in Eliade ed. 12:438).

28. Wainwright in Eliade ed., 3:453.

29. John Carman and Vasudha Narayanan, *The Tamil Veda: Pillan's Interpretation of the Tiruvaymoli* (Chicago: University of Chicago Press, 1989), p. 76.

30. Caman and Narayanan, pp. 76-77.

31. Nancy Ann Nayar, *Poetry as Theology: the Srivaisnava Stotra in the Age of Ramanuja* (Wiesbaden: B. Harrassowitz, 1992), p. 229.

32. Nayar 1992, p. 228.

33. Nayar 1992, p. 231.

34. Nayar 1992, p. 238.

35. Nayar 1992, pp. 239-40; 246.

36. Nayar 1992, pp. 244-45.

37. K.K.A. Venkatachari, *The Manipravala Literature of the Srivaisnava Acaryas: 12th to 15th Century A.D*. (Bombay: Ananthacharya Research Institute, 1978), p. 117.

38. Venkatachari, p. 118.

39. Nayar 1992, p. 232.

40. Wainwright in Eliade, ed. 3:453.

41. Mary Magdalene, a woman associated with Jesus, is portrayed more realistically than Jesus. Was this because Antal and Mary were marginal as women, and therefore no one initially cared about suppressing the details of their lives to fit a preconceived genre? This may account for the presence of more personal detail when the later hagiographers eventually created their sacred biographies some time later.

42. Frederick W. Danker, "Biblical Exegesis" Christian Views, in Eliade, ed. 2:149.

43. McBrien in Eliade, ed. 12:441.

44. McBrien in Eliade, ed. 12:440.

45. McBrien in Eliade, ed. 12:441.

46. Wainwright in Eliade ed. 3:453 speaking of the Communion of the Saints in 1Cor. 6:11 (Pt. 2:4-10), The Virgin Mary and the Saints may be considered in this regard.

47. McBrien in Eliade, ed.: 12:441.

48. McBrien in Eliade, ed.: 12:441.

49. There is considerable nuptial imagery in Christianity, which has borrowed language and themes from the Song of Songs. According to Origen, Christ is the spouse of the soul (RV. 22:17; 2 Cor. 11:2; Eph. 5:25-27).

50. Panikkar, p. 304.

51. Panikkar, p. 308.

52. Panikkar, p. 308.

53. Panikkar, p. 304.

54. Panikkar, p. 305.

55. See John Braisted Carman, The Theology of Ramanuja: An Essay in Interreligious Understanding (New Haven: Yale University Press, 1974).

56. Conference organized by David Goicoechea, Brock University, St. Catharines, Ontario, Canada 1996.

Love Stronger than Death and Panikkar's "And" (Jesus - Arjuna - Thich Nhat Hanh)

David Goicoechea

Raimundo Panikkar is convinced that a loving attitude must be an ecumenical attitude. He has spent his life living out and thinking about the "and" between *agape and bhakti and karuna*; between secularism *and* worship; between *cosmos* and *theos* and *anthropos*. He does not approach this "and" primarily as a thinker of comparative religion or comparative philosophy. For him it is a matter of living out and experiencing the "and" together with thinking it. He thinks that the secular person or the Christian or the Hindu or the Buddhist will each throughout their lives go through many moments of growth and thus live out many moments of the "and." Meeting each other and learning from each other can facilitate this spiritual growth. It can aid them in discerning and appropriating the divine will or way. It can build up a society with better opportunities for persons. Religious life has to do with spiritual growth and this takes place within the individual, communally in worship with others, in the spiritual reading of others, in working and serving with others. Panikkar's "and" is the existential "and" of living love that has within it the comparative "and" which thinks through differences, tensions and complementarities.

In this paper I want to reflect on three texts from the angle of Panikkar's "and"—the *New Testament*, the *Bhagavad Gita* and Thich Nhat Hanh's *Being Peace*. Reading

Panikkar has brought me to appreciate how the "and" that is within these texts might indicate what is most important about the "and" that can be between them. Of course, these texts are complex and so are Panikkar's so I will focus on the "and" within them and between them only from the perspective of love. But love too is vast so to reduce it further I will consider it from the aspect of "the love which is stronger than death." That haunting statement from the *Song of Songs* is perhaps its most potent. What might it mean?

Panikkar's "And" Within the New Testament

Judeao-Christian-Islamic thinkers have always wrestled with the "and." How do the *Torah* and the Writings and the Prophets fit together? How do the Hebrew Bible and the New Testament fit together in the Christian Bible? How do Abraham and Moses and Jesus and Mohammed fit together? The Alexandrians from the time of the Septuagint to Philo and to Clement seemed especially keen in their ecumenical setting on working out such an "and." They arrived at the formulae of typology and of *praeparatio evangelica*. Paul seems to have used that of typology and Matthew anticipated the *praeparatio* approach. But in any case if you consider the New Testament conceptually and sociologically it would appear that you could distinguish at least nine different philosophies or ways of practising *agape*. Paul began writing out his views of love in connection with the *resurrectionist* Jesus in the fifties. The *Q* text must have already been formulating its view of *agape* and the *insurrectionist* Jesus in the sixties. Mark's text with its *agape* of the *directionist* Jesus came on the scene at the time of the destruction of the temple in the early seventies. Matthew's *correctionist* Jesus with his traditional prophetic *agape* must have come on the scene in the late seventies. John's special kind of *erectionist agape,* so different from Paul's and *Q*'s and Matthew's could have appeared in textual form in the early eighties and Luke's could have appeared in the later eighties with its joyous love for the lost and marginalized: tax collectors, sinners, the poor and wom en. Then there would be the epistles belonging to the Pauline school such as Ephesians and Philippians. Next there would be the Catholic epistles such as the letter of James. Finally, there would be the letter to the Hebrews. Each of these would have their distinctive kind of *agape*. James, for example, is almost a kind of universal wisdom text that could appeal to anyone even the secular to practise the works of love.

So what you can see within the New Testament if you look at it with the eyes of Panikkar is many "ands"—the "ands" between the love of Paul and *Q* and Matthew and John and Luke and James etc. The early church like our society and perhaps any society in the second half of the first century went through several decades of rapidly changing social situations. The Holy Spirit called forth from out of the Christian community going through these new challenges various nuances of *agape* to meet the demands of the times. Of course, this variety of kinds of *agape* had within a kind of unity, the kind upon which Panikkar always insists, for the many without the one can become only anarchically destructive. So to begin focusing upon early Christianity's one-many unfolding after the manner of Panikkar's existential way we might now consider that love which is stronger than death. Jacques Derrida can guide us in this death contemplation.

In his book, *The Gift of Death*, Derrida distinguishes the Heideggerian, the Levinasian and his own, the Derridean, ways of Death contemplation or of receiving the gift of death. Heidegger sees death as only his own possibility and as his last possibility. When I die even if loved ones are with me I will in an essential way be dying alone. Even if two people are dying together in the same place they are each going through their own dying. No one can die for me or with me.

My death if I authentically anticipate it, if I really see what it is going to be like, individualizes me. If I interpret my death as my own it will individualize me. Since my death is my last possibility it can make all of my possibilities between now and then appear more meaningful as I see them in the light of my last possibility. Thus my death can not only individualize me but it can free me to choose more responsibly each possibility that I choose or do not choose within the totality of my life that reaches out to my death.

But Levinas contemplates death in another way. He thinks that it is not my own death that gives me the gifts of subjectivity and responsibility. It is the death of the suffering other, of the suffering widow, orphan or alien that I am trying to postpone, that makes me responsible. Before any representation or decision or commitment I am already rendered responsible to the other who claims me by his or her pleading look as a mother is claimed by her child. If the mother does not respond to the child the child will die. Levinas sees this elemental response which postpones the other's death as the gift of responsible subjectivity. For Levinas it is this elemental response that is stronger than death, that is stronger than the death of the other or that can at least postpone it.

Derrida has a third conception of a love that is stronger than death. His sensitivity makes him aware that when he is making a decision for one person or group of persons he is making it against another person or group of persons. If you have a sense of absolute love, then you would want to love all persons because each person is wholly other. You would want to embrace all of existence. But because you are finite, loving one in many ways means that you cannot love others. As he puts it, if you take care of one cat well it will render you incapable of caring for the many other cats. So the death that makes me responsible is not so much mine or the suffering other's, but the death that I bring about for the other. Abraham's sacrifice of Isaac is universally pertinent. Each of us sacrifices what is dear to us because of our limitations before the unlimited others. If I take responsibility for responsibility by seeing its implications then I will be made aware in guilt that I sacrifice others by my decisions. It is our awareness of slaying others in sacrifice that most of all makes us aware of what kind of responsible subjectivity we have.

In returning now to the New Testament texts it seems safe to say that *agape* in general has to do with the two great love commands: Love the Lord your God with your whole heart, mind and soul and your neighbour as yourself. Already here we see the "and" uniting love of God "and" love of neighbour. But what kind of "and" is this? How is it to be lived out and how is it to be represented?

The three earliest texts have a strong apocalyptic context. In Paul the emphasis is not so much upon our love of God but upon God's love for us and our love of neighbour. This has to do with a near Heideggerian approach to love and death. The apocalyptic urgency of my own death and the immanent collapse of the present order directs my caring in such a way that I might be saved or that I might become individualized and responsible so as to be fit for the new age. Paul was saved in his conversion which he interpreted as an imitation of the death and resurrection of the saviour. He went out to teach others that they likewise needed to let the old personality within them die that the new person might be born. Love most of all for him was that which saved him from sin and the wages of sin which is death. The *Q* text which is shared by Matthew and Luke presents an insurrectionist Jesus instead of a resurrectionist Jesus who raises us up as he was raised up. The Jesus of *Q* has both a Jewish apocalyptic and a Jewish wisdom background as does Paul's Jesus; but *Q*'s Jesus is cynical rather than stoical. The *agape* of *Q*'s Jesus expresses itself by saying that unless you hate your mother and father, your brother and sister, your wife and even your neighbour you will not be able to be my disciple.

Q's love is primarily an absolute love for the absolute and only with that in a near Heideggerian way can I be saved or authentic. The community of Mark's text experiences apocalyptic *aporia* and disappointment. Many, including such leaders as Peter and Paul, were being killed and were dying. How was this to be interpreted? The meaning of the Messiah was becoming mysterious and a hidden secret. The church of Mark had to discover a new direction. As John the Baptist went up to Jerusalem and was put to death, and as Jesus went up and was put to death, so will we often be put to death. But the balanced love for God and neighbour which became the synoptic *agape* could let this witnessing love be stronger than death for Jesus' love made sense of such death. As social life began to stabilize, the *agape* of Matthew's Jesus could restore institutions for it was the fulfilment of the law and the prophets. *Agape* in the community of John was the result of realistic decisions that it can only really grow and serve in small communities. We must love the brethren of our little community and not worry so much about outsiders. Luke emphasized Jesus' joyous love for the prodigal son and the lost sheep and for tax collectors, prostitutes and sinners, and had almost the opposite of John's restricted love within the beloved community. And so it went. There is not a single *agape* in the New Testament. As Panikkar would point out, there is an existential development of loves which have many and strong differences. There is an atonement based *agape* that is self-sacrificial, the kind Anders Nygren formulates. There is a trinitarian based *agape* that is even narcissistic in a good sense and which proclaims a healthy love and development of the self which can then be a model for love of others. Some feminists today oppose an emphasis on self-sacrificial love which Nygren and Levinas bring out and prefer a love that emphasizes self-fulfilment and not only self-sacrifice. They prefer the *agape* of Aquinas and D'Arcy who build out of John's trinitarian *agape* rather than out of the suffering servant's atonement *agape*. Especially as mothers they have plenty of self-sacrificial love and deeply feel the need for a self-development love.

Panikkar's "and" insofar as it is existential, emphasizes how each individual and each community must go through many stages of growth in love just as the new testament communities did. We are able to grow by meeting others and by being presented with new challenges. Love needs to go out to others and to receive from others is ecumenistic.

Panikkar's "And" Within *The Bhagavad Gita*

The Bhagavad Gita is a text of death contemplation of exactly the Derridean type. Arjuna's great existential and dramatic question about death is not about his own death or only the suffering and death of another, but rather the suffering and death that he brings to others. Arjuna is on the battlefield. He looks across at the foe. His loved ones make up that army—friends, relatives, neighbours. He asks: Should I kill my people for kingdom? Derrida makes clear how this question is a universal question that we all have to face. It is just like Abraham's question: Should I kill Isaac for God? Throughout our lives we all have to make difficult decisions and they are difficult because they involve sacrificing others. Some might look at Arjuna's and Abraham's dilemma and say it is a non-starter. Who would ever think of doing such ghastly deeds? But Derrida's philosophy and especially his book, *The Gift of Death,* show clearly that this question could be exactly the question of us all, the working out of which leads us to a responsible subjectivity.

The *Bhagavad Gita* again illustrates what we have been calling the existential dimension of Panikkar's "and." *The Gita* consists of Arjuna getting three major answer's to his question and the development and integration of those answers. Panikkar would think that this dramatic unfolding according to the "and" is also universal with us all. We can each go through dramatic stages in the unfolding of our spiritual lives. But *The Gita* can bring out a second aspect of Panikkar's "and," namely, that it is not only existential but also oppositional. Panikkar's philosophy of love's ecumenism emphasizes not only that our spiritual growth will bring us to others, but also that as we are led to appropriate the ways of the other that appropriation will involve great opposition even as great as that of Arjuna and Abraham. The *Bhagavad Gita* even though it appears to be a text which harmonizes the various *yogas* when looked at with the eyes of Panikkar can reveal the "and" of opposition.

Throughout the drama of *The Gita,* Lord Krishna helps Arjuna to answer his question and thus take responsibility for his destiny. To be as simple as possible perhaps we can say that Arjuna is lead to see three great answers: the one of *karma yoga,* the one of *jnana yoga* and the one of *bhakti yoga.* "Should I kill my people for kingdom?" At first Krishna focuses on the action of "killing" and the motive "for kingdom." Krishna says "yes," you have to act and thus to be involved in killing. Even if you decide not to act it is a decision and it will have many negative effects that amount to killing. So go ahead and fight. But do it for the right motive. Do not kill for kingdom. Kill in the spirit of sacrifice, out of duty and for the sake of maintaining the world order. Your decision to fight or not does involve you in a terrible dilemma and aporia, but you must be true to yourself. One way or another you will cause suffering or death. While other persons are not called upon to fight because it would not be true to their nature, to fight is your vocation, so kill. Of course, not for kingdom alone or for your own selfish ends, but for the good of all out of duty and sacrifice.

Then Krishna gives a second answer, that of *jnana yoga*, which is connected with the non-dualistic *Advaita Vedanta* outlook rather than the dualistic Sankhya philosophy from which the *karma yoga* answer comes. This time Krishna concentrates on the "I" of "Should I kill my people for kingdom?" Arjuna is brought to see the great *jnana* or wisdom of the *Upanishads* that his "I" or "Ego" is really the great "Self" or "*Atman*." Meditation and analysis both reveal that he, Arjuna, is *Atman* and that his noble friend-foe is *Atman* and that each being is *Atman*. Arjuna is bonded with his very foe because they are his friends, his uncles and his teachers who have brought him to be just what he is. But they are also each a part of an interconnected Self. They should each feel: "I that is we." Arjuna sees that each of his foe and every other is *Atman* and that *Atman* is *Brahman*. He hears the tolling of the bell as it were and he knows that it tolls for each of them because they are each part of the main. Arjuna sees that it is not "I" that is going to kill. It is just the great Self that kills. It is *Brahman*. His anxiety about his duty arises from a delusion about himself. The weight of his killing should not rest only on his ego. That would be the view of a mis-perceived, inflated ego. He must be humble and honest and see that his decision for some will have to be against others. He does have to fight for kingdom and for maintaining its order. But really it is *Brahman*'s way of doing things.

He has learned how to cope with the slaying of others according to the discipline of right action and according to the discipline of wisdom. But then he experiences the event of the vision in chapter eleven which reveals the way of *Bhakti yoga*. In his vision he sees the cosmos as a monster that is terribly frightening. It has many arms and heads and armies of humans in a great colossal commotion are being chewed up and devoured. Arjuna is fascinated for a moment by one detail. He sees a particular little human caught between two teeth of the monster writhing, squirming and then dangling as it is being crunched and devoured. Arjuna is frightened out of his mind and he runs around the monster in the oblivion of a terrible panic, praising the monster and begging for mercy. Then a calm comes into the midst of his anxiety. He begins to receive of *Bhakti*. He prays: "I beg thy grace, O Glorious Lord! As a father to his son, as a friend to his friend, as a lover to his beloved, be gracious unto me, O God." This is the *bhakti* or devotion that is given to Arjuna. He becomes aware that it is a matter of grace or favour. It alone is stronger than death, this terrible death that he has a hand in bringing about. This vision confirms and makes real for him that it is really the great *Atman* or *Brahman* that slays. It is not just his little ego that is the agent. *Bhakti* lets him have the *jnana* (wisdom) to see that he can best act in the spirit of sacrifice and to maintain the world order.

The next seven chapters of *The Gita* after the chapter of the vision go on to show how the "and" works between *karma yoga* and *jnana yoga* and *bhakti yoga*. Purushottoma in the spirit of *Bhakti* and *Prasada* (of devotion and grace) is able to unite the purush of *karma yoga's* Sankhya way and the *Brahman* of *jnana yoga's* Vedanta way. *Brahman* as the womb of Purushottoma is but one part of the threefold root of the upside down peepal tree. Purush is the second part of the root which comes out of the main root of Purushottoma. Krishna in his speech is always very peaceful and harmonious in uniting *karma yoga* and its nuances with *jnana yoga* and its and *bhakti yoga*. *The Gita* in its conceptual and imagined formulation has the spirit of *bhakti* which is connected with its root word *Bhaj* which means union, sharing, partaking, communion, committed and loyal love. But the force of the text shows a great struggle and opposition. Panikkar brings out this aspect of the text and of *Bhakti* when he writes in his article, *Advaita and Bhakti* (*Journal of Ecumenical Studies*, Temple University, Spring 1970, vol. 7), p. 302.

> If love is not to remain an empty word, it implies a certain tension between the lover and the beloved, or at least a certain distance between them. In fact, *Bhakti* etymologically means either separation (from Bhanj) or dependence from (bhaj).

Even if most Sanskrit scholars might not emphasize the relation of *bhakti* to *bhanj*, Panikkar makes a very good point. Any existential "and" has to be an oppositional "and" and the drama of *The Gita* in presenting Arjuna's dilemma in chapter one and Arjuna's vision in chapter eleven shows just how much opposition and struggle there is in living out the way of *karma yoga, jnana yoga* and *bhakti yoga* at once. Arjuna's struggle has to do with the opposition between his own *karma yoga* and his own *jnana yoga*. He is called upon as a Kshatriya to fight and kill. But he has strong Brahminic leanings and therefore does not want to fight and kill. The "and" of *Bhakti* was occasioned by the opposition between Arjuna's way of duty and his way of wisdom.

Panikkar's "And" Within Thich Nhat Hanh's *Being Peace*

Buddhism began with a Levinasian kind of death contemplation. When Prince Gautama went out of his palace into the city he saw a beggar, he saw a sick man, he saw a dead man. He was struck by *dukkha*, by the suffering of sentient beings and he wanted to alleviate that suffering. He wanted to postpone the death of others. So with his life he became responsible for the welfare of plants, animals and humans. Of course, to bring *ananda* or joy and peace to others he had to become joyful and peaceful himself, but how that is done brings us to the story of the "and" between myself and plants and animals and humans. Buddhism itself has gone through many, many stages of finding the love or *Karuna* that is stronger than death. There has been the *Hinayana* and the *Mahayana* and the *Yogacara* and the *Zen,* etc. But the essential meaning of the "ands" within Buddhism can also be found in Thich Nhat Hanh's wonderful little book, *Being Peace.*

If you read *Being Peace* with the eyes of Panikkar you find the centrality of the "and" at each moment. With Buddhism a third aspect of Panikkar's "and" becomes evident and that has to do with what he calls the principle of complementarity which is the healthy tension that makes life dynamic and keeps it from stagnating. This law works with a force of its own:

> When priest and monk were part and parcel of society, their estrangement was equally understood.... When all was sacred, the forms of worship had to affirm themselves by setting apart some places and times especially dedicated to its exercise.... When on the other hand difference was considered the basic principle.... When the secular asserted itself over against the sacred, then identity was consciously stressed. The real love for God is service to man, godliness is cleanliness, work is worship etc.

So the principle of complementarity is that structure of the "and" that not only necessitates difference, opposition and tension but thereby makes integration possible and a challenge. Thus there is the challenge of integrating, worship and ordinary human life or of integrating life into worship.

The very heart of Buddhism and thus of Nhat Hanh's book, *Being Peace,* has to do with this law of complementarity or with what the Buddhists call *pratityasamutpada,* (dependent co-arising). The first chapter of *Being Peace* is entitled *Suffering is Not Enough*. Life is dreadful; but it can also be wonderful. There is *Dukkha* but *Ananda* is possible and is the challenge. We need the dreadful to push us on toward the wonderful.

But that is only one aspect of dependent co-arising. Not only are the opposites dependent on one another, everything is. Thich Nhat Hanh shows that this piece of paper is dependent on the trees from which it came. They were dependent on water, air, sun and earth. The paper is also dependent on the logger, the truck driver, the paper maker, etc. But the paper is not only dependent on all of those, they are dependent on it. Paper makes reading possible and that makes technology possible, which lets logging be and forestry be. The tree is dependent on the earth and the earth is dependent on the tree. The earth needs the return of the leaves each fall to build it up.

So if we humans have understanding, if we become awake to the interconnectedness of all being and of all persons we will have *Karuna* or compassion for all. Thich gives an example of how the *Karuna* which is rooted in dependent co-arising works. He says that when he was working at Plum Village in France, which is still the center of his meditation and work, he received many letters of tragedy from the boat people. One time a twelve year old girl was raped by a sea pirate. She then threw herself into the sea and drowned. Thich tells us that in his meditation he saw that he was the girl and that he was the sea pirate. He found it very important not only to love the girl with compassionate *Karuna* but also to love the sea pirate with compassionate *Karuna*. He knew that but for the grace of God there go I. He understood how the coming to be of the sea pirate had to do with our society. To merely condemn the pirate would only add to violence and negativity. Nhat Hanh became awake to the connection that the sea pirate is dependent on the monk and the monk is dependent on the sea pirate. This insight into dependent co-arising is what brings him to what he calls "engaged Buddhism." In chapter six of *Being Peace* he tells us how he founded the order of Tiep Hien Buddhism which is dedicated to reconciliation.

In the Vietnam of his day there was a terror just as colossal as the vision of Arjuna; it was the Vietnam war. Millions of people were being killed and there was great suffering. Given the notion of dependent co-arising, Nhat Hanh and his fellow Buddhist monks were called to their sacred task of meditating in such a way so as to enable a reconciliation between communists and capitalists. It was very important for them never to take sides and be a capitalist to the exclusion of being a communist or a communist to the exclusion of being a capitalist. Their being awake to *anatman* guided them along this middle way of neither this ideology nor that ideology. Their *Karuna* or loving compassion went out to each person equally whether he or she be communist or capitalist.

Buddhist meditation is basically a five step process which enlightens the meditator to his or her own emptiness which at the same time is the great fullness. First the meditator focuses upon external things and detaches himself from any fixated idea about the hold of externals. Secondly, by focussing on perceptions he detaches himself from their hold. Thirdly, he focuses on mental formations and lets go of them. Fourthly, he becomes one pointed in focusing upon his breathing, for example, and then he relinquishes his hold on that. This leaves him fifthly in the emptiness of sunyata's calm. Here in this sunyata there is *pratityasamutpada*. His emptiness is dependent co-arising. The paper by being no paper element can be water, air, sun, earth, logger, truck, driver, etc. By being neither communist nor capitalist nor any other fixed idea the Buddhist can be co-dependent with the sacred emptiness of each person who need never be just a communist, capitalist, etc. These two principles of the emptiness of the desiring fixed self and thereby the momentary mix with all, clarify complementarity for the Buddhist. The daily meditation which brings about *anatman* and *pratityasamutpada* is the source of Thich Nat Hanh's "Engaged Buddhism." I would imagine that Panikkar has faced these two refined concepts about Buddhist subjectivity which opens Buddhists to their kind of ecumenistic approach. But I have not read what he thinks about their non-substance and non-causality. When he says that he is a Buddhist I would imagine that his principle of complementarity could admit of the Buddhist explanation. However, it must be asked if he would still retain some trace of personhood for theos and for *andros* but perhaps not for cosmos. And is not the term "*andros*" suspect insofar as it might exclude "*gyne*"?

Panikkar's "And" Between Jesus, Arjuna and Thich Nhat Hanh

In any case, Panikkar's ecumenism is not primarily an intellectual exercise. The intellectual is for him very important. It has been a major part of his vocation to bring to conceptual formulation his ecumenical experience. But the point of emphasizing that his "and" is existential in its tension and complementarity is to make clear that he has a living faith, hope and love that cares first of all for persons, however you might conceive of them.

In *The Unknown Christ of Hinduism,* Dr. Panikkar argues that it is the love within our own existential journey that makes of us ecumenists. A person's openness to the Divine Will can allow them to be lead to all sorts of surprising new ways of loving. This paper has merely illustrated Panikkar's insight within the New Testament, within *The Gita* and within *Being Peace*. But now we might reflect upon the "and" between Hinduism, Buddhism and Christianity that allows

Panikkar to say: "I 'left' as a Christian, 'found' myself a Hindu and 'return' a Buddhist, without having ceased to be a Christian."

Deep within Panikkar's faith there is the hope that love will be stronger than death. Panikkar is convinced that this love will be given to us by grace and that this belief in a grace given love is the great unifying belief of Hinduism, Buddhism and Christianity. Panikkar left on his journey as a Christian. Like St. Paul and Arjuna and Thich Nhat Hanh, he must have met death and mourned the dead many times, constantly in fact. His after all was the Spain of Picasso's *Guernica* and he lived through the Second World War and he knows well the suffering of peoples around the globe. Like St. Paul he must have been knocked off his horse by the Holy Spirit of Jesus and brought to a life of loving care for his people which meant all people just as it did for Paul. And that *agape* came to have for him many nuances just as it did in the New Testament.

Then, he "found" himself a Hindu. He found that the Holy Spirit led him to the Hindu faith and to Hindu texts such as *The Bhagavad Gita*. Like Arjuna he no doubt saw the destructive side of decisions. He no doubt felt like Abraham at times being called upon to sacrifice his loved ones. And at such times he deeply knew that what the spirit of Jesus had done for Paul and for himself, Ishvara had always done for Hindu's. Ishvara as Lord Krishna could touch him through *The Gita* in ways that not even the New Testament had touched him. In fact, he must have found that *The Gita* could open him to new, hidden graces within Christianity's scriptures, sacraments and traditions. The *Gita* could let him in the spirit of prasada's *bhakti,* in the spirit of a grace given love, proceed in his decisions out of duty, in the spirit of sacrifice and for the sake of maintaining a world order. Perhaps the *Gita* best of all taught him to cope with the death that he meted out by his decisions.

Then, he "returned" a Buddhist. No wonder of it! What Christian who ever discovered the Buddha could not be a Buddhist. The Buddha saw the suffering and death of others so clearly. The Buddha himself was a *Bhakta* in every way, in his revolutionary ways, and in all that made his revolution possible: his enlightenment, his understanding, his compassion, his community of peace and joy. Panikkar no doubt was touched by certain *Bodhisattvas*, even like Thich Nhat Hanh. He found that he could not do without Buddhist meditation and Buddhist formulation. He knew that his own Spanish St. John of the Cross was very much a Buddhist.

And he knew that the Buddhist metaphysics of no-self and dependent co-arising had to always be remembered. He knew that Buddhist meditation was a way of mourning that could make strong any mourner and could love the mourned and other mourners. How could he not always be "returning" a Buddhist?

And so Panikkar's "and" is an existential "and" that his love for himself and his own has revealed to him. How could he love himself and his own without loving all others? How could his love not become ecumenical. And Panikkar's "and" is an oppositional "and." As he matured and came to see with Arjuna the ghastly implication of love's decisions he found a love that could even valorize opposition itself. And yet Panikkar's love could always be complementary. For no matter how great the opposition—even if it be in Vietnam between the communists and the capitalists or even if it be in our own heart over the twelve year old girl and the sea pirate—Panikkar's love believes that such opposition is a challenge making possible a better love for each other and further spiritual growth. Panikkar's "and" arises from the creativity of a dynamic love that lets ever old and ever new forms of love come forth.

Agape and Spontaneity: An Exploration of Panikkar's Approach

Young-chan Ro

Agape, the highest form of love in the Christian tradition, has been the hallmark of Christianity, the norm of Christian life, and the way of *being* Christian. Love is not only a form of "action" but more importantly it is a way of "being." In love, we find both "the way I am" and "the way I do." Love overcomes the dichotomy of "being" and "doing," and the duality of ontology and ethics. Moreover, being is primacy to doing; being is not only the foundation of doing, but a primordial state of ontological unity.[1] In this sense, *agape* is an ontological reality expressed in an ethical form of love. Christian ethics, a theological formulation of what Christians ought to do, is an integral part of Christian ontology, namely, what Christians ought to be. Christian theology must combine ethics and ontology. For this reason, Karl Barth, for example, never wrote a separate section or a volume on Christian ethics when he wrote his *Church Dogmatics*.

This paper is an exploration of the significance and implication of Raimundo Panikkar's insight and vision in relation to the idea of *agape*; especially in expanding Panikkar's idea of "spontaneity" as a "way of being" and relating this idea to the idea of "piety" as a "way of being authentic." The Christian notion of *agape* can be reinterpreted and expounded to reveal a deeper meaning in relation to the idea of "spontaneity," "liberty," or "freedom." First, in the traditional and conventional understanding, *agape* was considered primarily an ethical virtue or a moral principle. *Agape,* however, is profoundly an ontological principle which has an enormous ethical significance and moral implication. I would like to explore the significance of *agape* from both the ontological and the ethical perspectives. *Agape,* the highest form of action, "doing for the sake of doing without expecting anything in return," (a similar idea of *bhakti* in Hinduism) is unconditional and "sacrificial" love. Love, however, is a state of being not a mere form of action. We can "love" someone without "being in love" but when we are in love, we "know" what love is. In other words, the knowledge of love or the epistemology of love is dependant on the ontology of love. Love is known through "being in love." The English expression " I *am* in love" is thus more primordial and profound than "I love you." Love is a state of being in which I *discover* myself as well as yourself in the state of "being in love." We can perform a certain action when we are in a certain state of being. Our action, which is not connected to our being, becomes artificial and thus is hypocritical.

"Spontaneity" is a form of human action and behavior that is connected to our being and the expression of our being. Dogen, the Japanese Zen master reminds us, "If you want to obtain a certain thing, you must first be a certain man, obtaining that certain thing won't be a concern of yours anymore." Here, Dogen was talking about *obtaining* enlightenment. *Enlightenment* is not something we can posses but a state of being in which we are possessed. Love is also a state of being possessed. *Agape* is a state of being possessed by divine love, unconditional, sacrificial love, and "creative love" as Panikkar puts it.

The *expression* of love, if we use Panikkar's mode of thinking, is an *explosion* of being in love. For Panikkar, being is not a static but a dynamic process which is explosive.[2] The Christian *agape* in this sense is the expression of divine being and explosion of divine love. In *agape,* divine act and divine being are totally integrated. Panikkar's nondualistic approach helps us explore a deeper implication of the Christian idea of *agape* from the highest ethical norm to the most profound way of understanding divine being, the way of being God. For Panikkar, *Being* is not a static concept but a dynamic process: "Being has an untapped reservoir, a dynamism, an inner side not illumined by self-knowledge, reflection, or the like."[3] When *being* becomes a mere being, it loses the life and vitality of *being*. The very structure of *being* or the constitutive elements of *being* contains an aspect of the verb. For Panikkar, a *being* is intrinsically both a noun and a verb at the same time. This is the power of being. Panikkar's ontology suggests that *being* becomes *being,* so every instant of *being* is *becoming* "being."

Panikkar's vision and insight in this way of understanding *being,* his ontology, provides a new way of interpreting the theological implication of *agape*. *Agape* is not only what God *does* for us but also what God is in terms of His relation to us. In this sense, "God is love" (1 John 4:7-8). Here, we see that the being of God is known to us through love because "God is love." In this respect, love is a unique mode of being God. The way of being God and the knowledge of God are interrelated. *Agape,* in this sense, is the total integration of knowledge, being, and act of God. In other words, *agape* as a state of being, existed prior to the conceptual division of "ontology," "epistemology," and "ethics," etc. These divisions are highly artificial and the result of Western philosophical conceptual scheme. Man as Panikkar uses it with capital M means the human being and not the male. East Asian languages such as Chinese, Korean, and Japanese do not necessarily classify or distinguish in terms of gender or number to denote "human being.")

The Christian understanding of *agape* reveals the nature of God beyond the conventional attributions of God: omnipresent (being), omnipotent (act), omniscient (knowledge). This division is largely due to the Western philosophical and intellectual categories influenced by the Greek tradition. Christian theology, especially the doctrine of God, is to be reconstructed in light of the integration of these three categories. The writer of *First John* has certainly provided the foundation of a new understanding of God through the idea of love which has a power to overcome the division of God's being, knowledge and act.

In this respect, Panikkar's *cosmotheandric* (universe-God-human) vision again provides a new foundation for understanding God. Since love is relational, we cannot conceive of God's love in isolation. God's love *expresses* itself in relation to humanity, nature, and the universe. The being of God, the knowledge of God, the act of God are to be understood in relation to humanity, nature, and the universe. God's way of being depends on the way God relates to human being, nature, and the universe. If we take *agape* as a unique way of being God, then *agape* is a unique way of expressing His self-sacrifice through *creation, incarnation, and consummation*: God's self-expression and self-explosion were as the creation of the *universe*; God's self-sacrifice in relation to *humanity* and reconciling Man to God through Jesus Christ was the incarnation; God's presence in all being and living in the Spirit is the consummation. In this way, *agape*, in terms of the Trinitarian model, is the power of creation, and the source of reconciliation, the fulfillment of the destiny of all beings. *Agape* is the way of being God, the way of how God manifests Himself in nature, and the way of how God acts towards human beings. *Agape* is the principle of integration of divine being and divine act, and divine knowledge. This knowledge is not merely an intellectual knowledge but "experiential" and "empirical" knowledge. *Agape* is the love in which Man can "know" God. This knowledge is uniquely an experiential knowledge. We cannot *know* God simply by studying the doctrines of God theologically or the concept of God philosophically. The knowledge of God is not entirely conceptually constructed but experientially understood. The mystery of God reveals to us through *agape*. In other words, the experience of *agape* is a unique mode of understanding God. In *agape*, the way of being God, the act of God and the *way* of knowing and experiencing God are all integrated.

Agape and "Spontaneity"

Divine love is divine spontaneity. Coerced love is no longer a love, acting is a pretension. Love is not something to be made but a spontaneous flow of *being* in love. Spontaneity is not an irresponsible arbitrary action but an *appropriate* action without deliberation. Spontaneity is a way of doing in accordance with nature, the way it is. This is the kind of action which is most fitting and proper and yet un-deliberate and most appropriate kind of action in the given circumstance. Spontaneity as the highest form of action, doing without "doing" in the Taoist tradition;[4] it is the most "refined" yet most "natural" form of human behavior. "Refinement" not in the sense of artificial articulation but in the sense of fulfilling or perfecting the potential and thus being completely "spontaneous." In this sense, "spontaneity" and "refinement" are not necessarily contradictory to each other or mutually exclusive of each other. "Refinement" is not an artificial activity but a sincere and honest self-expression. In this sense, "spontaneity" is a way of *being* itself in a most responsible way, the form of action which reflects the way of nature.

Divine being by nature exists by himself/herself/ itself. In this respect, the being of God is God's being. It is not that our conceptual scheme and philosophical category "being" characterizes God, but on the contrary, God defines His "being." This is God's freedom. Panikkar has already asserted this line of thinking.[5] God creates "being" and God is the source of being. Being is the outcome of God's spontaneity. God's spontaneous self-expression in relation to Man, nature, and the universe is *agape*. In this respect, *agape* is God's mode of being in relation to his creatures since the creation is the *spontaneous* manifestation of His love, *agape*. This spontaneity is God's freedom. *Agape* is God's freedom and spontaneity. *Agape* is the most authentic and primordial form of "relation" found in love.

Being is Relational

Being is defined in relation to itself and other beings. God's being, in this sense, is also relational. God exists in relation to the cosmos, human beings, and nature. Panikkar's "cosmotheandric" vision[6] reflects this relational structure of being which integrates God, human being, and the cosmos, and the very nature of this relationship is *agape*. *Agape* was the principle of being and the force or the energy of God's creation. "The Fall" is the distortion and destruction of this original and primordial relationship which was created by God and exercised by God. *Agape* is the defining characteristic of the relationship in which God related to other beings in His creation. For this reason, the incarnation is a restoration of *agape* through Jesus Christ. The event of Jesus Christ is the most concrete historical—

manifestation of divine love, *agape*, which gives a new structure, is a new order to make a "new being": St. Paul said, Jesus Christ is a foundation of a new creation (or a "new being"): "Therefore, if anyone is in Christ, he is a new creation; the old has passed away, behold, the new has come" (2 Corinthian 5:17). Jesus Christ laid a new ontological foundation for new being and new creation. New being and new creation are the result of the restoration of the original unity of the "cosmotheandric" relations through the reconciliation between God and Man; Man and nature. *Agape* is the new structure of being based on "cosmotheandric" unity. *Agape* is a new ontological structure which is fully manifested in the event of Christ. The incarnation, in this sense, is a new creation. But this new ontological structure is nothing but restoring God's original creation, God's spontaneity. The ontological structure of *agape* is *reconciliation* and restoration. St. Paul says:

> All this is from God, who through Christ reconciled us to himself and gave us the ministry of reconciliation; that is, in Christ, God was reconciling the world to himself, not counting their trespasses against them, and entrusting to us the message of reconciliation (2 Corinthian 5:18-19).

Reconciliation is the fulfillment of agape, and agape is the force for creating a new being: Being in *relation* to the cosmos, God, and human (Man), a cosmotheandric being in Panikkar's vision. The incarnation, in this sense, is God's way of restoring the original and authentic way of being. The authentic structure of being is *relational*. When a being exists in isolation, it becomes meaningless and empty; a being is defined in relation to other beings. A being is also *revealed* in relation to other beings.

Love *(Agape)* Relates and Reveals

Love *relates* us to other beings and *reveals* ourselves in relation to other beings. *Agape,* God's way of being, God's spontaneity, relates God to us by revealing himself to us. The revelation, in this sense, is an act of love (agape) manifested in the event of Christ. *Agape* reveals the very nature, the ontological structure of God to us by *relating* to us. The revelation is fundamentally relational. In *agape* we are able to relate to each other in the most genuine and authentic way. By relating with each other we are able to reveal ourselves to each other. Relating without revealing is an artificial act. The relation which does not require revealing is a mere functional and mechanical *connection* but it is not a relation, it does not relate to the very nature of our being. Relation without revealing, function without being, connection without interaction, is purely mechanical connection, i.e. connecting different parts of a machine. This kind of thinking or mind-set is based on a "mechanical model" which assumes that the foundation of being is fundamentally individualistic. On the other hand, an "organic model," which assumes the foundation of being as a "relation" or an "interaction," is based on the idea of being as "holistic." The "organic model" intends to *expose* the intrinsic unity of beings while the "mechanical model" tries to *impose* the extrinsic connection of different entities. The "organic model" sees "being" as a vital, dynamic, and a living organ while the "mechanical model" "being," as parts to be assembled.

The very nature of *agape* as the highest form of love, and love itself, is *revealing*. Love reveals itself in "relation of *being* in love," and in "loving." Love "reveals" itself only through love. The mode of being "in love" and its *modus operandi* is *agape*. From the Christian perspective, Jesus Christ is both the revelation of God and the incarnation of

God at the same time. The Incarnation was possible through the Revelation, and the Revelation was actualized in the Incarnation. God's spontaneity in expressing and revealing divine love is *agape,* and this *agape* is Jesus Christ. In this respect, the *incarnation* and the *revelation* becomes one and the same in *agape.* Reconciliation is the reestablishment of "relationship," God to Man, Man to God. This "relationship," of God and Man, has also provided the foundation for the relationship with other human beings. Through loving we discover "love" and "being in love." *Agape* reveals what love is and through this love we "discover" ourselves.

Panikkar's insightful interpretation of the phrase: "Love your neighbour as yourself" illuminates an ontological and a revelatory aspect of love: "For me this is an ontological and not just a moral principle." Panikkar compares the Hebrew and Christian understanding of this statement, which is primarily a legal and an ethical one, to the Hindu, the Buddhist, and the Chinese scriptures which emphasize an ontological and revelatory aspect of love: "Love you neighbour as yourself" is understood as "love you neighbour as *your* self," and unless you reach that kind of identity, all your love for the other person is make-believe, artificial, for the sake of possessing or for the sake of something else.

Love is neither a possession nor an utility but *being your* self, (a true sense of "spontaneity" through which we can develop a sense of identity of *my*self with *your*self). Panikkar's ontological approach to "love" is directly related to his hermeneutics of revealing: "Love your neighbor as your self amounts to saying *know, discover, realize* your neighbor as your self, because as long as this saving of knowledge of the *self* has not dawned upon you, you cannot truly love the neighbor as your self."[7] The discovery, the knowledge, and the understanding of *your* self is a part of *your* being. In this respect, *your* being is extended, enriched, and enlarged in the revelation of *your* self in your neighbour. For this reason, *being* yourself is unceasing, dynamic, yet "spontaneous" process of discovering your "self" through love.

Liberty and Spontaneity

True spontaneity is also freedom for Panikkar. Freedom is being in a state of spontaneity, just like being in love, it is a liberating experience, participating in the spontaneity of being. This liberation is not a state of aimless and directionless wandering, but a way to participate in being "spontaneous" as a "self" discovery or discovering "self." This is a liberation from "self-centeredness" and "self-orientedness" to a deeper, authentic, "self" which is ever expanding, enlarging, growing, and transforming. In this respect, "liberation" is an ontological process rather than a mere social and political process of finding freedom. In this respect, the concept of liberation such as *moksha, nirvana* or *enlightenment* has to be ontologically structured beyond the social and political sense of liberation.

The social and political liberation, though not entirely separable from the ontological or soteriological sense of liberation, alone cannot achieve the genuine freedom. Because the social and political sense of liberty assumes a dialectical frame work of thinking and thus it has to go through dialectical process, it may not lead us to liberation in the ultimate sense. Soteriological and ontological sense of liberation, however, does not negate the political and social significance of liberation yet it also does not identify political liberation with the liberation of salvation.

Love is liberating force. Social force, military power, revolutionary movement may liberate "certain groups," "certain classes," "certain people," to a "certain" degree through a dialectical process of struggle. Love is a liberating force both internally and externally. Love can liberate us from the external forces or bondage of others and from the internal force or bondage of our own. Love makes us free – free from fear and suspicion and makes us beings spontaneous. We can not become spontaneous unless we experience divine love (*agape*) or *bhakti* in Hinduism or *karuna* in Buddhism.

Unless we are in true love, we cannot be totally spontaneous and care free. Love in this respect is a state of being grasped by "faith." (I will not go into the discussion of the meaning of "faith" because it can be yet another subject matter.) Spontaneity is a natural outcome of being in a state of love, faith, and hope that are the fundamental structures of our being. When we lose these three dimensions of being, we not only lose the spontaneity of being but being itself. In this respect, liberation is restoration and recovery of being. The life with absolute spontaneity and liberty is the life with faith and love:

> Therefore I tell you. Do not worry about your life, what you will eat, or about your body, what you will wear. For life is more than food, and the body is more than clothing ... consider the raven: they neither sow nor reap.... Consider the lilies, how they grow: they neither toil nor spin; yet I tell you, even Solomon in all his glory was not clothed like one of these (Luke 12:22-27, NRSV).

Being carefree is a form of freedom from "care," a liberation from daily concern and living with spontaneity. Spontaneity is a form of liberation.

Love, Liberation and Spontaneity

Liberation without love is a mere external transformation and social and political revolution but not liberation; liberation with love is an internal transformation or self-transformation which extends to external transformation. External transformation may take a form of social and political liberation while internal transformation is spiritual and religious liberation. These two forms of liberation require love. Expounding in this love is "piety." Piety is a way of accepting and participation in "spontaneity" with sincerity and integrity. For Panikkar, the most spontaneous act is the act of prayer, contemplation, and worship. In this sense, "piety" is not an extraordinary act but the most ordinary way of accepting the mystery of life and responding to this mystery in a spontaneous way.

Notes

1. In order to understand the primacy of "being" over "doing," see, Raimundo Panikkar's insight found in his book, *Blessed Simplicity*, New York: The Seabury Press, 1982, p. 45.

2. Raimundo Panikkar, *Blessed Simplicity: The Monk as Universal Archetype*. New York: The Seabury Press, 1982, p. 123.

3. Raimundo Panikkar, *Invisible Harmony*, Minneapolis: Fortress Press, 1995, p. 159.

4. "In-action" or "*Wu-wei*" in Taoism is not absent or negation of action but a spontaneous action.

5. See Panikkar's exploration of this issue in his discussion of the myth of Prajapti. Cf. Raimundo Panikkar, *Myth, Faith and Hermeneutics: Cross-Cultural Studies*. New York/Ramsey/Toronto: Paulist, pp. 70-72.

6. For a comprehensive discussion of Panikkar's "cosmotheandric" vision, see his *The Cosmotheandric Experience: Emerging Religious Consciousness*. Maryknoll, New York: Orbis Books, 1993.

7. Raimundo Panikkar, "Chosen-ness and Universality: Can Christians Claim Both?" *Cross Currents*, p. 317.

The Three Worlds of Raimundo Panikkar: A Personal Introduction

Scott Eastham

I have always considered it my part simply to present Raimundo Panikkar, not to make representations about him. I've been translating him (sometimes), and editing his English (often), for 25 years now. My relationship with Panikkar is in certain ways so close that I can not "objectify" him, "throw" him "out there" before me as an object of thought or analysis. It's more like love: He is part of me and I in some ways of him, or at least of his writings as they appear in English.[1] I see him always standing more behind me, or beside me, than in front of me. I see us looking at something of intense interest together, trying to discover just how to say "it," whatever "it" may be, so clearly and resonantly that it will not be misunderstood. To under-stand one another, says Panikkar in his favorite English pun, is to "stand under" the same *mythos*, the same horizon of intelligibility. That myth "goes without saying." Putting it into words is another matter: "What carries ... the conscious passage from *mythos* to *logos* is not the concept, but the symbol."[2] Our relationship, then, may be in some measure symbolic: We are "thrown together" *(sym-ballein)* in various roles – teacher and pupil, thinker and poet, *hotr* and *rsi*, spirit and the word. Yet none of these paired analogies is adequate. Maybe we have ever always just been friends.... I have marveled over the years how others are able to make splendid articles out of the *distance* between Panikkar's thought and their own. For me, this is difficult. I lack perspective. I don't stand "over against" Panikkar's thought. And yet I am certainly not him. I could not even pretend to his gifts, not just in languages or intellect or the depth of his cross-cultural and inter-religious experience, but in what one can in fairness only call holiness. Panikkar is one of a kind. Sometimes I feel like I've discovered Ali Baba's cave of treasures, but have only been able to share my discovery piecemeal with a very few people—a diamond necklace here, a few gold coins there, a pearl or two in my pocket for emergencies.

I see what we do together at its best as a form of congealed dialogue. He speaks in some other language, or writes in rough-edged English.[3] I respond by using my own words for what I think he's saying. He responds to my response, usually in surprising ways. I take in his response and try to make it accessible to the English-speaking reader, and the whole process begins all over again. We must often go through half a dozen drafts at least before we are both halfway satisfied, but the process really is endless. I may declare myself satisfied (or just tired!), but he never is. He is always revising. Writing, I have learned from him, is mainly rewriting. Panikkar considers the self-critical power that comes with literacy (all the world a perfectable text) one of the lasting legacies of the West.[4] Something usually intervenes—time, space, a publisher's deadline—to bring to a halt a process that properly speaking can never close itself off. My interpretation has become part of the text I'm interpreting, so much so that it is often difficult to see in retrospect where his words leave off and mine begin. The ideal is a kind of transparency.

Another way to look at this process is as one of discovering, in the act of writing itself, what *needs* to be said. To do this, you have to know what *has been said.* Even to prepare the footnotes for a Panikkar article, you must sometimes review entire literatures in several languages. He will leave a reference open – "cf. Divus Thomas" – and I will soon be ransacking the library only to find that the passage he refers to exists only in Latin. I will find someone to translate it into English. He will inevitably be dissatisfied with the shortcomings of the translation, and retranslate in a tricky way that requires me to stretch the English to encompass some kind of *triple entendre*, etc., etc. We are then testing out *what can be said,* rejecting the more extravagant and flashy metaphors – "I have the ambition to be read in a hundred years, cf. Plato," he once wrote in the margins next to a contemporary metaphor I had tried out – in hopes of arriving at what Pound used to call *le mot juste,* the "right" word. In the final analysis, it may be this very process of sorting out between what *has been said,* and what, possibly, *can be said,* that lets us close in on the very thing that *needs to be said.*

I once asked him, What is it you're doing? What are you up to? "I am trying to free people from the bonds of space and time," he replied. Is that all?! In a certain sense, it is. "Holy and wise people," he wrote recently, "are those who hold open the possibility of dialogue with us despite all the barriers of space and time."[5] To broaden and deepen that dialogue, Panikkar has spent his life. It's a kind of a love affair, is it not? What draws one thinker to another, what pulls them (and us) into the same orbit? What indeed is a living cultural tradition but this "pull"? Extend the question: What binds together the entire reality? Is there not love at the heart of the non-dual, trinitarian structure of the real? Between Father and Son, between Sky and Earth, and between people as well, there is "the love that moves the sun and the other stars," as Dante concluded the *Paradiso.* Love is that living pulse, the "rhythm of being," the dynamic polarity, the give and take – always "open" to what "occurs" to us in the encounter. And it is a fruitful love; as he likes to say, a "mutual fecundation." At his best, I have found, Panikkar's sentences actually do what they are talking about in the same words and at the same time as they are talking about "it." This is always difficult to convey in translation, but I do not agree with Joseph Prabhu that Panikkar is "lost in translation."[6] Many times he has declared the translation an improvement over the original language draft, precisely because the dialogical process of editing has deepened it. Instead of the corrosive hermeneutic of suspicion so popular today in the "postmodern" academic world, Panikkar's is—as Gerard Hall has recently emphasized—a hermeneutic of trust and, ultimately, of cosmic confidence in the integrity of the entire reality.[7] Panikkar means by this not some sort of individualistic optimism, but nothing less than our share, our portion of the very confidence of the creation itself. When I first heard him, I supposed that this famous fellow Panikkar must have a very complicated notion of faith to so freely traverse so many religions and philosophies and cultural styles. It is not so. Rather, the basic sort of faith he calls "cosmic confidence" seems to be at the root of Panikkar's own ability to penetrate to the core of more than one religious tradition.[8] Faith is, as he says, a "constitutive human dimension," precisely the dimension of "openness" to the mystery of life itself.[9]

The encounter of religions is the prime spiritual imperative of our time, and Panikkar is of course the world-renowned pioneer in this area. He is, to my knowledge, the only Hindu-Christian-Buddhist recognized by all three traditions. For fifty years, his has been the calm, steady voice calling for dialogue between the great religious traditions of the world. His example has sometimes been emulated, never surpassed. We should quickly review the scope of his work, so that we may then focus on what I see as its *omni-triangulated* structure.[10]

Panikkar's contributions to the comparative study of religion and philosophy can scarcely even be summarized; it's like trying to pick out individual colors from the rainbow. In early books like *El Concepto de Naturaleza* and *Ontonomia de la Ciencia,* he sought to bridge the gap between traditional ways of knowing *(scientia)* and those of modern science. As the author of *The Unknown Christ of Hinduism,* he sought to extend the noble ideal of ecumenism from an in-house discussion amongst Christians to a genuine dialogue between religions. In *The Silence of God,* he counterposed the religious atheism of the Buddha to the challenge posed by secular atheism in the West, at a stroke widening the intelligibility of the earliest Buddhist texts and deepening the contemporary "death of God" theology. In *The Trinity and the Religious Experience of Man,* Panikkar sketched a nondualistic understanding of the symbolic character of the entire reality, as experienced uniquely by Christian and Hindu religiousness. His *Worship and Secular Man* addressed the often aggravated interface between the religious traditions and the modern secular world, to the enrichment of both. *The Intra-religious Dialogue,* widely used for graduate seminars in religion, opened up the "rules of the game" in the dialogical theatre where all these views may encounter one another in mutually enhancing ways, without minimizing their differences. In his monumental *Vedic Experience,* Panikkar tried to render accessible to the modern reader the most primordial stratum of human religious experience, through the *Vedas* themselves. There are many anthologies of his essays in several languages, but in English it is *Myth, Faith and Hermeneutics* that brings together the major essays which best illustrate his method of understanding the truth of more than one religious tradition "from within." More recently, *The*

Cosmotheandric Experience summed up his more than fifty years of multi-religious experience in a powerful synergy of God, Man and Cosmos – the three "worlds" of my title.

Panikkar is today widely hailed as a leading light in the urgent effort to articulate a cross-cultural philosophy of peace; his volume *Cultural Disarmament,* published just last year, highlights this issue. Modernity boils down to a war of the worlds: the cosmic, the human, and the divine dimensions of reality are pitted each against the others.[11] Peace-making stems from dialogue, and must reconcile not only one human group with another, but these three constitutive dimensions of the real. Two recent collections of Panikkar's articles – *Invisible Harmony,* and *A Dwelling Place for Wisdom* – have helped make his work more accessible to the general reader in English. His *Ecosophy,* to date available only in Spanish, takes the eco-*logical* movement one step further, into a full and reciprocal dialogue with the many voices of the Earth herself – wind and water, tree and rock – so long muted in the Western psyche. And now there is the new volume, edited by Prabhu, *The Intercultural Challenge of Raimon Panikkar,* a book in which Panikkar responds directly to interlocutors from around the world. I need hardly add that Panikkar not only writes about religion but lives a genuinely religious life. Anyone who knows him personally will know why Kerenyi remarked, upon first meeting Panikkar, on the "direct religiosity" of the man. He embodies the cross-cultural and inter-religious encounter he writes about. Panikkar is, so to speak, the encounter of religions in person.

In the Spring of 1989, Panikkar delivered *The Gifford Lectures* at the University of Edinburgh. He was the first Spaniard, the first Catalan, the first Indian and the first Asian to be so honored, and his lectures marked the Centennial of that renowned series. Those lectures, now in preparation and soon to be published as *The Rhythm of*

Being – The Radical Trinity, may prove to be both a watershed in the philosophy of religion and an earthquake for theology. They amount, in his words, to nothing less than an attempt "to liberate the Divine from the burden of being God." These lectures, concentrating and surmounting the work of a lifetime, may well represent the 20th Century's most original contribution to our understanding of the Divine.

The Three Worlds: A Guided Tour

When I first heard Panikkar speak, as a graduate student at the University of California at Santa Barbara in the early '70's, most of what he said seemed to me abundantly clear, almost commonsensical. You need the other to know your own myth. Dialogue cannot be constrained by rules of the game laid down from one side or the other. No single religious or cultural tradition exhausts the millennial human experience. Nobody has a monopoly on being human. These things seemed to me altogether straightforward, even if he spoke with an accent, even if he used a few neologisms nobody had heard before. I was astounded to discover that otherwise quite intelligent and quick-witted people found Panikkar utterly dumbfounding. They simply did not understand him. It was then that I took up the task of editing him. It seemed to me that if his English were straightened out a bit, nobody could fail to understand him. And yet many people still do find his thinking and his writing incomprehensible—too "dense," I'm told, too "demanding," with "too many references."

Certainly Panikkar requires a great deal of his readers, if only to keep up with his thinking in writings where every sentence moves the argument forward, and little space is wasted on exposition (if you need it, the notes are there ...). But there seems to be some other problem. Panikkar is still difficult for scholars and readers who have invested the time to get to know his work and his vocabulary, who have spent years studying one or more of the several traditions he has made his own. It seems he wants people to think around one more corner than they're willing to go. Prabhu provides a clue to such misunderstandings in his Introduction to *The Intercultural Challenge:* "Panikkar simply doesn't think straight."[12] True enough. This "non-linear" thinking of his (which is also, bear in mind, not just circular), may be at the bottom of some of these misunderstandings. I want to try to get at what it is. Let me use a bit of a poem I wrote many years ago, mainly in response to *The Trinity and the Religious Experience of Man,* to illustrate both the elegance of Panikkar's thinking, and its elusiveness:

On the Track
MARGA,
trail of an animal,
track of the cat: snow leopard
padding over the high Himalayas ...

karmamarga:
Way of the Father: to create;
via activa, way of action,
salvation by acts.

bhaktimarga:
Way of the Son: to love,
via amativa, way of devotion,
by services rendered.

anamarga:
Way of the Spirit: to comprehend,

via contemplativa, way of knowledge,
intuition of Mystery.[13]

It is not overstating the case to say that Panikkar's work stems from one, threefold intuition: the fruit not of reflection but of mystical experience, he tells us, "not the vision of a vision but merely a vision."[14] In the instance I refer to in this poem, he was aligning core Hindu and Christian intuitions. He does so by establishing what he later came to call the *homeomorphic equivalence*[15] of the Christian trinity (Father, Son, Spirit), with the three *margas* (action, devotion, knowledge) of the Hindu tradition—breaking out of the longstanding tendency to compare the Christian trinity with the three Gods Shiva, Vishnu and Brahma (mistaking the trinity for a species of tri-theism probably tells us more about the interpreter than it does about Hinduism). Yet Panikkar's trinitarian/advaitic vision does not stop unfolding here.

To see what he's doing in its full range, we may spread out before us a kind of map that charts the way his vision of the three worlds appears in different fields, and comes to light in various of his own works. Such a chart is provisional, of course, and much too abstract on its own. Its warrant is Panikkar's own affirmation that "the divine, the human, and the earthly—however we may prefer to call them—are the three irreducible dimensions which constitute the real, i.e., any reality inasmuch as it is real."[16] This is his *cosmotheandric* intuition, *tout court.* Accordingly, I have found it useful to correlate Panikkar's "triads" on these lines when preparing larger works like *Myth, Faith & Hermeneutics* where several of them appear to partially overlap but never entirely fuse. The result demonstrates, I think, a consistency to his work, an underlying coherence to his thinking, a synthesis not "systematic" but organic. In short, if I were conducting a guided tour to the high points of Panikkar's thought, I would have at least to stop at the following way-stations:

Panikkar's Three Worlds: Connecting the Connections

THOU ART-	I AM-	IT IS[17]
anthropos-	*theos-*	*kosmos*
the human	- the divine-	the world[18]
Humanities	- Religion-	Science[19]
noumenon-	*mysterion-*	*phainomenon*
Mind-	Spirit-	Body
inner/subjective	center\whole	outer\objective[20]
Theory	- Way	-Praxis
logos-	*pneuma-*	*mythos*[21]
text	- texture-	context[22]
the true	- the good	the beautiful
ta noetika	- *ta mystika-*	*ta aesthetika*[23]

It is crucial to realize that the relations here are more real than these "poles." Each is or is capable of being the middle term for the other polarities of the relationship: sheer, i.e., radical, relativity. Already we are at least one step beyond the binary oppositions of dialectical thinking. Yet all too often, as we shall see in the next section, these relations are conceived monistically (law of the jungle) or dualistically (jungle of the law) and not as a threefold unity, i.e., neither one nor many but what I can only call "omnitriangulated."[24] Still, it is all too neat, as only abstractions can be. Such a schema is a caricature because it leaves out the living context, and pretends to put all the terms on the same playing field, or framework, which in fact is part of the schema and not a separate field. The cosmotheandric intuition has no center, Panikkar reminds us,[25] or rather, each term is capable of "centering" the relationship between the others. I am not trying to present a skeleton key to reality, merely an outline of congruencies in Panikkar's work. He himself approvingly cites Abhinavagupta to the effect that there is no key to reality, and none needed. And why not? Because it is not locked.[26]

The "three margas" poem works because the Christian trinity as Panikkar interprets it is indeed very close to the three "paths" of Hinduism, but as homeomorphic equivalents—to use Panikkar's own language for functional analogies discovered within diverse cultural traditions—neither are they the "same." Such a "list" will always be defective, and slightly deceptive, since the contexts diverge so wildly: You can't just say "The 'myth' is the 'Father' who is as 'good' as 'I am' ..." without falling into either tautology or absurdity. Yet such a "list" of the three worlds may be helpful as a kind of map so long as one factors in the appropriate context of each formulation, or refers to the Panikkar pieces where each "triad" is explicated. The threefold pattern is not simply repeated, the way it is expressed varies according to context, but it's *there.* The co-ordination of these "triads" does not reduce them to a mono-focal pattern from a single privileged "perspective" or "higher" instance, but indicates structural and functional analogies betwixt and between the triadic structures of Panikkar's essays. These are homeomorphic equivalents internal to his own works. My excuse for such an "algebra" is that as an editor, I found I needed a thumbnail sketch of how all the "triads" fit together ... but in each case I also found that it amounts to a creative act to think in this way. The next question we must face, however, is a good deal trickier: Just how are we to understand the integral relationship of these three worlds to one another?

Ontonomy: Neither One nor Two nor Many

If Panikkar's work fits together as nicely as my "map" of the three worlds would seem to claim where, then, lies the difficulty people find in reading him? As would any *advaitin,* Panikkar suggests it lies in the limitations of the human mind itself. He speaks often lately of "the inertia of the mind." And most people do tend most of the time to think either monistically or dualistically, so that it seems a strain to follow efforts like Panikkar's to give both schemas of intelligibility their due, and then leave them behind.

Why is it the human mind seems so bent on thinking in ones and twos? It may well be because each of us has two brains, or rather, two distinct lobes to our single brains, connected by a massive bundle of fibers called the *corpus colossum.* There is tremendous gain in such an arrangement, but certainly built-in limitations as well. The most basic limitation is that you cannot think monistically and dualistically at the same time.

The left lobe is analytic, and ultimately dualistic; it relies on the principle of non-contradiction: A_B.

"When looking for an ultimate reality ... the way of thinking based mainly on the principle of non-contradiction will obviously look for something different from everyday experience: the Ultimate will then be considered transcendent, wholly Other, superior, difference, cause, mover ... and the like. This procedure will lead to the 'God' of the Abrahamic religious traditions." [27]

The right lobe perceives *Gestalt* patterns, and is ultimately monistic; it relies on the principle of identity: A=A.

> When looking for an ultimate reality, the way of thinking based mainly on the principle of identity will obviously look for something self-identical in our common experience: the Ultimate will then be considered immanent, the real One, basic, intrinsically identical, condition of possibility and the like. This will lead to the Brahman of the indic religious tradition. [28]

And the balance between these views is presumably what Renata Adler once called *sanity,* "the most profound moral option of our time." Neither principle of intelligibility is exhaustive; neither even accounts for the existence of the other principle. Both must be considered necessary, but lopsided, approaches to the trinitarian and advaitic integrity of reality (including but not limited to the mind's awareness of that reality).

Panikkar's work is notable precisely because he never seems to lose the balance. He elucidates it as follows...

> The history of mankind as well as the history of human consciousness individually and collectively, i.e., from the point of view of its personal development, could be conveniently understood and heuristically expounded under the three headings of 1) heteronomy, 2) autonomy and 3) ontonomy. 1) By *heteronomy* we understand a world view, as well as an anthropological degree of consciousness, which relies on a hierarchical structure of reality, which considers that the regulations in any sphere of being come from a higher instance, and are

> in each case responsible, so to speak, for the proper functioning of that particular being or sphere of being.[29]

Words associated with the heteronomic attitude from diverse fields would be, for instance, authority, tradition, and stability. Philosophically, it emphasizes the reality of Being over the dynamism of becoming. Sociologically, the emphasis is on the obligations to the collectivity (state, corporation) over the individual, biologically it focuses on the pattern rather than the variations; in physics, order takes precedence over randomness. From the outside, heteronomy presents itself as a monism; from the inside, it appears as a dualistic pyramid of values with somebody or something *else*, some single principle (God, King, or Country) at the "top."

2) "By *autonomy* we understand the world as well as the human being to be *sui iuris,* i.e., self-determined and determinable, each being a law unto itself. This autonomy means that any injunction from outside, even if it is said to come from above, is regarded as an abusive imposition." [30]

Words associated with the autonomic attitude would be, for instance, liberty, progress, and energy. Philosophically, it emphasizes the dynamic reality of becoming rather than static Being. Sociologically, the emphasis will fall on the importance of the "rights" of the individual over those of the collectivity; biologically the variations will be perceived as more important than the pattern; in physics, randomness will predominate over order. From the inside, the autonomic attitude insists on its own internal consistency and unity; from the outside, it appears in a dialectical arena where dualistic competition prevails—for votes, dollars, numbers, etc.

3) "By *ontonomy* we mean that degree of awareness which, having overcome the individualistic attitude as

well as the monolithic view of reality, regards the whole universe as unity so that the regulation of a particular being is neither self-imposed nor dictated from above, but a part of the whole discovering or following its destiny. Ontonomy is the realisation of the *nomos,* the law of the *on,* being, at that profound level where unity does not impinge upon diversity, but where the latter is rather the unique and proper manifestation of the former. It rests on the specular character of reality, in which each 'part' mirrors the whole in a way proper to it." [31]

Ontonomy is less well known, but under other names no less a perennial human attitude. Its most common formulation is as the Great Middle Way, and while quite as prevalent down the ages as the other two attitudes, it is today muted in the cacophony of the conflictual modern world. It is all too easily mistaken for a mushy middle, a weak compromise, instead of the tensile polarity, crackling with the creative sparks of life and light, that Panikkar has in mind. Words associated with the formulation of this "third way" in our own century might be the holism of Smuts [32] or the bionomics of Rosenstock-Huessy.[33] Panikkar himself associates it with the radical *freedom* of the spirit, with the category of *growth* (in the history of religions, not in urban sprawl), and occasionally *synergy.* Despite the prefix *on*-(being), it makes more sense to say in English that this is the intuition that Life transcends both the mental category of Being and that of becoming. Sociologically, it portends the co-evolution of the person in community, without reifying either the collectivity as a state or institution (Church, e.g.), or the solipsism of the individual. Biologically, the organism will be perceived to exist in the interplay between pattern and variation; and in physics, it will appear as neither an open system nor a closed system, but as a stochastic system (or perhaps a "strange attractor" in chaos theory). From the inside, the integrity of the part comes to the fore, but it is always perceived to exist precisely as a *part-* icipation in the larger harmony of the whole; indeed, inside and outside cease to be little more than heuristic devices.

Panikkar himself sums up this non-dual attitude very thoroughly and completely, which is one of the reasons I have hesitated over the years to add anything at all:

> [Ontonomy] stands for the recognition neither of heteronomy, i.e., the regulation of the activity of a particular being by laws proceeding from another higher being, nor of autonomy, i.e., the affirmation that each field is absolutely self-normative and patron of its own destiny. Ontonomy is intended to express the recognition of the inner regularities of each field of activity or sphere of being in the light of the whole. The whole is, in fact, neither different from nor merely identifical with any one field or sphere. Ontonomy rests on the assumption that the universe is a whole, that there is an internal and constitutive relationship between each and every part of reality, that nothing is disconnected and that the development and progress of one being is not to be at the expense of another —[34]

But again, we must be careful with abstract schemas. Some of the categories I mention here are not even Panikkar's, but beyond this, there is the built-in *enantiadromia,* the Heracleitan tendency for each extreme attitude to "flip" into its opposite. Example: The totalitarian regime (heteronomy) "creates" the (autonomous) revolutionaries by its repressive measures; but, once in power, the revolutionary council soon enough revolves around to become the new dictatorship. Heteronomy and autonomy are like *yin* and *yang*, each containing the seed of its contrary. The polarity is constitutive, so that if you "push" either attitude to extremes, it "flips" into its opposite. Such a schema as that above lays out what is ultimately the ontonomic constitution of the real: It is this whole, or nothing—just an epistemological strategy in our minds, or a political tactic, or whatever.

Ways of West & East: The Rhythm of the Real

The dynamic of life pulses between the "poles" (terms, limits) of our powers to understand, but we "feel" there is a rhythm to this dance. We can get a "feel" (feeling, *sentimiento*[35]) for it because we are always already not only part but parcel (vehicle, embodiment) of the dance itself. Panikkar understands "rhythm" not as a metaphor at all, but as the most basic character of Life itself: It is all rhythm. Hence the title of his Gifford lectures, *The Rhythm of Being.* The following paragraph emerged from Panikkar's hand on the revised manuscript of those Lectures, where it now concludes the section introducing the word "rhythm." It displays, in a nutshell, not only the "three worlds" we have been discussing, but a concentrated digest of their ontonomic interrelationship. It is as near as I know to a succinct summary of the whole of Panikkar's thought—or better put, of his life, his words, and his spirit:

> In sum, we discover rhythm when we experience the subjective difference of an objective identity.... But we could equally have said: the objective difference of a subjective

> identity. Identity and difference, subjectivity and objectivity, are overcome. In other words, the experience of rhythm is the experience of the neither-identity-nor-difference of the Real. This is precisely the advaitic experience: neither monism or identity, nor dualism or difference. Neither the subjective nor the objective views are real. Being itself is advaitic, it is rhythmic....[36]

I suppose I am myself an example of how Panikkar's insistence on the *pisteuma*—the core of belief at the center of any religion and therefore of any religious study—applies as well to getting to know his own work.[37] You've got to share the belief of the believer to some extent and in some degree, so that whoever you are interpreting can at least recognize themselves in the interpretation (Panikkar's "golden rule" of hermeneutics[38]). This is risky; it requires a leap of faith.

Since I am contributing to proceedings with an "East/West" theme, I might illustrate this by remarking that my compass seems to show East and West turning up where they aren't supposed to be. I am writing now from Aotearoa, in Maori "the Land of the Long White Cloud," specifically the North Island or "Maui's Fish" in New Zealand. The "West," which used to be Europe and later North America, is way over to the east of me. And the mysterious "East" is pretty much northwest of where I stand. Obviously, geographic East and West are relative to one's position.

When my family and I moved to New Zealand, Panikkar sent me a card welcoming me to Asia (from his home in Calalunya!). I recalled him saying long ago in "The Supreme Experience" that as we approach the year 2000, we know very well that the typically Western spirit can be found all over the globe, just as traditionally Eastern ways of looking at things are gaining ground in the so-called West.[39]

So have East and West any meaning anymore? Yes, a deeply human one. Panikkar suggests that if there is to be a real cross-fertilization between cultures, we need to discover both horizons in ourselves. In each of us there is a kind of East and West, although one aspect usually predominates.

In every human being there is an orient, he says, a horizon never reached, always just beyond or behind our experience, an innocence, the bright and spirited hope which rises each day with the sun: *the morning knowledge.*

Every one of us has likewise an occident, a horizon reached after the day's experiences, a maturity, the sadder but wiser spirit of the setting sun, where values materialize and material things are valued: *the evening knowledge.*

East and West, self and other, identity and difference, immanence and transcendence.... We may learn from Panikkar that in each of us lies not only the chasm between these antinomies, but also and above all the bridge.

Notes

1. Not all of his writings, of course; many hands have gone into editing Panikkar's English over the years. The uniquely valuable contributions to Panikkar's English "voice" over the years by, e.g., Mary Rogers, N. Shanta, Leonard Swidler, Christine Hopper, Madelon Bose, Robert Barr, H. J. Cargas, and very many others cannot be overestimated. I can speak, not for them of course, but only from my own experience of the man and his writings. I have worked with Panikkar on dozens of his articles, and several books: *Myth, Faith and Hermeneutics; The Intrareligious Dialogue; Blessed Simplicity; The Cosmotheandric Experience;* and soon, *The Rhythm of Being.*

2. Quotation abridged from the Introduction to R. Panikkar, *Myth, Faith and Hermeneutics,* New York (Paulist Press), 1979, p. 6.

3. Panikkar in fact knows the *words* of English far better than most English-speakers, but he knows them as a linguist and philologist, from their roots and associations in other languages. What he does not have is a native speaker's feel for the tongue, though he has astutely observed that "the genius of English is its simplicity" and tries to write accordingly.

4. Cf. R. Panikkar, "Manifesto for the Quincentennial," in *Compass,* Vol. 10, No. 5, Nov.-Dec. 1992, pp. 27-29: "If Europe loses its self-critical sense, it renounces one of its most precious conquests, acquired through reflection on its own errors."

5. R. Panikkar, "The Encounter of Religions: The Unavoidable Dialogue," introductory article for the German journal, *Dialog der religionen,* Nr. 1, 1991, pp. 9-39, which will be included in the newly expanded edition of R. Panikkar, *The Intrareligious Dialogue,* New York (Paulist Press) 1978, due to be re-issued this year.

6. Cf. Joseph Prabhu, Ed., *The Intercultural Challenge of Raimon Panikkar,* New York (Orbis) 1996, Introduction, "Lost in Translation – Panikkar's Intercultural Odyssey," pp. 1-21.

7. Cf. Gerard Hall, *Raimon Panikkar's Hermeneutics of Religious Pluralism,* Ann Arbor, Michigan (University Microfilms International) 1994, Ch. VI, "A Dialectical, Hermeneutical and Rhetorical Reading of Panikkar's Dialogical Project," pp. 261-322. Hall's work, soon to be published by Catholic University Press, Washington, D.C., is the most comprehensive, insightful, and readable review of Panikkar's work presently available in English.

8. Cf. "The Invisible Harmony – A Universal Theory of Religion or a Cosmic Confidence in Reality?," recently reprinted as the final chapter of R. Panikkar, *Invisible Harmony – Essays on Contemplation and Responsibility,* H. J. Cargas, ed., Minneapolis (Fortress Press) 1995, pp. 145-82.

9. Cf. "Faith as a Constitutive Human Dimension," Ch. VI of *Myth, Faith & Hermeneutics, op. cit.*, pp. 187-229.

10. I borrow the term "omnitriangulated" from R. Buckminster Fuller's *Synergetics, Explorations in the Geometry of Thinking*, and *Synergetics 2* (with E. J. Applewhite), New York (Macmillan) 1975, 1979. For Fuller, inventor of the geodesic dome and other formidable design concepts, the triangle *is* structure, and structure always triangulated: "By structure, we mean a self-stabilizing pattern. The triangle is the only self-stabilizing polygon. By structure, we mean omnitriangulated. The triangle is the only structure.... Only triangularly structured patterns are regenerative patterns. Triangular structuring is pattern integrity itself. This is what we mean by *structure*" (°610.01-03, p. 319).

11. I have dealt with "the three worlds at war" at greater length elsewhere; cf., e.g., S. T. Eastham, "How Is Wisdom Communicated?—Prologue to Peace Studies," *INTERculture*, Journal of the Intercultural Institute of Montréal, Vol. XXV, No. 2, Spring 1992, pp. 1-45. French edition, "Comment communiquer la sagesse?," *INTERculture*, Cahier 115.

12. J. Prabhu, ed., *The Intercultural Challenge of Raimon Panikkar, op. cit.*, Preface, p. ix.

13. Cf. S. T. Eastham, *The Radix, or The Original Radical Poem*, New York/ Bern (Peter Lang) 1991, III/1 "On the Track," pp. 153-159. The concordance of Panikkar's "three worlds" below is also adapted from a later part of the same poem.

14. R. Panikkar, *The Cosmotheandric Experience—Emerging Religious Consciousness*, S. Eastham, ed., Maryknoll, New York (Orbis) 1993, p. 15.

15. Cf. R. Panikkar, *The Intrareligious Dialogue, op. cit.*, "Introduction: The Rhetoric of the Dialogue," pp. xii-xxviii.

16. R. Panikkar, *The Cosmotheandric Experience, op. cit.*, p. 60.

17. Cf. "The Threefold Linguistic Intrasubjectivity," *Intersoggettività*

Socialità Religione, M. M. Olivetti, ed., *Archivio di Filosofia,* Roma, LIV, 1/3, 1986, pp. 593-606.

18. Cf. Panikkar, *Cosmotheandric Experience, op. cit.*

19. As is well-known, Panikkar's holds three doctorates—in the sciences, philosophy, and theology.

20. Cf. R. Panikkar, "There is No Outer without Inner Space," in *Concepts of Space, Ancient and Modern,* K. Vatsyayan, ed., New Delhi (Abhinav) 1991, pp. 7-38.

21. Cf., e.g., R. Panikkar, *Myth, Faith & Hermeneutics, op. cit.,* "The Philosophical Tradition," pp. 335-48.

22. Cf. R. Panikkar, "Philosophy and Revolution: The Text, the Context and the Texture," *Philosophy East and West,* Honolulu, Vol. XXIII, No. 3, 1973, pp. 315-22.

23. These last two "triads" are derived from the forthcoming volume of Gifford Lectures, R. Panikkar, *The Rhythm of Being – The Radical Trinity,* New York (Orbis) and London (SCM), 1998(?), Ch. V, "The Radical Trinity."

24. "Aristotelian logic cannot think in threes. From Aristotle's law of contradiction, also called the law of the excluded middle, to the binary logic—0 or 1—in our computer programs, our mind sets up its systems in pros and cons, in either-or's," writes James Hillman in *The Soul's Code,* New York (Random House) 1996, p. 129. Yet "thinking in threes" is precisely what Panikkar obliges his readers to do.

25 Panikkar, *Cosmotheandric Experience, op. cit.,* p. 77.

26. Cf. Panikkar, *The Rhythm of Being, op. cit.,* Ch. VI, "The Cosmotheandric Invariant." Cf. also, Panikkar, *Myth, Faith & Hermeneutics, op. cit.,* Ch. VIII, "Silence and the Word. The Smile of the Buddha," pp. 257-76.

27. R. Panikkar, "Singularity and Individuality, The Double Princi-

ple of Individuation," *Revue Internationale de Philosophie,* No. 111-12, fasc. 1-2, 1973, pp. 141-66. Quotation from p. 147.

28. *Ibid.*

29. R. Panikkar, *Worship and Secular Man,* New York (Orbis), London (Darton, Longman, Todd) 1973, p. 28.

30. *Ibid.*

31. *Ibid.*, p. 29. Cf. also Panikkar's *Ontonomia de la Ciencia.,* Madrid (Editorial Gredos) 1961.

32. Cf. Jan Christian Smuts, *Holism & Evolution,* New York (Macmillan) 1926, Ch. 5, "General Concept of Holism."

33. Cf. Eugen Rosenstock-Huessy, *Out of Revolution – Autobiography of Western Man,* Norwich, Vermont (Argo Books) 1969, esp. Ch. 18, "Farewell to Descartes," pp. 740-53.

34. R. Panikkar, *Worship and Secular Man, op. cit.,* pp. 41-42.

35. Panikkar's first published book was *F. H. Jacobi y la filosofía del sentimiento,* Buenos Aires (Sapientia) 1948.

36. Panikkar, *Rhythm of Being, op. cit.,* Introduction, 3(a).

37. Cf. Panikkar, *The Intrareligious Dialogue, op. cit.,* Ch. III, "Epoché in the Religious Encounter," pp. 39-52.

38. Cf. Panikkar, *Myth, Faith & Hermeneutics, op. cit.,* p. 105.

39. *Ibid.*, pp. 309-310, paraphrased in the reflection below.

Post-Scrypt

Re-Arming the Remains of *Bhakti, Karuna, Agape*

Marko Zlomislić

I will speak words of truth and the words of divine law shall be on my lips
Taittiriya Upanishad

The named is the mother of the myriad creatures.
Tao Te Ching

With human cords I ever draw them forward,
leading them with strings of love;
Hosea 11: 14

The heart in mourning prompts us to think.
E.M. Cioran, *Tears and Saints*

The picture shows the Blessed Mother of Međugorje.[1]

In the 1980's at the outset of Yugoslavian and Serbian aggression against Kosovar Albanians and Croatians living in Hercegovina she appeared to a group of children. So we are told.

Mary gave and continues to give them her message of peace. Do you believe in *it*; in the *it* that is peace?[2]

Millions have gone there to pray for peace. But going there or anywhere to pray for peace is not enough when there is no peace here where we stand.

In what follows I want to remember the mother and what it might mean to give love and compassion.

Today when tanks and commandos of the one "God" surround the Church of the Nativity and soldiers of the other one "God" hide inside its walls and the politicians of the nation that proclaims "In God We Trust" sell weapons to anyone with enough cash and currency and then feigns ignorance or innocence, I ask[3]:

What remains of *Bhakti, Karuna, Hesed, Agape, Ramah, Love, Ljubav* except the radical forgetting of compassionate for-giving?

Bhakti, Karuna, Agape; these are words that have become intellectualized and disarmed by the so called religious.[4]

This disarming is alarming.

I wish these words to be re-armed without being militarized.[5]

If what is ethical about ethics is compassion then the present state of affairs shows that we have not encompassed ourselves with compassion.

Compassion is the compass showing us what must not be passed over as the other stands before us.

Compassion is said to be an understanding of suffering and the commitment to promote its alleviation.

But the intellectual can say "yes, I have understood suffering and therefore it is alleviated."

The religious could say "yes, I practice compassion but only towards those I have yet to bind (*ligare*) and abuse."

I agree with Panikkar when he writes that a cultural disarmament is necessary if there is to be peace.[6]

But does such a view go far enough? Is it a cause for alarm?

When Loyola put down his weapons of war did he pick up the weapons of religion as a supplement? What was the goal of his *Jihad*?

Disarmament cannot proceed if one view is exchanged for another especially if that view is imposed by a faulty, i.e. literal reading of scripture and by the spray and spread of bullets and bombs. This type of disarmament only bring harm.

If we take into the account the millions upon millions who say that they have practiced or practice *Hesed, Bhakti, Karuna, Agape, Ramah* then why does there continue to be so much suffering-in-the-world? Might one say that humanity has not evolved beyond its stone-age aggression? The tools used to carve out the world quickly became the tools used against the other.

The exemplars of Abraham-Jesus-Buddha-Mohammed-Ghandi have not been followed.

The truths of *Tat Tvam Asi*[7] – The Kingdom is Here-*Om mani padme hum*[8] remain to be put into practice.

In this age where everything can be revealed; where everything is therefore already always apocalyptic what remains as that which is still veiled?

What remains of *Bhakti-Karuna-Agape*?

An infinite number of remains remain to be remembered and mourned over from time immemorial to the present second and all its divisions.

Forty thousand children die every day because of the lack of food and medicine.[9]

Suffering remains, even while it is recognized as a first noble truth.

Forgiveness remains to be given.

The radical forgetting of forgiveness at the heart of compassion is more destructive than the forgetting of Being.

Ghandi whose *bhakti* revolution taught us much said that peace between countries must rest on the solid foundation of love between individuals.

With *bhakti* we realize the interconnectedness between *Atman* and *Brahman*.

With *bhakti* we are like Krishna at Devi's breast; like Isaac at Sarah's breast; like Jesus at Mary's breast.[10]

The mother nourishes us and teaches her children to be heard and seen; like the young Jesus teaching at the Temple.

Krishna teaches Arjuna that the true devotee has no ill will toward any being; is friendly and compassionate; free from egoism and self-sense; even- minded in pain and pleasure; is patient. The true devotee is ever content; self-controlled; unshakeable in determination; with mind and understanding given up to the Supreme Lord. The true devotee does not shrink from the world and if free from emotions, agitation and attachment. The devotee is pure, skillful in action; has no expectations; is unconcerned and untroubled.

Why are there so few devotees?

The *Maitri Upanishad* gives the answer:

"If men thought of God as much as they think of the world, who would not attain liberation?"

Here the *Maitri Upanishad* gives us a distinction between two types of devotion. To be devoted to the things of this world is bondage and *maya*; to be delivered from them is *moksa*.

In the Buddhist *Mahayana* tradition the *Boddhisattva* is attuned to suffering and answers with a constant outpouring of *karuna*.

Compassion sees things exactly as they are and is not afraid to speak things as they are.

Karuna is the soft and noble heart of spontaneous action reached through the six *paramita's* of generosity, morality, patience, perseverance, meditation and discriminating awareness.

Every practice and all the positive actions that these practices generate are dedicated to the benefit of all beings.

Compassion is a genuine fearlessness[11] that does not allow for nonsense, stupidity or oppression: like Christ chasing the money-lenders out of the temple like Ghandi on his march to the sea and like the words of Dr. Martin Luther King.

Karuna is the being-nailed to the present moment.

It is here that we are exposed to desolation in order to find out what cannot be annihilated

The six *paramitas* of the *Boddhisattva* show us the way to the other shore which is no other than here.

One might develop attachment or desire for the other shore of nirvana.

Such attachment is as deadly as honeyed razor so the Buddha gave the teaching on groundlessness.

This teaching known as the *Heart Sutra* contains the paradox that form is emptiness and emptiness is form.

Emptiness if no other than form.

Form is no other than emptiness.[12]

The *Heart Sutra* challenges us to throw away any conclusions so that an attitude of openness can be maintained.

This is the state of fearless, futureless and hopeless *karuna*.

Unless there is detachment even from the goal of achieving enlightenment there can be no release from *samsara*.

What remains is the situation to serve others.

Jesus through a universal (*kathalikos*) ministry taught that the Kingdom is Here. Yet those who call themselves his disciples act as if he still has to come again. Some wait to be raptured into the sky while they turn the Bible into a self-help prosperity manual.[13]

Jesus' performance on the cross between the two criminals illustrated that the ground of groundlessness is golgotha. Buddhism states that to live is to be willing to die over and over again.

The Buddhist *Heart Sutra* resonates in Jesus's teaching of non-attachment which leads to openness.

We remain non-attached out of love to go beyond that which prevents us from becoming fully human and fully awake.[14] Nietzsche was aware of Jesus' teachings even if Paul forget them.

With *Bhakti* we go beyond self, family, other.

With *Karuna* we go beyond hinayana, mahayana, tantra.

With *Agape* we go beyond joy, sorrow, glory.

The common ground in this trinity is the cultivation of non-attachment, compassion and emptiness.[15]

Those who count themselves as followers of these traditions have not followed the ground of the teachings they have been given.[16]

Their fundamentalism cannot be located in the *sutras*, scriptures and strings of their respective traditions.

There is a thirst for compassion even while nuclear or biological weapons are made and satellite systems are deployed in the name of deterrence.

Buddhist statues are blown up in the name of the Prophet along with the trade towers. It is always the other that remains guilty; never the I that accuses the other of performing acts I have already committed against the other in so many different ways.

Jets and helicopters rain bombs and machine gun men surround synagogues, schools, churches, mosques and hospitals.

Suicide bombers take the lives of innocents. The land is on fire. Nuclear devices are detonated as "scientific experiments." Confusion is dispensed by the fuse of anger that creates fracture and fissure.

Sanctions that kill millions of children are put in place by an organization called the United Nations.[17]

Webs are woven and optic fibers connected so that communication can take place in front of screens where we surf the waves of virtual togetherness in the compartments of our inhuman spaces that give:

Inequality
Discrimination
Injustice
Cruelty
Poverty
Despair
Absurdity
Suffering.

Bhakti- Karuna-Agape:

Here we are joined at the cross-roads
with Oedipus and his Father
with Cain and Abel
with Jesus and Judas
with Abraham and Isaac[18]
with Moses and Mohammed
with Mao Tse Tung and the Dali Lama
with JFK and Castro
with Bush and Bin-Laden
with dictators and saints
with all our dead

and everything that remains dead within us because of the radical forgetting of compassionate forgiving.

When a Krishna Gotami came to the Buddha to restore the life of her dead child the Buddha said, "There is only one way to heal your affliction, Go down to the city and bring me back a mustard seed from any house in which there has never been death."

Krishna Gotami returns with empty hands and Buddha teaches her the doctrine of impermanence.

> Buddha's mustard seed teaches impermanence.
> Christ's mustard seed teaches faith.
> Meditation is the road to enlightenment.
> Faith is the road to salvation.

Do these slogans prevent dialogue?

The three-fold Hindu understanding of the essence of God as

> *sat-cit-ananda*[19]

finds it parallel in the Buddhist

> *sambhogakaya- nirmanakaya-dharmakaya*[20]

which can be compared to the Catholic[21] nature of God as

> Father-Son-Holy Spirit

It is thought provoking that there is a three fold process at the heart of these traditions. This alone would make Hegel happy.

A fourth dimension in this explication of compassion is the mother.

The mother opens the triangle of *Bhakti-Karuna-Agape* into an open ended square that emanates its compassion.

The mother always already present in her absence is:

Devaki
Kuan Yin
Sophia
Eve
Mary
Majka
Mater

To think what remains of *Bhakti-Karuna-Agape* is to think what remains of the mother.

The mother is devoted without expecting reward.[22]

Her works of devotion do not need approval.

The mother gives hospitality not brutality.

The mother does not abuse.[23]

The mother says "I am here."

The mother is a treasure because her heart is always open.

Miriam, the sister of Moses guarded his safety, his security and his vulnerability. In her devotion and self-less service she gave fully.[24]

Rumi says, " Woman is a ray of God. She is not that earthly beloved: she is creative, not created."

Love is what awakens. It makes enlightened.

Scheler taught us that love is creative. Love is a spontaneous opening in which new values are created.

Love is that which tears opens the doors of the fortress of death.

Heal me.

Ave Maria

Zdravo Marija
Milosti Puna...

God said to me, " You are my child, for today I gave birth to you."
Psalm 2:7

But what do I love when I love my God?
St. Augustine, *Confessions*

Great Love does not desire love—it desires more.
Nietzsche, *Thus Spoke Zarathustra*

For my Mother Ljubica
and for my
Grand-Mothers Mara and Dragica

Notes

1. The village of Međugorje is located in Bosnia- Hercegovina, not far from the village of Rakitno where I was born in 1966.St. Jerome's Church in Međugorje was targeted by the Yugo-Serbian Army in the early 1990's with cluster bombs. It was not damaged. In the Croatian language Međugorje means, "between the mountains." The word "Between" remains an important ethical, religious and political word deserving further reflection.

2. I will have to return to this Freudian question by giving a non-Lacanian answer.

3. In Thomas Merton's words, "The God of peace is never glorified by violence."

4. As E. M. Cioran writes in *Tears and Saints*, " The most obscure mumbo-jumbo is closer to God than the *Summa theologiae*; and a child's simple prayer offers a greater ontological guarantee than all ecumenical synods."

5. Like the shafts of love that penetrated St. Teresa's heart.

6. In the words of Thich Nhat Hanh in *Living Buddha, Living Christ*, "We humans can be nourished by the best values of many traditions." There is a danger with the notion of cultural disarmament insofar as it could be read otherwise. China could say that it was practicing cultural disarmament when it invaded Tibet and various Lamas fail to apply the teaching of karma to the situation of their invaded and brutalized homeland.

7. Thou art That.

8. The Jewel is in the Lotus.

9. This while global corporations go "bankrupt" after "losing" $30 billion or while pharmaceutical companies withhold medicines from Third World Nations in the name of profit or while banks and credit card companies record huge profits by hiking borrowing rates or charging you "service fees" to withdraw your money. More needs to be written about how "the law" allows corporations and financial institutions to steal without penalty.

10. Kierkegaard's *Fear and Trembling* could be read as a meditation on the breast. See the *Exordium* where Johannes de Silentio distinguishes between the blackened breast, the virginally concealed breast, the sorrowful breast and the supplemental breast.

11. As Lao Tzu states, " Now, it's because I'm compassionate that I therefore can be courageous."

12. This mantra is *gate, gate, paragate, parasamgate Bodhi Svaha.*

This mantra can be translated as *groundlessness, groundlessness, more groundlessness, even beyond groundlessness, Fully Awake, Amen.*

13. The tele-evangelist mantra is "The end is near so give us more money" Readers can see this for themselves on the TCT. (Total Christian Television) Network which has excellent late-night entertainment value. A particular slogan I found intriguing was "Suffering from Truth decay? Brush up on your Bible!" If Truth is something that decays then no amount of Bible brushing is going to fix or fill the immense cavities of misunderstanding and misinterpretation being disseminated on these networks in the name of "knowing the Lord who gives financial prosperity." Does Truth decay when it is enclosed in the *biblia*?

14. As Thomas Merton writes in *Thoughts in Solitude,* "To live as a rational animal does not mean to think as a man and live as an animal."

15. Merton writes, "You pray best when the mirror of your soul is empty of every image except the Image of the Invisible Father. This image is the Wisdom of the Father, the Word of the Father, *Verbum spirans amorem*, the glory of the Father."

16. Again Merton's insights are poignant, "Laziness and cowardice are two of the greatest enemies of spiritual life ... they fear the future because they place no trust in God."

17. As Slavoj Žižek points out in *The Fragile Absolute- or, why is the christian legacy worth fighting for?*, "The notorious Iraqi 'weapons of mass destruction' offer another example of the *objet petit a*: they are an elusive entity, never emperically specified ... expected to be hidden in the most disparate and improbable place, from the (rather logical) desert to the (slightly irrational) cellars of presidential palaces (so that when the palace is bombed, they may poison Saddam and his entire entourage); allegedly present in large quantities, yet magically moved around all the time by workers; and the more they are destroyed, the more all-present and all-powerful they are in their threat, as if the removal of the

greater part of them magically heightens the destructive power of the remainder...."

18. Abraham's name means "compassion." He bound Isaac whose name means "joy and laughter." The *akeda* teaches us that the time for human sacrifice had come to an end. In other words, the time for sacrificing joy in the name of compassion had terminated. This reading takes us beyond Kierkegaard's *Fear and Trembling*.

19. Manifestation, consciousness, bliss.

20. The springing forth of energy out of the ground of emptiness; the continuous crystallization of that energy into form; the unconditioned from which all thing arise. The Sanskrit word *Kaya* means "body" but can also signify "dimension, field, or basis."

21. From the Greek word *Kathalikos* or Universal which was the lineage established by Jesus which I distinguish from its Roman and Greek versions and from the lineages established by Luther, Calvin etc. I follow the distinction between Catholic and Christian as formulated by St. Augustine. In Book VI of his *Conf--essions,* he writes "And she [his mother] found out that I too was in grave danger because of my despair of discovering the truth. I told her that I was not a *Catholic Christian*, but at least I was no longer a Manichee." (my emphasis).

22. As Nietzsche writes in *Thus Spoke Zarathustra*, "You love your virtue as the mother her child: but when was it heard of a mother wanting to be paid for her love?"

23. As Dame Julian of Norwich (1342-1415) writes, "To the property of Motherhood belongeth kind love, wisdom and knowing."

24. In the words of the Baal Shem Tov, "When you serve God through God's compassion, you empower yourself with greater strength, elevate your mind with higher thoughts and soar with the angels. This is what is called, "complete service."